Work, Working and Work Relationships in a Changing World

This book is concerned with the rapid and varied changes in the nature of work and work relationships that have taken place in recent years. While technological innovation has been a key contributor to the nature and pace of change, other social and market trends have also played a part, such as increasing workforce diversity, enhanced competition and greater global integration. Responding to these trends alongside cost pressures and the need for continued responsiveness to the environment, organizations have changed the way in which work is organized. There have also been shifts in product markets with growing demand for authenticity and refinement of the customer experience, which has further implications for how work is organized and enacted. At the same time, employees have sought changes in their work arrangements in order to help them achieve a more satisfactory relationship between their work and non-work lives. Many have also taken increased responsibility for managing their own work opportunities, moving away from dependency on a single employer.

The implications of these significant and widespread changes are the central focus of this book and in particular the implications for workers, managers and organizations. It brings together contributions from an international team of renowned management scholars who explore the opportunities and challenges presented by technological and digital innovation, consumer, social and organizational change. Drawing on empirical evidence from Europe, North America and Australia, *Work, Working and Work Relationships in a Changing World* considers new forms of service work, technologically enabled work and independent professionals to provide in-depth insight into work experiences in the 21st century.

Clare Kelliher is Professor of Work and Organisation at Cranfield School of Management, United Kingdom.

Julia Richardson is Professor of Human Resource Management at Curtin Business School, Curtin University, Australia.

Routledge Studies in Human Resource Development
Edited by Monica Lee, Lancaster University, UK

HRD theory is changing rapidly. Recent advances in theory and practice, how we conceive of organisations and of the world of knowledge, have led to the need to reinterpret the field. This series aims to reflect and foster the development of HRD as an emergent discipline.

Encompassing a range of different international, organisational, methodological and theoretical perspectives, the series promotes theoretical controversy and reflective practice.

Global Human Resource Development
Regional and Country Perspectives
Edited by Thomas N. Garavan, Alma M. McCarthy and Michael J. Morley

On the Nature of Human Resource Development
Holistic Agency and an Almost-Autoethnographical Exploration of Becoming
Monica Lee

Identity as a Foundation for Human Resource Development
Edited by Kate Black, Russell Warhurst and Sandra Corlett

Positive Ageing and Human Resource Development
Edited by Diane Keeble-Ramsay and Andrew Armitage

Work, Working and Work Relationships in a Changing World
Edited by Clare Kelliher and Julia Richardson

Also published in the series in paperback:

Action Research in Organisations
Jean McNiff, accompanied by Jack Whitehead

Understanding Human Resource Development
A research-based approach
Edited by Jim Stewart, Jim McGoldrick, and Sandra Watson

Work, Working and Work Relationships in a Changing World

Edited by Clare Kelliher and
Julia Richardson

Routledge
Taylor & Francis Group

NEW YORK AND LONDON

First published 2019
by Routledge
605 Third Avenue, New York, NY 10017

And by Routledge
2 Park Square, Milton Park, Abingdon, Oxon, OX14 4RN

First issued in paperback 2020

Routledge is an imprint of the Taylor & Francis Group, an informa business

Library of Congress Cataloging-in-Publication Data
A catalog record for this book has been requested

ISBN 13: 978-0-367-73212-7 (pbk)
ISBN 13: 978-0-8153-7153-3 (hbk)

Typeset in Sabon
by Apex CoVantage, LLC

Contents

Figures and Tables

Figures

Tables

Preface

Work, working and work relationships each play a dominant role in our lives, impacting on how, where, when and with whom we interact. They also impact directly on organizational structures and processes, and national and international relationships. Recent years have witnessed far-reaching changes being made to the nature and organization of work, and to work relationships, driven at least in part by increased competitive pressures, growing global integration and developments in information and communication technologies. These changes and the way in which they are experienced are the subject of this book. It is primarily aimed at scholars seeking to understand both the complexity and diversity of change and the implications for individuals, organizations and society more broadly. The findings reported in each of the chapters will also be of value to those concerned with the development of work-related policy and to managers and human resource professionals facing the challenge of designing and implementing new forms of work and work relationships in a changing world.

This volume, *Work, Working and Work Relationships in a Changing World*, is a follow-on text to our previous edited book, *New Ways of Organising Work: Developments, Perspectives and Experiences*, published by Routledge in 2012, which had stemmed from a sub-theme entitled 'New Ways to Work: Organizing Work and Working Practices' at the European Group on Organization Studies (EGOS) conference in Barcelona in 2009. Many of the changes to the meaning and organization of work covered in that book have become more pervasive, alongside moves away from traditional work arrangements and relationships. In the intervening years, we have continued conversations with many of the original contributors as well as starting conversations with the new contributors to this book.

While the dynamics of change in the contemporary workforce are the subject of increasing debate, there is still a paucity of literature in this area (partly due to the pace of change), with corresponding calls for more theoretical development. As the calls for theoretical development have increased, so too have calls for more diversity in the field, with growing awareness of the complexity and diversity of current work forms and relationships. A key aim of this book is to answer those calls and to signal areas for further exploration.

The publication of this book would not have been possible without the co-operation and support of many people. First, we would like to extend our sincere thanks to all the scholars who contributed to the book, for providing well-written chapters, based on rigorous research, illuminating various aspects of changes to the nature and organization of work and work relationships. We are also grateful to them for making our lives easier by meeting deadlines and for prompt responses to our comments and queries. Second, we would like to pay tribute to Jayne Ashley for her assistance throughout the project and for her help in putting the final manuscript together. Third, we would like to thank David Varley at Routledge, who approached us with the idea of a follow-on volume, for his enthusiasm and support for our proposal and advice during the early stages. We would also like to thank Brianna Ascher who took over from David midway through the process and to Mary Del Plato for her help during the production process. Finally, we would like to thank our families and friends who supported us throughout and tolerated our own new ways of working, adopted in order to complete this project.

Clare Kelliher
Julia Richardson
August 2018

1 Work, Working and Work Relationships in a Changing World

Clare Kelliher and Julia Richardson

Introduction

Since the turn of the 21st century, there has been much discussion about the changing world of work among scholars, public policy makers, managers and employees. Much has been written about the subject in scholarly and practitioner publications alongside increasing interest in the broader media. A central concern has been changes in the nature and organization of work and the relationship between organizations and the individuals who carry out work for them, be it as employees or contractors. These changes have also been connected to implications for society in general, including the implications for public spending, education and economic performance. For example, Brynjolfsson and McAfee (2014) have warned that increasing job automation could disrupt labour markets, leading to greater inequality and, ultimately, social unrest. There has also been concern that a broader range of jobs have become more precarious and characterized by increased job insecurity and work intensification (Hassard & Morris, 2018; Huws, Spencer & Syrdal, 2018; Rubery et al., 2018). On the other hand, recent industry reports have suggested that such changes will also lead to the creation of new jobs and potentially to new, improved ways of working with greater opportunities for learning and development (e.g. Deloitte, 2018; Price Waterhouse Coopers, 2017; World Economic Forum, 2016). This view aligns with Schumpeter's (2012) notion of 'creative destruction', as was reported to have occurred following earlier industrial revolutions. For the short and medium term, therefore, the extant debate seemingly points towards both challenges and opportunities in the world of work.

Given the embeddedness of work in society, any change in the nature of work, working arrangements and relationships invariably has some impact, positive and/or negative, on a range of stakeholders and with respect to personal and professional relationships and interactions, individual identities and institutional dynamics. In this context, concerns also emerge about 'the future of work' and the implications of what has been referred to as the Fourth Industrial Revolution (Schwab, 2016) for organizational, industrial and societal sustainability. A recent World Economic

Forum (WEF, 2016) survey of chief human resource officers and senior talent and strategy executives of leading global employers proposes that current changes will "lay the foundation for a revolution more comprehensive and all-encompassing than anything we have ever seen" (2016, p. v). Whilst there is still much uncertainty about the implications of these changes, they are seen as stemming from widespread social, economic and political changes, including rapid developments and innovations in information and communication technology, digitization and artificial intelligence (AI), greater global integration, demographic changes and increasing market pressures. There is a growing awareness of the need to respond to, or at least map out, what the changing nature of work, working arrangements and relationships might involve and their potential implications at societal, institutional and individual levels.

Drawing on nine empirical studies located in five different countries, this book aims to respond to some of these issues. As a precursor to each of the chapters, in this introductory chapter, we present an overview of the driving forces behind some of the dominant changes in work, working and work relationships. We begin by examining technological developments and innovations and the refinement of product and service offerings. We then turn to the use of greater flexibility in when and where work is carried out along with an increasing concern for work-life balance and well-being, followed by an examination of the changes in the structure of employment and in expectations of professionals, specifically, human resources managers. The aim of this chapter, therefore, is to set the scene for the remaining chapters of the book.

Technological Development and Innovation

Technological development and innovation, such as the ubiquity of mobile Internet connection, growth in the use of AI, robotics, quantum computers, 3-D printing, nanotechnology, the Internet of Things (IoT) and autonomous vehicles are argued to incur fundamental changes in the way in which businesses and societies work and how individuals lead their lives. The 2016 WEF Report (2016), for example, argues that technological disruptions have been significant drivers of industrial change, particularly the expansion of low-cost computing power and the mobile Internet. It also draws attention to the significance of technological developments and innovations still in nascent stages, in particular 3-D printing and artificial intelligence, which it predicts to be "well underway in specific industries in the years leading up to 2020" (WEF, 2016, p. 9). A Price Waterhouse Coopers (PWC) report proposes that "we are living through a fundamental transformation in the way we work. Automation and 'thinking machines' are replacing human tasks and jobs, and changing the skills that organizations are looking for in their people" (2017, p. 3). Similarly, a survey of 11,000 business and HR leaders by

Deloitte (2018) found that almost half of respondents reported that their organizations are "deeply involved in automation projects, with 24 percent using AI and robotics to perform routine tasks, 16 percent to augment human skills and 7 percent to restructure work entirely" (2018, p. 75). A key theme in these debates is the extent to which technological development and innovation changes not only how work is done but also where and by whom it is done. Furthermore, the PWC report emphasizes that whereas many commentators have focused on the impact of technology and particularly automation on jobs and workplaces, the "real story is far more complicated" (2017, p. 7). As such, they call for more attention to be paid to "the manner in which humans decide to use that technology" (p. 7) and exploration of the human-technology interface.

Several of the chapters in this book respond to that call by examining circumstances where organizations provide opportunities for individuals to work in different ways through the use of technology, such as telework and in turn providing opportunities for them to divest expensive office space (Beauregard, Canonico & Basile, Chapter 2; Wessels & Schippers, Chapter 5; Peters & Van der Heijden, Chapter 6). As these chapters show, although this has created (welcome) opportunities for employees to work away from the workplace, it is also often characterized by high-intensity workloads. The digital workplace can also serve as an important strategic asset for dealing with organizational complexity, uncertainty and ambiguity as demonstrated in Chapter 9 by de Meulen, Dery and Sebastian and by Anderson and Kelliher in Chapter 10. In some contexts, organizations have used technological development and innovations to replace jobs, to the concern of public policy makers and to employees and their representatives. Several studies conducted in recent years, propose that up to a third of current jobs will be lost to automation in Western economies in the next two decades (e.g. Berriman & Hawksworth, 2017). This is expected to be particularly the case in manufacturing and production roles, as a result of what the WEF report (2016) refers to as 'substituting technologies' such as AI, 3-D printing and robotics. Nevertheless, it is notable that the report also provides considerable room for optimism where technological development and innovation gives rise to job creation through Big Data Analytics, mobile Internet, the Internet of Things and robotics. In a related vein, the Deloitte Report (2018) indicates that "leading companies increasingly recognize that these technologies are most effective when they complement humans, not replace them" (p. 76). It also notes that there is growing recognition that AI tools require human oversight with 'tens of thousands' of employees needed to monitor, train and augment the use of technology, and argues that "Many of today's fastest growth areas for jobs are in fields such as health care, sales and professional services that are essentially human, but that can be aided and augmented by machines" (Deloitte, 2018, p. 41).

Elsewhere, the Foundation for Young Australians Report (2018), with the specific aim of exploring workplace opportunities for future generations in Australia, indicates that although technological advancement may limit growth in some job sectors, it will spur growth in others when coupled with the 'human element' of the future workplace. This reinforces the idea that while some jobs may be threatened by technological development and innovations, others are predicted to grow. Furthermore, it would seem not only to be a matter of job destruction or creation, since many existing jobs are likely to change with respect to how they are done and by whom. Organizations may utilize technology to enable employees to work collaboratively, accessing people and projects regardless of their location. This development is a dominant theme in the reports cited earlier and demonstrated by Anderson and Kelliher in Chapter 10.

Refinement of Product and Service Offerings

A further important trend impacting contemporary work and work relationships is that of increasing product differentiation, a strategy being adopted by many service companies in order to improve their competitive position. Whereas Ritzer's 'MacDonaldization of Society' (2009) speaks to the increasing standardization of products and social processes, more recent trends reflect what may be understood as an 'authentic turn' towards a search for greater authenticity and individualism in both production and consumption. According to philosopher Andrew Potter, "The demand for the honest, the natural, the real—that is the authentic—has become one of the most powerful movements in contemporary life" (2010, p. 4). Although he acknowledges that the broader demands of the market economy are more directly met by mass production, he argues that the presentation of authenticity is fast becoming an industry in itself.

The search for increasing authenticity has also been identified by others. The WEF report (2016) cited earlier, notes increased consumer concerns about ethical and privacy issues, with a greater emphasis on food safety, labour standards, animal welfare, carbon footprint and product origins. Likewise, a recent Price Waterhouse Coopers Consumer Insights Survey (2018) reports an increase in physical store shopping, which they attribute to a desire for more sensory and social experiences. Thus, while shoppers are making increasing use of digital technologies, they also have increasing expectations that their products and services are characterized by high levels of customization, particularly with regard to service expectations. For individual workers and their careers, Mainiero and Sullivan (2006) have suggested that the need for authenticity is a powerful driving force with an increasing number of individuals seeking to 'find their own voice' in their careers, rather than simply meeting the demands of an employer. The Deloitte (2018) report takes a critical approach to the 'up or out' model of careers and calls for greater acknowledgement that an increasing number of workers are looking for opportunities to learn and express themselves in their work rather than fitting into a 'cookie-cutter' linear career structure. Svejenova (2005) also identified an increasing trend in individuals looking for ways in which to experience a sense of authenticity, both in how they work and in the nature of the products they are working with and providing for their customers.

Yet, the demand for more customized products and services increases alongside the continued expansion of the mass market. Thus, for example, where food and beverages are concerned, as with many other industries, such as clothing, travel and tourism, we see a trend towards a bifurcation of mass production and customization. The implications of this are also reflected in the experiences and opportunities of those working in these industries, which is the focus of Chapters 7 and 8 of the book. Knox, in Chapter 8, focuses on the Australian café sector and examines the experiences of workers in both speciality (quality-based) and standard (cost-based) outlets, showing differences in ways of working and required skills. Clarke, Weir and Patrick in Chapter 7, focus on the emergence of craft beer and examine the role of the Cicerone as a certified expert in the keeping, serving and food pairing of beer, comparing their role to those of wine sommeliers.

Use of Time-Spatial Flexibility and Increasing Concern for Work-Life Balance

An important influence on contemporary work practices and work relationships is the increasing use of time and spatial flexibility, where a growing number of employees having access to flexible work practices, which allow choice over where and when they work. This trend has been closely connected to increasing demands for a more satisfactory work-life balance and enabled by advances in technological development and innovation. Specifically, the ubiquity of the Internet allows many workers to fulfil their work responsibilities away from the traditional workplace, in remote locations and outside of traditional working times. In this regard, an individual worker may not be in the same physical space as their employer or their colleagues, or working at the same times, even though they may be in regular contact via the use of technology and specifically technology enhanced communication systems.

Technological advances and innovations have also enabled time flexibility, allowing individuals to perform their work outside of regular hours. This has created a situation where individuals can work according to their own time and spatial preferences, as examined by Wessels and Schippers in Chapter 5 and Peters and Van der Heijden in Chapter 6. For work-life balance, the advantage of this form of flexibility is that it can reduce negative (time-based and strain-based) work-life interference and enhance positive work-life spillover. However, it is notable that the extent to which better work-life balance is achieved in reality is also influenced by factors such as whether the individual works part or full-time and whether they have elected to work part time or whether they unable to secure full-time work. It may also be that working remotely results in work intensification (Kelliher & Anderson, 2010), in part because time saved on commuting is used to extend working hours and because there are no 'healthy distractions' by work colleagues (Richardson & McKenna, 2013). Furthermore, individuals working remotely may overcompensate with output to make up for lack of physical visibility (Richardson & Kelliher, 2015)

Changes in the Structure of Employment

A further trend impacting work, working and work relationships is the widespread change in the structure of employment. This has, in part, been facilitated by technological development and innovation which has, according to a recent Union NSW study in Australia, "unlocked new, innovative and efficient ways of working and doing business" (p. 1). There is evidence of greater distancing and/or detachment of the organization and the worker, resulting in a more transactional employer-employee relationship. The increasing use of zero-hours contracts, temporary agency contracting and more workers engaged in what has become known as the 'gig' economy (Unions NSW, 2018; Taylor et al., 2017; Rubery, Keizer & Grimshaw, 2016) are illustrations of this trend. A recent report commissioned by the UK government, *The Taylor Review of Modern Working Practices* (Taylor et al., 2017) and the *Recruitment and Employment Confederation* (REC) (2017) in the UK estimated that around 1.2 million individuals were engaged in agency work, and 905,000 individuals (2.8% of those in employment) were on zero-hours contracts, with the majority being young people aged between 16–24. This also reflects a more transactional relationship between the employer and the employee, where work opportunities may be unpredictable and are allocated and completed with no long-term allegiance between the employer and the employee.

These new types of working relationships are frequently seen as poorer quality employment (Moore & Newsome, 2018; Rubery et al., 2016) and of principal benefit to the employer, allowing them to avoid a longer-term commitment and the payment of work-related benefits such as health care and pension contributions. Focusing on the casualization of academic staff, some scholars (Williams & Beovich, 2017; Crimmins, 2016) have noted that this has caused widespread job insecurity and a reduction in employment related benefits, such as sick and holiday pay and entitlement to parental leave and pay. Furthermore, it has been suggested that, even where hourly rates of pay are higher for casual and part-time employees, it may be difficult to secure a 'living wage' due to the limitations of work available (Ilsøe Larsen & Felbo-Kolding, 2017). Precarious work has also been found to have a detrimental impact on well-being (Moore & Newsome, 2018), particularly where those involved have limited autonomy and income. A recent Australian Study of the Internet-based 'Airtasker' (Union NSW, 2018) also notes that the increased prevalence of digitally enabled, gig-based work erodes labour standards and removes the legal safety net. It is argued that such companies, by classifying their workers as independent contractors, have "used a cloak of innovation and progress to reintroduce archaic and outdated labour practices" (p. 1).

Whereas the negative dimensions of these trends is a cause for concern, some have suggested that these emerging forms of work relationships also grant greater control to the individual worker who can take charge of their own work experiences, selecting who they wish to work for and how long, rather than becoming dependent on a single employer (Richardson, Wardale & Lord, 2018). There are also arguments to suggest that this working arrangement may give greater negotiating power to the individual worker in times when their skills are scarce, or when demand exceeds supply. Furthermore, Wood, Lehdonvirta and Graham (2018) suggest that in some cases gig workers may be able to support each other and share information in order to enhance their work opportunities and experiences. According to a McKinsey report (2016) there are 'tens of millions who put together their own income streams and shape their own work lives' (2016, p. 8) in this way. A key concern here, however, is the extent to which the individual worker has elected to engage in this way of working, or whether they are doing so because they are unable to find permanent work elsewhere. McKeown in Chapter 4 deals directly with individual volition by investigating the notions of 'entrepreneurial pull' and 'unemployment push' as dimensions of the rapid expansion of professionals moving into self-employment. Moreover, as McKeown points out, these forms of work, working and work relationships are directly influenced by changes to the broader institutional context of work.

Changing Role of (Human Resource Management) Professionals

In line with the continued reduction in the proportion of the workforce employed in manual jobs and the growth in knowledge work in many economies, there has been an increased focus on the role of professional workers. This has included discussion about what it means to be professional and as a result what is expected from professional workers (Muzio, Brock & Suddaby, 2013). Being professional has tended to mean behaving in a seemingly rational manner, not allowing emotions to colour judgement or behaviour, implying that professionals are required to engage in emotional labour managing their emotions as part of their work role

(Clarke, Hope-Hailey & Kelliher, 2007). However, more recently, there have been calls for leaders and professionals to be more authentic and bring their true selves into their professional roles (Kreiner, Hollensbe & Sheep, 2009; Ramarajan & Reid, 2013). This sets up a potential tension between the differing expectations placed upon them, on the one hand, to be detached and on the other to engage emotionally. This tension has perhaps always been relevant for human resource management professionals, and particularly so in the light of increasing objectification, driven by a pro-market focus (Dundon & Rafferty, 2018), at the same time as a need to create greater emotional bonds and engagement with employees to facilitate individual and organizational performance.

Furthermore, concern has been expressed about the extent to which management practices, and HRM practices in particular have become overly formulaic and less able to respond to changes in the nature of work and work relationships (Alvesson & Gabriel, 2013; Harley, 2015). Dundon and Rafferty (2018) warn of the risk of impoverishment of HRM and HR practitioners themselves are increasingly concerned about the longevity of their profession and its ability to navigate the future workplace, leading to calls for a "quantum shift in mindset and skills" (Vorhauser-Smith & Cariss, 2017, p. 210) to keep up with the changing nature of work. It is noteworthy that because of the very nature of its role, the HRM profession has a direct role to play in the introduction of changes to work and work relationships.

The trend towards an individualistic and market-led approach to managing people has led to the increasing use of 'people analytics', said to offer 'new opportunities to better hire, manage, retain and optimize the workforce' (Deloitte, 2018; Chartered Institute of Personnel and Development, 2018). Advances in technology have enabled organizations to collect an increasing amount of personal and business data about their employees. For example, the Deloitte Human Capital Trends survey reported that 84% of respondents viewed people analytics as the second-highest rank trend in terms of importance, just behind the need for more collaboration between senior 'C-Suite' management. Data collected through people analytics has been used to monitor individual performance and inform organizational reward systems. This increasing capacity to monitor individual performance has been a subject of interest to management and HRM scholars (Moore & Hayes, 2017) who have raised concerns that 'minute-by-minute' monitoring may be stressful for employees, with a detrimental effect on well-being. Concerns have also been expressed about how such data is managed, particularly with regard to confidentiality, transparency and privacy. In the Deloitte Human Capital Trends Survey (2018), 64% of respondents reported that they are "actively managing legal liability related to their organizations' people data" (p. 90). A recent Economist Intelligence Unit (2018) report recommends that in order for the HR profession to make better use of the potential of people analytics and thus avoid its respective pitfalls they need to work more closely with IT departments.

These developments have led to concern being raised that the 'human' element of human resources management may be giving way to the 'management' element resulting in 'data-driven decisions' that may fail to account for the more nuanced dimensions of effective human resources management. This failure is especially likely given the reported dearth of HR professionals with sufficiently honed skills to be able to accurately interpret and apply large bodies of data (SHRM, 2018). This adds weight to arguments about the need to ensure active human oversight in how technologies are being used as a tool in human resources management. The 2018 Deloitte Global Human Capital Trends report makes the recommendation that

> Organizations need to understand the trade-offs involved in the accelerating collection and use of employee and workforce data. . . . While this is a relatively new challenge for HR, it is rapidly, and rightly, becoming a top priority.
>
> (p. 93)

At the same time, there are increasing demands for emotion work, particularly in the context of managers being expected to establish strong emotional bonds with their profession and work, their employees and frequently their customers and clients (Pettinger, 2005). Bolton and Houlihan (2007), for example, have called for 'thicker' relationships between HR professionals and other organizational members, characterized by close personal connections and affective commitment. Thus, for HR professionals, we observe two seemingly opposing trends emerging— the increasing use of data and the quantification of human behaviour in the workplace and the increasing requirement for workers to be emotionally connected and engaged with both their work and their employing organization. Addressing this theme, in Chapter 3 Linehan and O'Brien examine the expectations placed upon HR professionals in contemporary workplaces and with particular reference to the management of emotions. They present data showing that being 'professional' involves navigating the traditional norms of rationality, as well as the expected norms of emotionality, albeit the latter in a constrained sense.

Having explored some of the key influence on the changing nature of work, work organization and work relationships, we turn now to the structure of the book and the contribution of the respective chapters.

The book is divided into four parts. The first part "Career Opportunities and Experiences in the Contemporary and Future Labour Market: A Double-Edged Sword?" addresses changing working arrangements and relationships, and their related opportunities and limitations. Each of the chapters in this section addresses the experiences of a particular group of workers: teleworkers, human resource managers and independent professionals, examining their respective work experiences and in particular the tensions between their working arrangement or work relationship and their expectations and aspirations. In Chapter 2, "The Fur-Lined Rut: Telework and Career Ambition", Beauregard, Canonico and Basile examine the relationship between telework and career ambition, exploring how teleworkers involved in high-intensity telework have lower levels of career ambition than their office-based counterparts and/or those who have a more even balance between working remotely and in the workplace. In reporting their findings, the authors make a strong case for the need for more careful succession planning and work oversight at a time when an increas ing number of employees are demanding greater flexibility over where and when they work. In Chapter 3, "Performing the Ideal Professional: Insights From Worker's Accounts of Emotional Labour in Contemporary Workplaces", Linehan and O'Brien examine the challenges of meeting the expectations of being an 'ideal professional' as human resources managers. Adding to the extant literature on the professionalization of management occupations (Wright, 2008; Hodgson, Paton & Muzio, 2015), the authors question contemporary discourses about the desirability of displaying authentic selves and emotions in the workplace, arguing that the professionalization of human resource management places greater restrictions on the potential for authentic expression of the self. Echoing Wright's (2008) earlier arguments, they suggest that increasing professionalization brings a more restricted and prescribed view of what it means to be a human resources professional. In Chapter 4, "Working as an Independent Professional: Career Choice or the Only Option?", McKeown explores the growth in the number of professionals entering self-employment to become independent workers. A key concern in this chapter is the extent to which institutional and organizational forces impact on both the decision to enter self-employment and subsequent experiences of working independently. The chapter demonstrates that whereas the decision to enter self-employment may be seen as individually driven, it may in practice be impacted by changing contextual forces.

The second part of the book "*Making the Most of Flexible Work Practices: The Need for Spatial Job Crafting and Boundary Management*" offers insight into strategies for the effective management of flexible work practices. In doing so, it answers calls for more practical solutions or frameworks to meet the challenges of contemporary work practices. In Chapter 5, "Reflecting on and Proactively Making Use of Flexible Working Practices Makes All the Difference: The Role of Spatial Job Crafting", Wessels and Schippers provide insight into how employees can make the most of flexible work arrangements and relationships. A key contention is the need for individual proactivity in how work space is managed to support increased work engagement and innovation, whilst at the same time retaining the freedom to work outside traditional work space and time. In Chapter 6, "Bounded Flexibility: The Influence of Time-Spatial Flexibility and Boundary-Management Strategies on Women's Work-Home Interface", Peters and Van der Heijden argue that time-spatial flexibility can reduce negative work-home interference. They also suggest that effective boundary-management strategies can facilitate positive experiences in each domain, thus contributing positively to overall well-being and work performance.

The third part of the book *"Professionalization in the Service Industry: Cicerones and Baristas"* examines the consequences of broader consumer trends in service industries and their implications for job opportunities and experiences. In this regard, it builds on the extant literature on the professionalization of managerial occupations, which has been described as an attempt to improve the status and power of the respective occupational community (Wright, 2008). It considers themes relating to greater differentiation and demand for authenticity and individualism in service offerings as an alternative to mass production. In Chapter 7, "Craft Beer, Cicerones and Changing Identities in Beer Serving", Clarke, Weir and Patrick examine the emergence of craft beer and the related work opportunities with a specific focus on the experiences of Cicerones engaged in 'beer work'. The chapter makes a particular point of exploring the emergence of prosumption and professionalization within an emerging sphere and the implications for individual occupational identity. In Chapter 8, "Wake Up and Smell the Coffee: Job Quality in Australia's Café Industry", Knox examines the café sector as an example of differentiated service work. This chapter demonstrates how the nature of work differs between standard cafés, aimed at mass consumption and the new speciality cafés. Speciality cafés redefine the role of the server, giving rise to increased skill and the development of new occupational identities as baristas located within an emerging profession. A key concern in this chapter is the extent to which bifurcation and professionalization within an industry creates the need for specific policy development to support the expansion of these new work opportunities.

The fourth and final part of the book *"Harnessing Technological and Digital Information: The Need for Workforce Agility"* reconnects the reader to management practices by examining how changes to ways of working and work relationships are implemented at organizational level. Specifically, it draws on two case studies to demonstrate managerial thinking, processes and subsequent outcomes in achieving workforce agility. In Chapter 9, "Digital Workplace Design: Transforming for High Performance" van der Meulen, Dery and Sebastian develop a framework outlining a range of design and management elements of the digital workplace. The authors demonstrate how, taken together, these elements impact on organizational performance and how successful organizations gain competitive advantage from effective and efficient digital workplace design. A key message in the chapter is the need for more holistic rather than piecemeal approaches to the implementation of digital workplace design. This message is also connected to the need for top and middle management buy-in together with consistent support from related key stakeholders, including IT, HRM, facilities and communications. In Chapter 10, "Agile Working: The Case of TechSci, Global Technology Company", Anderson and Kelliher examine the implementation of workforce agility in a global technology company. They examine the organization's understanding, interpretation and enactment of workforce agility, followed by an exposition of how it was implemented. A key theme in the chapter is the extent to which implementation of new working arrangements and relationships invites both tensions and opportunities. This is connected to the need for nuanced and sensitive employee consultation when embedding agile working into an organizational context.

Chapter 11, "Observations and Conclusions on Work, Working and Work Relationships in a Changing World", the final chapter of the book, reflects on the findings presented in each of the chapters. Drawing the key themes together and identifying avenues for further enquiry.

References

Alvesson, M., & Gabriel, Y. (2013). Beyond formulaic research: In praise of greater diversity in organisational research and publications. *Academy of Management Learning and Education*, 12(2): 245–253.

Berriman, R., & Hawksworth, J. (2017). Will robots steal our jobs? The potential impact of automation on the UK and other major economies. *UK Economic Outlook*, March 2017. Available from www.pwc.co.uk/economic-services/ukeo/pwcukeo-section-4-automation-march-2017-v2.pdf.

Bolton, S., & Houlihan, M. (2007). Risky business: Re-thinking the human in interactive service work. In Sharon Bolton & Maeve Houlihan (Eds.), *Searching for the Human in Human Resource Management Theory, Practice and Workplace* (pp. 245–262). London: Palgrave MacMillan.

Brynjolfsson, E., & McAfee, A. (2014). *The Second Machine Age: Work, Progress, and Prosperity in a Time of Brilliant Technologies*. New York, NY: W.W. Norton & Company.

Chartered Institute of Personnel and Development (CIPD) (2018). Available from www.cipd.co.uk/knowledge/work/trends/uk-working-lives

Clarke, C., Hope-Hailey, V., & Kelliher, C. (2007). Being real or really being someone else?: Change, managers and emotions at work. *European Management Journal*, 25(2), 92–103.

Crimmins, G. (2016). The spaces and places that women casual academics (often fail) to inhabit. *Higher Education Research & Development*, 35(1), 45–57.

Deloitte (2018). The Rise of the Social Enterprise, *2018 Deloitte Global Human Capital Trends Report*.

Dundon, T., & Rafferty, A. (2018). The (potential) demise of HRM? *Human Resource Management Journal*, 28, 377–391.

Economist Intelligence Unit (2018). *Why HR is Becoming a Numbers Game*. Available from http://transformingbusiness.economist.com/hr-becoming-numbers-game/ [Accessed 25.08.2018].

Foundation for Young Australians (2018). *The New Work Reality, FYA New Work Order Report Series*. file:///C:/Users/jules/Dropbox/Reports/FYA/FYA_TheNewWorkReality_sml.pdf.

Harley, B. (2015). The one best way? "Scientific" research on HRM and the threat to critical scholarship. *Human Resource Management Journal, 25*(4), 399–407.

Hassard, J., & Morris, J. (2018). Contrived competition and manufactured uncertainty: Understanding managerial job insecurity narratives in large corporations. *Work, Employment and Society, 32*(3), 564–580.

Hodgson, D., Paton, S., & Muzio, D. (2015). Something old, something new?: Competing logics and the hybrid nature of new corporate professions. *British Journal of Management, 26*, 745–759.

Huws, U., Spencer, N.H., & Syrdal, D.S. (2018). Online, on call: The spread of digitally organised just-in-time working and its implications for standard employment models. *New Technology, Work and Employment, 33*(2), 113–129.

Ilsøe, A., Larsen, T.P., & Felbo-Kolding, J. (2017). Living hours under pressure: Flexibility loopholes in the Danish IR-model. *Employee Relations, 39*(6), 888–902.

Kelliher, C., & Anderson, D. (2010). Doing more with less? Flexible working practices and the intensification of work. *Human Relations, 63*(1), 83–106.

Kreiner, G.E., Hollensbe, E.C., & Sheep, M.L. (2009). Balancing borders and bridges: Negotiating the work-home interface via boundary work tactics. *Academy of Management Journal, 52*(4), 704–730.

Mainiero, L., & Sullivan, S. (2006). *The Opt-Out Revolt*. Mountain View, CA: Davis-Black.

Manyika, J., Lund, S., Bughin, J., Robinson, K., Mischke, J., & Mahajan, D. (2016). *Independent Work: Choice, Necessity and the Gig Economy*. McKinsey Global Institute.

Moore, S., & Hayes, L.J.B. (2017). Taking worker productivity to a new level? Electronic monitoring in homecare: the (re)production of unpaid labour. *New Technology, Work and Employment, 32*(2), 101–114.

Moore, S., & Newsome, K. (2018). Paying for free delivery: Dependent self-employment as a measure of precarity in parcel delivery. *Work Employment and Society, 32*(3), 475–492.

Muzio, D., Brock, D.M., & Suddaby, R. (2013). Professional and Institutional change: Towards an institutionalist sociology of professions. *Journal of Management Studies, 50*(5), 699–721.

Pettinger, L. (2005). Friends, relations and colleagues: The blurred boundaries of the workplace. *The Sociological Review, 53*(2), 37–55.

Potter, A. (2010). *The Authenticity Hoax*. New York: Harper.

Price Waterhouse Coopers (2017). *Workforce of the Future, the Competing Forces Shaping 2030*. Price Waterhouse Coopers.

Price Waterhouse Coopers (2018). PwC Global Consumer Insights Survey (2018). Available from www.pwc.com/gx/en/industries/consumer-markets/consumer-insights-survey/new-consumer-habits.html [Accessed 25.08.2018].

Ramarajan, L., & Reid, E. (2013). Shattering the myth of separate worlds: Negotiating non-work identities at work. *Academy of Management Review, 38*(4), 621–644.

Recruitment and Employment Confederation (2017). Available from www.rec.uk.com/ [Accessed 3.09.2018].

Richardson, J., & Kelliher, C. (2015). Managing visibility for career sustainability: A study of remote workers. In A. De Vos & B. I. J. M. Van der Heijden (Eds.), *Handbook of Research on Sustainable Careers* (pp. 116–130). Cheltenham: Edward Elgar.

Richardson, J., & McKenna, S. (2013). Reordering spatial and social relations: A case study of professional and managerial flexworkers. *British Journal of Management, 25*(4): 724–736.

Richardson, J., Wardale, D., & Lord, L. (2018). The "double-edged sword" of a sessional academic career. *Higher Education Research and Development*, forthcoming.

Ritzer, G. (2009). *The McDonaldization of Society*. Los Angeles: Pine Forge Press.

Rubery, J., Grimshaw, D., Keizer, A., & Johnson, M. (2018). Challenges and contradictions in the "normalising" of precarious work. *Work Employment and Society, 32*(3), 509–527.

Rubery, J., Keizer, A., & Grimshaw, D. (2016). Flexibility bites back: The multiple and hidden costs of flexible employment practices. *Human Resource Management Journal, 26*(3), 235–251.

Schwab, K. (2016). *The Fourth Industrial Revolution*. London, UK: Penguin.

Schumpeter, J.A. (2012). *Capitalism, Socialism and Democracy* (1st edition.) London, UK: Routledge.

SHRM (2018). What's Next: Future Global Trends Affecting Your Organization— Use of Workforce Analytics for Competitive Advantage. Available from http://futurehrtrends.eiu.com/report-2016/challenges-obstacles-and-pitfalls-in-the-implementation-of-workforce-analytics/ [Accessed 25.08.2018].

Svejenova, S. (2005). The path with a heart: Creating the authentic career. *Journal of Management Studies, 42*(5), 947–974.

Taylor, M. (2017). *Good Work: The Taylor Review of Modern Working Practices*. UK: UK Government.

Unions NSW. (2018). *Innovation or Exploitation, Busting the Airtasker Myth*. New South Wales, Australia: Unions NSW.

Vorhauser-Smith, S., & Cariss, K. (2017). *Cliffhanger: HR on the Precipice in the Future of Work*. Melbourne, Australia: PageUp People Limited.

Williams, B., & Beovich, B. (2017). Experiences of sessional educators within an Australian undergraduate paramedic program. *Journal of University Teaching & Learning Practice, 14*(1). Available from http://ro.uow.edu.au/jutlp/vol14/iss1/13/

Wood, A.J., Lehdonvirta, V., & Graham, M. (2018). Workers of the internet unit? Online freelancer organisation among remote gig economy workers in six Asian and African countries. *New Technology and Employment, 33*(2), 95–112.

World Economic Forum (WEF). (2016). The future of jobs, employment, skills and workforce strategy for the Fourth Industrial Revolution. *Global Challenge Insight Report*.

Wright, C. (2008). Reinventing human resource management: Business partners, internal consultants and the limits to professionalization. *Human Relations, 61*(8), 1063–1086.

Part I

Career Opportunities and Experiences in the Contemporary and Future Labour Market

A Double-Edged Sword?

2 "The Fur-Lined Rut"
Telework and Career Ambition

T. Alexandra Beauregard, Esther Canonico and Kelly A. Basile

Introduction

For many knowledge workers, teleworking is the new normal. Telework refers to the practice of working away from the office for some part of the work week, while keeping in contact using information technology (Bailey & Kurland, 2002; Allen, Golden & Shockley, 2015). This practice is growing in popularity on both sides of the Atlantic, with research from the Trades Union Congress demonstrating that the number of employees who report "usually" working from home increased by 19% between 2005 and 2016 in the United Kingdom, and US Census Bureau data showing that the number of American employees working on a regular basis from home grew by 115% between 2005 and 2015 (Calnan, 2016; Global Workplace Analytics, 2017). This trend is also represented in other parts of the world; for instance, Argentina has seen teleworkers increase from 320,000 in 2004 to approximately 2 million in 2014 (Munhoz, 2016), while 19% of non-agricultural workers in India's formal economy work at least one day a week from home (Eurofound and the International Labour Office, 2017). In Japan, where "face time" in the office has typically been an important element of workplace culture, the Ministry of Economy, Trade and Industry is promoting trial "telework days" in an effort to reduce the harmful effects of the long-hours culture as well as to prepare for the 2020 Olympics when commuting to work is likely to be significantly disrupted (Reuters, 2017). The expansion of telework can be attributed to the benefits that it brings for both employees and employers; research consistently finds that working from home is associated with increased levels of job satisfaction (Fonner & Roloff, 2010; Gajendran & Harrison, 2007), and organizations report significant cost savings due to reduced overheads. For example, Sun Microsystems found annual savings of $64 million in real estate costs and $2.5 million in electricity bills as a result of its telework program, and IBM has reported annual savings of $100 million from reduced office space (Caldow, 2009; Lavey-Heaton, 2014).

Flexible working arrangements that enable employees to vary the timing and location of the hours they work are often portrayed as a way to keep talented women in the workforce, or as a means more generally for working parents and carers to continue climbing the career ladder while simultaneously fulfilling their family commitments (Hewlett, 2007). In support of this view, there is some empirical evidence of a positive association between career ambition and the use of flexible working arrangements in the Netherlands (Dikkers, van Engen & Vinkenburg, 2010). However, a substantial amount of research in Anglo Saxon contexts suggests that there is a general perception among employees that the utilization of such arrangements has a negative effect on career advancement (Beauregard, 2011). This is particularly the case for flexible work arrangements that reduce visibility in the office, such as telework.

According to signaling theory, when decisions need to be made with incomplete information available, managers will use observable characteristics (such as physical presence in the workplace) to form inferences about unobservable characteristics (such as organizational commitment and productivity) among their employees (Spence, 1973; Leslie et al., 2012). Visibility at work often serves as a signal for work dedication and quantity, and quality of work output (Bailyn, 1997) and is thus a factor in decisions regarding promotion or development opportunities. Work by Elsbach, Cable and Sherman (2010) differentiates between expected visibility, which refers to being seen at work during regular work hours, and extracurricular visibility, which refers to being seen at work outside of regular work hours. Their research demonstrates that employees who enact expected visibility are perceived as being dependable and reliable, while those who enact extracurricular visibility are viewed as committed and dedicated. If employees are indeed being assessed on both the amount and timing of their presence in the workplace, and are expected to be "extra" visible in order to be considered ambitious and hardworking, then it is hardly surprising that those who use telework arrangements are more likely than their office-based colleagues to report experiencing both reduced visibility in the workplace and reduced career development (Maruyama & Tietze, 2012), and to see themselves as more at risk of losing their jobs during organizational restructuring processes (Richardson & Kelliher, 2015).

Concern on the part of employees that taking up flexible work arrangements will jeopardize their career progression may be justified; past empirical research has shown that the use of flexibility policies can result in lower performance evaluations (Wharton, Chivers & Blair-Loy, 2008), and that employees who request flexibility are routinely stigmatized—particularly when they wish to work from home (Munsch, Ridgeway & Williams, 2014). Organizational cultures that emphasize the importance of being physically present in the workplace may therefore tacitly discourage ambitious employees from availing themselves of opportunities to work from home or another location outside the workplace (Beauregard, Basile & Thompson, 2018). The end result in such "face time"–focused organizations is the creation of a dual-track career path, whereby individuals focused on career advancement work a standard schedule and are based primarily in the workplace, and individuals who work remotely for reasons such as care responsibilities or health issues are not considered eligible for leadership positions.

In organizations with a culture more accepting of flexible work arrangements, however, employees may not perceive to the same extent that there are negative effects on career advancement of being less visible in the workplace. Usage of telework practices may, therefore, not be associated with employees' career aspirations, or with concerns that progression within the organization will be stymied by working from home on a regular basis. In fact, in some organizations, managers may actually attribute employee requests for telework resources as an effort to increase their ability to work more while also balancing home responsibilities (Leslie et al., 2012). In this chapter, we investigate this premise by presenting a case study that explores the link between telework usage and career ambition within an organization where remote working is an embedded practice and used by a significant proportion of the workforce. First, this chapter will describe the organizational context for the case study as well as the qualitative and quantitative methods utilized. Next, qualitative and quantitative results detailing the impact of telework on career ambition will be presented. Last, a discussion of the findings, their implications for managers and suggestions as to how organizations might address the challenges associated with telework and career ambition will be presented.

Organizational Context

The research took place in a medium-sized public sector organization that provides a range of advisory and other services to employers and workers in Great Britain. The organization employs just over 900 people and has offices in England, Scotland and Wales. Telework was introduced in the organization in the 1970s in response to both employee demand and cost reduction targets, the latter of which have resulted in the closure of a number of smaller, regional offices over the years since then. In the past decade, the practice of telework within the organization has expanded considerably, in part due to office closures but also because the nature of the work carried out by a large proportion of employees is highly suitable for working remotely: tasks require confidentiality, focus and minimal active supervision, and are performed independently, with little need for coordination with colleagues.

Flexible working practices, particularly telework, are entrenched in the organization's culture and widely used by employees. Approximately

11% of staff members are classified as "designated teleworkers". However, telework is used on an ad hoc basis by a much larger number of employees. An estimated 44% of employees work regularly from home for at least 20% of their working time in a typical week. For the purposes of this chapter, we differentiate between employees who work mostly from home (teleworkers), employees who work an average of two to three days away from the office (flexible workers) and employees who work mostly at the office but who may make occasional use of the opportunity to work from home (office-based workers).

While telework is offered to the majority of the organization's staff, managerial roles require occupants to be either office-based or flexible workers. Full-time telework is not available to managers. Employees who currently work from home for all or the majority of their working week would therefore need to adjust their working patterns and develop a greater presence at their local office should they be promoted to a managerial position.

Data Collection

This study formed part of a larger research project addressing a number of issues associated with telework, such as work-life conflict, enrichment and boundary management (Basile & Beauregard, 2016; Canonico, 2016). A mixed-methods approach was used to examine perceptions of career ambition among the organization's teleworkers. The first phase of the study employed a qualitative methodology, with the three researchers conducting 40 interviews among a purposive (Marshall, 1996) sample of employees representing the range of roles and hierarchical levels in the organization, as well as its geographical distribution. All interviews took place at the local offices of the participants and were face-to-face, semi-structured and of approximately one hour's duration. Interviews were scheduled on days when teleworkers were likely to come in to the office for team meetings in order to make participation in the study less burdensome. All interviews were recorded with the consent of the participants and subsequently transcribed in full.

Participants were asked about their official working arrangements, their typical working patterns with regard to location, their interest in taking up an office-based position in future if they currently worked from home and their career aspirations within the organization. Managers of teleworkers were asked about challenges or concerns associated with managing employees who worked from home, and at the end of the interview, all participants were encouraged to contribute any other information related to telework that had not yet been discussed but that participants felt it was important for the researchers to know.

Based on the findings from the qualitative component of the study, a quantitative, online survey was then developed in conjunction with organizational representatives to assess levels of career ambition, career orientation, personal life orientation, willingness to become office-based and (if applicable) reasons for unwillingness to take up an office-based position for the purpose of career progression. A pilot test of the survey was conducted with 12 employees prior to full-scale distribution.

Sample

The 40 participants in the qualitative component of the study were recruited to represent, as accurately as possible, the entire workforce of the organization. Participants hailed from three different geographical locations in Great Britain and were a mix of office-based staff (43%) and teleworkers and flexible workers (67%). Forty-six percent of interviewees were women.

A total of 514 employees completed the online survey, for a response rate of 56.4%. The demographic, organizational and geographical characteristics of the sample were very similar to those of the overall population of the organization's workforce. The majority of respondents were female (57.7%), the average age of respondents was 46.2 years and 73.3% were married or in a similar relationship. More than one-third of respondents (35.2%) had at least one child under the age of 18 living in their home. Nearly all respondents reported their ethnicity as white or white British (90.5%). Respondents represented the full range of job roles and levels within the organization, with 23% being line managers and average tenure within the organization was 11.4 years. With regard to working patterns, 54% reported being office-based, 27% reported working mostly from home and 19% worked an average of two to three days a week from home and the remainder in the office.

Measures

Career ambition was assessed with Dikkers, van Engen and Vinkenburg's (2010) measure. Sample items include "I have the ambition to reach a higher position in my line of work" and "I like to be challenged in my work". Respondents answered each item on a five-point Likert scale, with 1 = strongly disagree and 5 = strongly agree. Cronbach's alpha was 0.74.

Career orientation was measured with Lobel and St. Clair's (1992) career identity salience inventory. Following Song, Foo and Uy (2008), we used two of the original five items to assess career orientation: "The major satisfactions in my life come from my job" and "The most important things that happen to me involve my job". The same five-point Likert response scale was used. The reliability alpha for this measure was 0.77.

Personal life orientation was measured with another two of the original five items in Lobel and St. Clair's (1992) career identity salience inventory, again following Song, Foo and Uy (2008). These items were adapted to reflect respondents' personal lives in general rather than family lives in particular: "The major satisfactions in my life come from my family and friends" and "The most important things that happen to me involve my family and friends". Cronbach's alpha for this measure was 0.84.

Willingness to become office-based was assessed with one question, developed in conjunction with organizational representatives for this survey: "How willing would you be to take up an office-based position in the near future if it meant greater opportunity for career progression?" Respondents were asked to choose from three response options, where 1 = not at all willing, 2 = somewhat willing and 3 = very willing.

Reasons for unwillingness to take up office-based position for career progression purposes. Employees were asked to select, from a drop-down list or write-in box, the reason(s) why they would be unwilling to take on an office-based position for career progression purposes. These were developed from themes that emerged during the interviews (e.g., caring arrangements; commuting distance) and consisted of eight response options in addition to an "Other" write-in text box. The response options are listed in full in Table 2.5.

Data Analysis

Thematic analysis (Braun & Clarke, 2006) was conducted with the qualitative data. All three researchers followed an iterative process of reading and re-reading the interview transcripts in order to identify recurrent themes, which then became categories for analysis (Fereday & Muir-Cochrane, 2006). Initial codes were generated based on snippets of text that represented a particular concept or idea (e.g. the perceived comfort of working from home). Codes were then sorted into themes, with overarching themes categorized as "organizing themes" and sub-themes as "basic themes" (Attride-Stirling, 2001). The researchers then reviewed the themes for internal homogeneity and external heterogeneity (Patton, 1990) to ensure that basic themes fit together in a meaningful way and that there were clear and identifiable distinctions between organizing themes. A summary of these themes is presented in Table 2.1.

For the quantitative data, one-way analysis of variance (ANOVA), Tukey's honest significance difference (HSD) tests and t-tests were conducted to test differences in mean scores on the study variables between teleworkers, flexible workers and office-based workers.

Qualitative Findings

We explored the career goals of the participants in the qualitative study by asking if there were any other positions within the organization that interested them. Many of the interviewees did not express any aspirations in terms of career development. A number of employees spoke of enjoying the work they currently did and wishing to continue in that role, but many specifically cited the need to work from the office more often in senior-level roles as a "deal breaker" for them.

> *No, because I don't want to give up my teleworking.*
>
> (Louisa, teleworker)

This was particularly the case for employees who worked from home on a full-time basis. Individuals expressed concerns about their ability to readjust to an office setting, as would be required in a higher-level role.

> *I would find it hard to get back in to the routine of going back in to an office and staying all day in an office and then coming home. If I had to I could, but I probably wouldn't choose to do that again after being a teleworker so long with all the benefits.*
>
> (Timothy, teleworker)

> *You get so conditioned or so used to working for yourself in your own office that to come back and have to sit in open plan like that would be very challenging for me which is very worrying really because I may have to do that in the future.*
>
> (Leo, teleworker)

The perception that senior management roles demand office presence was challenged by a senior manager who thought that the organization was misleading employees when communicating requirements for promotion. He also thought this was a sign that the organization was not embracing teleworking as fully as it should be.

> *Half the problem is we don't help because we say if you get promoted, we assume you have to be in the office, where what they should be saying is that if you get promoted you still don't have to be in the office. . . . So we haven't, perhaps, taken the philosophy of [teleworking] . . . as far forward as we could have done. I think that is putting in these little barriers because you should be able to say I am promoting you, and by the way, I am perfectly happy with you being a homeworker.*
>
> (Hugh, flexible worker)

Another issue raised by participants were the difficulties associated with commuting to the organization's nearest office location to take on a higher-level role. Due to the office closures facilitated by telework, the distance between home and work increased a great deal for many employees. Both the length of the commute and the financial costs of travel were cited as deterrents to working in an office-based position.

I don't think I would like to come back to the office because of the amount of travelling, the expense and the time basically.

(Marina, teleworker)

I think one of the downsides of [telework] is that you can easily get into a very comfortable existence like the one I am in where you get used to not commuting, you get used to being your own boss. I am not sure that having done it for so long I could cope with the cost and getting up in the morning and the commuting and the hassle . . . so that is a consideration in terms of career progression. . . . It's too comfortable where I am. That's probably why I've been in the job for 14, 15 years.

(Dominic, teleworker)

Even for individuals who reported a desire to advance within the organization, weighing the financial and lifestyle implications of frequent commuting against the incentives of more challenging work and increased remuneration offered by a promotion often did not result in an attractive cost-benefit ratio.

I would be interested in promotion because I know I am capable of doing more than what I am doing in terms of challenging work. It is whether the promotion would still give me the flexibility that I've got now. As I mentioned earlier, from a financial point of view, I wouldn't be greatly better off, and if that meant that I had to come in to the office four or five days a week I would be significantly worse off. So there is no carrot for me to do it.

(Peter, teleworker)

It should be noted that reluctance to make major lifestyle changes for the sake of career advancement was not limited to teleworkers or flexible workers. There were a number of office-based workers who perceived that the trade-offs required for a more senior position, in terms of travel time to visit clients or other offices, increased responsibility or longer work hours generally, were too steep to make promotion an attractive proposition.

When asked if they envisioned themselves working for their current organization for a long time, few interviewees who made use of telework arrangements expressed any interest in leaving the organization to advance their careers. This intention to remain with their current employer was often linked to both a sense of contentment with their current job role, and the flexibility available to employees in their current position.

I've got no reason to go. The work suits me; it suits my skills. I know so many people here, and to me with all the flexibility, I know in reality I couldn't get this anywhere else, not now. So why would I go anywhere else?

(Joshua, flexible worker)

Some employees and managers reflected on the negative implications for the organization of wide employee take up and commitment to working from home. Telework was viewed as suppressing individuals' identification with the organization and their ambitions to progress their careers. These factors in turn were seen as depriving the employer of engaged, motivated workers ready to assume greater responsibility within the organization.

[P]eople put teleworking before their career aspirations. A lot of our grade, Grade 9, do work from home and wouldn't consider an office-based job because they prefer to work from home, so it can stifle that.

(Grace, teleworker)

The disadvantages to [the organization], I think it can and has created a culture whereby people are disengaged and don't feel an allegiance to [the organization], and also have got themselves in to a position where there isn't another better role for them to do locally because they may be living in an area where there are very little job prospects. So I think it encourages them to stay in jobs long past their sell by date, which is not healthy.

(Karen, manager and flexible worker)

In interviews with managers, the issue of succession planning arose repeatedly. Managers, several of whom used telework arrangements themselves, spoke of difficulties in replacing middle managers due to the reluctance of many individuals in the grade immediately below to consider putting themselves forward for promotion. A large proportion of employees in this grade worked from home for the majority of the working week, and the view of managers was that these working arrangements were either too comfortable, or too convenient with regard to combining work and family responsibilities, for employees to be willing to eschew them for the sake of career progression.

I think the other big issue for us is about succession strategies because there is a huge chunk of what should be our middle management tier that is actually, I think, losing interest in career progression within [the organization] because they've become so comfortable with literally working at home all the time.

(Graham, office-based manager)

> The [drawbacks of telework] are real issues of succession planning, the lack of people who are prepared to be managers, the lack of people prepared to move out of their role into [a] public facing role . . . this is one of the reasons why people don't want to do the supervisory role, they know that the hours are long, and if they've got children, they are going to have to get their own childcare.
>
> (Simon, manager and flexible worker)

One manager reflected on his own history within the organization compared to the career paths taken by his fellow new hires. Although he himself currently engaged in a mix of working from home and traveling each week, his erstwhile peers had taken up full-time telework arrangements years ago and continued to work from home today.

> On the day that I started, four other people started with me on that day in the same office. I am the only one who has ever done anything different in 12 years. Those four other people were all talented people who'd had serious jobs before they came here and were not less ambitious than I was, if you want to put it that way; we were a group of relative peers at the time, both in terms of our experience and our aspirations. It does make me wonder if that fur-lined rut is a bit of a drain on talent. I am sure that some of the people who have, with all due respect, sat in their bedrooms for the last 12 years wouldn't have done so and wouldn't have, necessarily, not progressed both through the ranks and into different, more varied and interesting careers if they hadn't had the facility to go teleworking.
>
> (Richard, manager and flexible worker)

The use of telework arrangements, especially on a full-time basis, thus appears to have a positive effect on employee retention but wields a negative impact on career progression at the individual level and succession planning at the organizational level. The overriding theme that emerged from the qualitative findings was the prioritization of telework over career progression for many employees who worked from home on a frequent basis. The themes discussed in this section are presented in Table 2.1.

Quantitative Findings

The means, standard deviations and intercorrelations among the study variables are reported in Table 2.2. While all respondents answered questions on career orientation and personal life orientation, willingness to become office based was only answered by employees currently designated teleworkers or flexible workers. Items measuring career ambition were positioned toward the end of the survey, and missing answers here are likely attributable to survey fatigue.

Table 2.1 Basic, Organizing and Global Themes

Basic Themes	Organizing Themes	Global Theme
Comfort of working from home		
Lack of privacy/own space		
Different routine	Perceived difficulty in readjusting to working in office	
Less autonomy		
Increased time commuting		
Increased financial cost of commuting	Reluctance to travel for work purposes more frequently	
Inconvenience of travel		Prioritization of telework over career progression
Satisfaction with current work role		
Reluctance to take on more responsibility	Low career aspirations	
No alternative options locally		
Cost-benefit analysis		
Contingent on continuing to work from home at least two days per week	Interest in promotion	
Disengaged employees		
Succession planning	Problems for organization	

Table 2.2 Intercorrelations Among Career Ambition, Career Orientation, Personal Life Orientation and Willingness to Become Office-Based Workers for Purposes of Career Progression Variables

Variable	M	SD	1	2	3
1. Career ambition[a]	3.80	0.58			
2. Career orientation[b]	2.45	0.74	0.24***		
3. Personal life orientation[b]	3.84	0.80	−0.06	−0.54***	
4. Willingness to become office based[c]	1.64	0.72	0.49***	0.19**	−0.13

Note. [a] N = 371. [b] N = 512. [c] N = 224.
** $p < 0.01$.
*** $p < 0.001$.

Table 2.3 One-Way Analysis of Variance of Career Ambition by Telework Status

Source	Df	SS	MS	F	p
Between groups	3	4.52	1.51	4.66	0.003
Within groups	369	119.30	0.32		
Total	372	123.81			

Note: N = 371

Table 2.4 Results of T-Test and Descriptive Statistics for Willingness to Become Office-Based Workers for Purposes of Career Progression by Telework Arrangement

		Telework Arrangement					95% CI for Mean Difference		
		Teleworkers			Flexible Workers				
	M	SD	n	M	SD	n		t	df
Willingness to become office based	1.41	0.62	74	1.70	0.72	132	0.10, 0.49	2.93**	204

Note: N = 224.

** p < 0.01.

An analysis of variance showed that there were significant differences in career ambition between different work arrangements, $F(3,369) = 4.66$, $p = 0.003$. These results are displayed in Table 2.3. Post hoc comparisons using the Tukey HSD test indicated that the mean career ambition score for teleworkers (M = 3.55, SD = 0.46) was significantly lower than that for office workers (M = 3.89, SD = 0.58). The difference between the mean score for teleworkers and for flexible workers (M = 3.79, SD = 0.59) approached significance ($p = 0.059$). There were no significant differences between the scores of office workers and flexible workers.

Analyses of variance did not reveal any significant differences between teleworkers, flexible workers, and office workers with regard to their average scores on career orientation and personal life orientation.

The survey asked employees who make use of telework whether they would be willing to become office-based workers for the purpose of career progression. An independent-samples t-test was conducted to compare answers to this question for teleworkers and flexible workers. There was a significant difference in the scores for teleworkers (M = 4.41, SD = 0.62) and flexible workers (M = 1.70, SD = 0.72); t (204) = 2.91, p = 0.004. These results are displayed in Table 2.4 and demonstrate that flexible workers are significantly more willing than teleworkers to take on an office-based position in order to advance their careers within the organization.

Table 2.5 Reasons for Unwillingness to Take Up Office-Based Position for Career Progression Purposes

Reason for Unwillingness to Take Up Office-Based Position for Career Progression Purposes	*Respondents Citing Reason*
I like the job that I have.	64 (31%)
I am not interested in career progression.	63 (31%)
It would be difficult to manage my home/ family commitments if I were to stop teleworking.	45 (22%)
My commute would be too expensive.	43 (21%)
My commute would be too long.	42 (20%)
I do not like the jobs that are available in the office.	19 (9%)
I do not like the office environment.	19 (9%)
I do not feel qualified to do another job.	6 (3%)
Other: Would not be able to work from office due to disability.	2 (1%)

Note: N = 206 (132 flexible workers, 74 teleworkers)

When asked to identify reason(s) why they would be unwilling to take on an office-based position for career progression purposes, the two options most frequently selected by teleworking employees were "I am not interested in career progression" and "I like the job that I have". Both these options were selected by 31% of respondents to this question. In comparison, 22% of respondents indicated that they would experience difficulties in managing their family commitments if they took on an office-based position, 21% reported that their commute to the nearest office would be too expensive and 20% reported that their commute would be too long. Results are presented in full in Table 2.5.

Discussion

Within our case study organization, employees who made heavy use of telework arrangements displayed considerably less career ambition than their colleagues who spent more time working at the office. These lower levels of career aspirations among teleworkers can be attributed to a number of factors. Working from home on a full-time basis is acknowledged by most organizational members as incompatible with holding a senior position; being promoted therefore necessitates committing to work from the office more often. However, the perception that a senior role would absolutely require office presence may be supported by an organization that values presenteeism among their top managers and does not fully adopt a flexible working culture. This lifestyle change does not appeal to many teleworkers, who value the convenience and comfort of their own work space at home and see more frequent work-related travel in a negative light due to the extra time and expense it incurs. The financial terms of a promotion are not always seen as compensating for the increased responsibilities of a more senior position and the economic and lifestyle costs of commuting to the office more frequently. The teleworkers in this organization clearly perceive a trade-off between holding a more senior position and their quality of life, which includes but is not restricted to work-life balance. Notably, none of the employees in the qualitative study made any mention of family commitments impacting their interest in career progression or lack thereof, and teleworking respondents in the quantitative study did not differ from their office-based colleagues with regard to caregiving responsibilities.

These findings may have theoretical implications as they run counter to several commonly accepted outcomes associated with flexible working practices. First, based on the traditional exchange relationship associated with flexible working practices, there is the presumption that employees who are offered high levels of autonomy in an organization are likely to reciprocate with higher levels of commitment to the organization (e.g., Wayne, Shore & Liden, 1997). However, one possible explanation is that the facilitation of non-work-related activities by telework actually leads to an increase in employees' normative commitment to, or desire to continue in, non-work roles (Allen & Meyer, 1990). Research suggests that antecedents to normative organizational commitment include socialization and investment (e.g., Meyer et al., 2002). Therefore, individuals in extensive teleworking roles may find that the increased investment and socialization in other non-work obligations afforded by the flexibility attributed to telework scheduling, leads to greater commitment in these non-work roles, in effect changing the balance of the exchange with work-related outcomes, such as career progression. Similarly, employee identification with work may be weakened by extensive teleworking. Research suggests that as individuals work from home more extensively, identification with home-related roles may increase (Thatcher & Zhu, 2006).

Another possible theoretical explanation of the impact of telework on career ambition may be related to the uncertainty associated with the changes in the exchange relationship that might arise out of more senior-level organizational obligations. Research has examined the impact of individual differences in positive or negative attributions toward reciprocity as well as uncertainty associated with reciprocity on the relationship between social exchange and affective commitment (Perugini et al., 2003; Shore et al., 2009). "Wary individuals either receiving or extending aid fear that others will violate the reciprocity norm through non-reciprocation of beneficial treatment" (Shore et al., 2009, p. 705). Those demonstrating higher levels of wariness may, therefore, experience less commitment to an organization despite high organizational efforts toward exchange. It might be argued that this wariness can be attributed not only to innate individual qualities but also to the contextual stability associated with telework. Teleworkers may be reluctant to change the nature of their exchange relationship with the organization due to the fear or uncertainty that the greater commitment engendered by taking on a more senior role might not be reciprocated in benefits to them personally.

Given that this study represents a snapshot of employee attitudes rather than having tracked them over a period of many years, it is impossible to ascertain if there is a genuinely causal relationship between telework and career ambition. It is entirely plausible that some employees may self-select into full-time telework arrangements because of pre-existing, low aspirations for career advancement. However, a strong possibility remains that over time, employees experience working from home as so positive a practice that otherwise attractive opportunities, such as career progression, are seen as relatively less appealing. In 2014, Possenriede, Hassink and Plantenga found in their study of a representative sample of the Dutch labor force that while use of occasional telework did not have significant effects on employees' career progression, working from home more often was associated with fewer training opportunities and fewer promotions. They attributed these findings to the reduced visibility of teleworkers in the workplace, which organizational leaders may take as a signal of low commitment and potential for advancement. Our findings cast those of Possenriede et al. (2014) in a new light. While employees in environments focused on "face time" may indeed suffer limited career progression opportunities as a result of working from home, those in more results-oriented organizational cultures that focus less on visibility may simply be opting out of advancement opportunities in order to maintain what they believe is a "prized" work arrangement. For employees whose organizational cultures fall somewhere in the middle—neither strongly focused on visible presence in the workplace, nor strongly emphasizing work results over location of work—working from home for the majority of each week may be associated with fewer opportunities for advancement in conjunction with reduced career ambition. Both drivers of career stagnation may operate in tandem.

Implications for Employers

Embedded flexible work arrangements such as telework may be seen by many as a very positive development, especially if these arrangements are decoupled from career progression processes and users of these practices have the same opportunities as office-based workers to pursue advancement and apply their talents on behalf of the organization. When such circumstances are in place, telework enables organizations to make full use of the skills of all workforce members and can have positive motivational effects on teleworkers. It appears, however, that organizations can have too much of a good thing. In the case study organization examined in this chapter, we see that employees who perform the majority of their work from home are self-selecting out of the managerial pipeline in order to avoid changing their work arrangements to come into the office more often.

There are potentially serious implications of these reduced career aspirations among teleworkers. Senior managers in the organization express concern that succession planning is rendered more difficult by having a large proportion of employees opt out of the promotion process. This is an especially problematic issue for organizations such as that featured in our case study, which have a very specific remit, whose work is not duplicated in other organizations, and who have no competitors per se. These organizations are reliant upon an internal labor market for staffing senior-level positions. When management positions require detailed knowledge of work performed at lower levels and this work is unique to a specific public sector organization, hiring in managers from the external labor market is difficult to do and is likely to result in suboptimal results, in terms of the time required for new managers to acquaint themselves with the operations of the organization and become fully productive in the role (Bidwell, 2011).

How Can These Challenges Be Addressed?

Despite the high-profile withdrawal or reduction in telework availability at firms such as Yahoo, Best Buy and Hewlett-Packard (Lavey-Heaton, 2014), working from home continues to increase due to both employee and employer demand. According to US census data, 50% of the US workforce holds a job that is compatible with at least partial telework and between 80%–90% would like to work from home on at least a part-time basis (Calnan, 2016). In the UK, informal surveys claim that nearly 24% of workers would rather be given permission to work from home one day per week than receive a pay raise (Institute of Inertia, 2017). Given these trends, some resolution to the challenges associated with telework and career progression is essential in order for organizations to retain, motivate and grow the roles of their top performing workers. In addition, telework serves an important role for employment of certain talent groups as well as in specific environmental contexts. For example, working from home is an important way for individuals with disabilities to access the labor market; at present, approximately 160,000 people with a disability work from home in the UK (TUC, 2016). However, if limited career development opportunities are available for employees working from home extensively, will individuals with disabilities lose the opportunity to progress into higher levels of the organizational hierarchy? Similarly, telework may be seen as a "go-to" resolution for organizations, such as public sector organizations, who may be subject to austerity measures and reductions in public spending which constrain their operating budgets and force difficult decisions, such as selling off office space and constraining the use of financial incentives for behavioral change. However, turning to extensive telework to resolve extensive space and incentive issues may reduce organizational growth and competitiveness.

Therefore, managers and employees alike must remember that telework needs to serve the dual agenda of benefiting both workers and employers in order to be effective (Bailyn, 2011). To that end, a happy medium needs to be found between the extremes of a traditional, office-based work arrangement on the one hand and a full-time work from home arrangement on the other. There is a growing body of research to suggest that the best outcomes for both employees and organizations arise when telework is undertaken on a part-time rather than full-time basis. For example, curvilinear relationships have been found between extent of telework and job satisfaction, productivity and both promotions and salary growth, with outcomes appearing to plateau or even decrease at extensive levels of telework (Golden, Eddleston & Powell, 2017; Golden & Veiga, 2005; Hoornweg, Peters & Van der Heijden, 2016). Organizations need, therefore, to be very careful about granting access to full-time telework for employees who would normally be considered eligible for eventual promotion. While working from home for the majority of each week may be appropriate for those who are nearing retirement or whose health conditions preclude them from office-based work, there should otherwise be requirements for teleworkers to spend at least two or three days per week at the office in order to retain them in the talent pipeline.

In addition to this measure, organizations may also wish to make telework usage contingent on an annual review carried out jointly by the teleworker and his or her line manager, rather than granting permission on an indefinite basis for employees to work from home. Is the working arrangement continuing to serve the dual agenda? What are the next steps with regard to career progression for the teleworker? How can the teleworker prepare for a more senior role in the organization? This preparation might require the teleworker to work in the office more often; it might require the organization to re-examine its requirements for managers to maintain a frequent physical presence in the office. Solving the problem of telework and career progression will require flexibility in terms of both thought and action on the part of employees and organizations.

References

Allen, T. D., Golden, T. D., & Shockley, K. M. (2015). How effective is telecommuting? Assessing the status of our scientific findings. *Psychological Science in the Public Interest, 16*(2), 40–68.

Allen, N. J., & Meyer, J. P. (1990). Organizational socialization tactics: A longitudinal analysis of links to newcomers' commitment and role orientation. *Academy of Management Journal, 33*(4), 847–858.

Attride-Stirling, J. (2001). Thematic networks: An analytic tool for qualitative research. *Qualitative Research*, *1*(3), 385–405.

Bailey, D. E., & Kurland, N. B. (2002). A review of telework research: Findings, new directions, and lessons for the study of modern work. *Journal of Organizational Behavior*, *23*(4), 383–400.

Bailyn, L. (1997). The impact of corporate culture on work-family integration. In S. Parasuraman & J. H. Greenhaus (Eds.), *Integrating Work and Family: Challenges and Choices for a Changing World* (pp. 209–219). Westport, CT: Quorum Books.

Bailyn, L. (2011). Redesigning work for gender equity and work-personal life integration. *Community, Work & Family*, *14*(1), 97–112.

Basile, K. A., & Beauregard, T. A. (2016). Strategies for successful telework. How effective employees manage work/home boundaries. *Strategic HR Review*, *15*(3), 106–111.

Beauregard, T. A. (2011). Corporate work-life balance initiatives: Use and effectiveness. In S. Kaiser, M. Ringlstetter, M. Pina e Cunha, & D. R. Eikhof (Eds.), *Creating Balance? International Perspectives on the Work-life Integration of Professionals* (pp. 193–208). Berlin: Springer.

Beauregard, T. A., Basile, K. A., & Thompson, C. A. (2018). Organizational culture in the context of national culture. In R. Johnson, W. Shen, & K. M. Shockley (Eds.), *The Cambridge Handbook of the Global Work-family Interface* (pp. 555–569). Cambridge: Cambridge University Press.

Bidwell, M. (2011). Paying more to get less: The effects of external hiring versus internal mobility. *Administrative Science Quarterly*, *56(3)*, 369–407.

Braun, V., & Clarke, V. (2006). Using thematic analysis in psychology. *Qualitative Research in Psychology*, *3*(2), 77–101.

Caldow, J. (2009). Working outside the box: A study of the growing momentum in telework. Institute for Electronic Government, IBM. Available from http://www-01.ibm.com/industries/government/ieg/pdf/working_outside_the_box.pdf

Calnan, M. (2016, May 20). Number of staff working from home passes 1.5 million. *People Management*. Available from http://www2.cipd.co.uk/pm/peoplemanagement/b/weblog/archive/2016/05/20/number-of-staff-working-from-home-passes-1-5-million.aspx

Canonico, E. (2016). Putting the Work-Life Interface into a Temporal Context: An Empirical Study of Work-Life Balance by Life Stage and the Consequences of Homeworking. Doctoral dissertation, London School of Economics and Political Science.

Dikkers, J., van Engen, M., & Vinkenburg, C. (2010). Flexible work: Ambitious parents' recipe for career success in The Netherlands. *Career Development International*, *15*(6), 562–582.

Elsbach, K. D., Cable, D. M., & Sherman, J. W. (2010). How passive "face time" affects perceptions of employees: Evidence of spontaneous trait inference. *Human Relations*, *63*(6), 735–760.

Eurofound and the International Labour Office (2017). *Working Anytime, Anywhere: The Effects on the World of Work*. Geneva: Publications Office of the European Union, Luxembourg, and the International Labour Office. Available from www.ilo.org/wcmsp5/groups/public/—dgreports/—dcomm/—publ/documents/publication/wcms_544138.pdf.

Fereday, J., & Muir-Cochrane, E. (2006). Demonstrating rigor using thematic analysis: A hybrid approach of inductive and deductive coding and theme development. *International Journal of Qualitative Methods, 5*(1), 80–92.

Fonner, K. L., & Roloff, M. E. (2010). Why teleworkers are more satisfied with their jobs than are office-based workers: When less contact is beneficial. *Journal of Applied Communication Research, 38*(4), 336–361.

Gajendran, R. S., & Harrison, D. A. (2007). The good, the bad, and the unknown about telecommuting: Meta-analysis of psychological mediators and individual consequences. *Journal of Applied Psychology, 92*(6), 1524–1541.

Global Workplace Analytics (2017). *Latest Telecommuting Statistics.* Available from http://globalworkplaceanalytics.com/telecommuting-statistics.

Golden, T., Eddleston, K. A., & Powell, G. N. (2017). The impact of teleworking on career success: A signaling-based view. *Academy of Management Proceedings.* DOI: 10.5465/AMBPP.2017.14757abstract

Golden, T. D., & Veiga, J. F. (2005). The impact of extent of telecommuting on job satisfaction: Resolving inconsistent findings. *Journal of Management, 31*(2), 301–318.

Hewlett, S. A. (2007). *Off-ramps and On-ramps: Keeping Talented Women on the Road to Success.* Boston, MA: Harvard Business Press.

Hoornweg, N., Peters, P., & Van der Heijden, B. (2016). Finding the optimal mix between telework and office hours to enhance employee productivity: A study into the relationship between telework intensity and individual productivity, with mediation of intrinsic motivation and moderation of office hours. In J. De Leede (Ed.), *New Ways of Working Practices: Antecedents and Outcomes* (pp. 1–28). Bingley, UK: Emerald Group Publishing.

Institute of Inertia (2017). The Institute of Inertia looks at the benefits of working from home vs the office. Available from www.comparethemarket.com/inertia/working-from-home-vs-the-office/.

Lavey-Heaton, M. (2014, March 10). Working from home: How Yahoo, Best Buy and HP are making moves. *The Guardian.* Available from www.theguardian.com/sustainable-business/working-from-home-yahoo-best-buy-hp-moves.

Leslie, L. M., Manchester, C. F., Park, T. Y., & Mehng, S. A. (2012). Flexible work practices: A source of career premiums or penalties? *Academy of Management Journal, 55*(6), 1407–1428.

Lobel, S., & St. Clair, L. (1992). Effects of family responsibilities, gender, and career identity salience on performance outcomes. *Academy of Management Journal, 35*, 1057–1069.

Marshall, M. N. (1996). Sampling for qualitative research. *Family Practice, 13*(6), 522–526.

Maruyama, T., & Tietze, S. (2012). From anxiety to assurance: Concerns and outcomes of telework. *Personnel Review, 41*(4), 450–469.

Meyer, J. P., Stanley, D. J., Herscovitch, L., & Topolnytsky, L. (2002). Affective, continuance, and normative commitment to the organization: A meta-analysis of antecedents, correlates, and consequences. *Journal of Vocational Behavior, 61*(1), 20–52.

Munhoz, M. (2016, August 2). Is Latin America ready to embrace a future of remote work culture? Available from www.nearshoreamericas.com/latin-america-picking-work/.

Munsch, C. L., Ridgeway, C. L., & Williams, J. C. (2014). Pluralistic ignorance and the flexibility bias: Understanding and mitigating flextime and flexplace bias at work. *Work and Occupations, 41*(1), 40–62.

Patton, M. Q. (1990). *Qualitative Evaluation and Research Methods*, 2nd edition. Newbury Park, CA: Sage.

Perugini, M., Gallucci, M., Presaghi, F., & Ercolani, A. P. (2003). The personal norm of reciprocity. *European Journal of Personality, 17*(4), 251–283.

Possenriede, D., Hassink, W., & Plantenga, J. (2014). Does face-time affect your career? *Discussion Paper Series/Tjalling C. Koopmans Research Institute, 14*(10). Available from https://dspace.library.uu.nl/bitstream/handle/1874/300231/14_10.pdf?sequence=1.

Richardson, J., & Kelliher, C. (2015). Managing visibility for career sustainability: A study of remote workers. In A. De Vos & B. I. J. M Van der Heijden (Eds.), *Handbook of Research on Sustainable Careers* (pp. 116–130). Cheltenham: Edward Elgar.

Reuters (2017, July 24). Japan launches "telework" campaign to ease congestion, reform work culture. *Reuters.* Available from www.reuters.com/article/us-japan-economy-telework/japan-launches-telework-campaign-to-ease-congestion-reform-work-culture-idUSKBN1A90ET?il=0.

Shore, L. M., Bommer, W. H., Rao, A. N., & Seo, J. (2009). Social and economic exchange in the employee-organization relationship: The moderating role of reciprocation wariness. *Journal of Managerial Psychology, 24*(8), 701–721.

Song, Z., Foo, M. D., & Uy, M. A. (2008). Mood spillover and crossover among dual-earner couples: A cell phone event sampling study. *Journal of Applied Psychology, 93*(2), 443.

Spence, M. (1973). Job market signalling. *Quarterly Journal of Economics, 87*, 355–374.

Thatcher, S. M., & Zhu, X. (2006). Changing identities in a changing workplace: Identification, identity enactment, self-verification, and telecommuting. *Academy of Management Review, 31*(4), 1076–1088.

Trades Union Congress (2016, May 20). Home-working up by a fifth over the last decade, TUC analysis reveals. Available from www.tuc.org.uk/news/home-working-fifth-over-last-decade-tuc-analysis-reveals.

Wayne, S. J., Shore, L. M., & Liden, R. C. (1997). Perceived organizational support and leader-member exchange: A social exchange perspective. *Academy of Management Journal, 40*(1), 82–111.

Wharton, A. S., Chivers, S., & Blair-Loy, M. (2008). Use of formal and informal work-family policies on the digital assembly line. *Work and Occupations, 35*(3), 327–350.

3 Performing the 'Ideal Professional'

Insights From Worker's Accounts of Emotional Labor in Contemporary Workplaces

Carol Linehan and Elaine O'Brien

Introduction

Who is the ideal professional worker in contemporary organizations, and how should s/he behave? Traditionally, rationality was the dominant administrative paradigm or 'frame of reference' (Shrivastava & Schneider, 1984) in organizations and workers were encouraged to construe themselves in ways that emphasized 'being effective', which in turn focused on the importance of rationality, technical skills and task-based competence (Bardon, Brown & Peze, 2017). The prevailing ideology and organizational practices encouraged workers to keep personal and professional domains separate, reinforcing the imperative of work primacy in images of the 'ideal worker' (Dumas & Sanchez-Burks, 2015). Also, as Acker (1990) argued, the ideal worker was required to demonstrate devotion to, and constant availability for, work. A shift from an 'over-rationalised' (Morgan, 1986) conception of organizational life to a recognition that emotional and relational competences are critical in shaping social transactions and contribute to the structure, culture and success of organizations (Fineman, 1993) has, however, resulted in changing expectations of the 'ideal worker'. A growing number of studies document organizational practices that now encourage employees to attend to their emotions (Bolton & Boyd, 2003; Lindebaum, 2012) and incorporate their personal selves into the professional domain (Kreiner, Hollensbe & Sheep, 2009; Ramarajan & Reid, 2013) as well as attempts to capture the sociality, energy and 'authenticity' of workers through encouraging them to 'just be themselves' (Fleming & Sturdy, 2011). Thus perhaps it is time to re-visit expectations of the 'ideal' professional, to examine if there really has been a shift away from the norms of rationality or has the 'ideal worker' image expanded to now include expectations of emotionality that may stand in contradiction to more traditional norms? In this chapter, we explore these questions and in doing so also consider what scope the worker in contemporary organizations may have to act in a way informed by personal as opposed to corporate expectations/ideals.

We argue that attending to the emotional labor required of professional workers will enable us to extend our understanding of the 'ideal' professional worker.

Hochschild (1983) developed the term emotional labor to describe the purposeful efforts workers engage in to conform to norms or display rules which dictate the kinds of emotions employees should and should not express in the performance of their job role. Specifically, we examine the kinds of emotional displays that are required of human resource professionals (HRPs). Our focus on emotion will highlight how work demands in contemporary organizations increasingly require professional workers to display particular emotions as part of their work role. By examining what are deemed to be appropriate and inappropriate emotional displays for HRPs, we tease out dimensions of the 'ideal worker' in contemporary work landscapes. In particular, we wish to attend to the struggles that workers face in living up to such ideals and the personal and professional consequences of deviating from them.

This chapter connects to the overall theme of the book by examining the insight using a lens of emotion can bring to understanding expectations about professional work and work identities in contemporary organizations. We explore how employees make sense of who they are and what it means to be 'professional' in the new organizational landscape where there has been a renewed interest in the area of emotionality (lots of talk about emotion, emotional intelligence, training managers and leaders in soft skills particularly around emotion, etc.) and where employees are encouraged to integrate their 'personal selves' into the professional domain (see Dumas & Sanchez-Burks, 2015; Qvotrup Jensen & Prieur, 2016) but where in practice (as we see from our data) emotions are still seen as irrational and disruptive elements that bias perceptions and interfere with the rational functioning of organizations and only 'appropriate' emotion is allowed.

Constructing the 'Ideal' Professional Worker

In post-bureaucratic organizations, as Alvesson and Robertson (2006) highlighted, control is not achieved predominantly by structure, rules and regulations but by norms, values and shared meanings. In this organizational landscape, Bailly and Léné (2015) explore a new archetype of the 'good worker'. They start from Edward's (1979) classic characterization of the 'good worker' as one who follows the rules, adheres to the spirit of the rules and exhibits loyal and committed behavior that results in workers internalizing corporates aims and values and explore if this still has relevance in contemporary organizations. They highlight that, while flexibility and uncertainty in contemporary workplaces have prompted a shift in the competences that are valued, moving away from adherence to rules towards greater use of relational and soft skills, the underlying corporate normative controls are still very much in operation. Bailly and Léné (2015) identify a new archetype of the good worker:

The personification of competences, a process whereby workers' occupational identities are made dependent on personal characteristics that are a more or less innate or natural part of their make-up, tends to make autonomy a question of personality or character.

(p. 186)

Qvotrup Jensen and Prieur (2016) also point to trends in contemporary work of emphasizing social skills, soft skills, emotional competence, etc., as evidence of a shift from practical or technical skills to an increasing commodification of personal traits or characteristics.

The ability to perform and communicate emotions has thus become a central asset on labor markets.

(p. 101)

The trend in contemporary workplaces to require from workers a particular display of character, including emotion, has been well documented in the emotional labor literature (see Grandey & Gabriel, 2015; or Hulsheger & Schewe, 2011 for reviews of this literature). The intersection of these literatures on ideal workers and emotional labor is useful to make visible the labor, or performance, involved in producing the appropriate and acceptable display of self and emotion in workplaces, rather than assuming that the personal characteristics displayed are simply innate or natural. It provides a useful lens with which to question the 'just be yourself' rhetoric of authenticity (see Fleming & Sturdy, 2011), which eclipses workers' efforts in producing the appropriate self and the degree to which such 'selves' are fashioned to meet corporate needs.

On the theme of fashioning an appropriate self, much of Alvesson's work (e.g. Alvesson & Willmott, 2002; Alvesson, 2010) has examined how individuals construct and sustain particular selves/identities from shared meanings in different types of organization. We position our understanding of professional identity construction within this type of social constructionist framework (see Alvesson, 2010 for an overview of common themes and metaphors across identity theories or Miscenko & Day, 2016 for a review of theoretical approaches) but build on such work via an emphasis on the 'feeling' actor (as well as a thinking, meaning-making actor) to fully explore the construction of professional workers' identities in contemporary landscapes of work. There are interesting complementarities between the concepts of emotional labor and identity as both take a performative view of the individual in context (Goffman, 1959) and both grapple with questions of relations between individual and organizational agency in shaping and regulating experiences, emotion and identity at work. We turn now to elaborate on this concept of emotional labor.

Emotional Labor and Professional Work

In her analysis Hochschild (1983) focused on the way in which work commercializes human feeling and how norms or 'feeling rules' in organizations shaped and controlled workers' emotions and emotion displays to meet organizational ends. Her work explores how employees are expected to manage their emotions and display organizationally prescribed emotions as part of their job role. She presented a largely negative picture of workers being exploited through the emotional labor demands of their job role and in choosing the word 'labor' she highlighted relations of domination and subordination implicit in work (Lee, 1998). She focused on organizational prescription and the display of inauthentic emotions that are used by management as a commodity that can be controlled, trained and prescribed in employee handbooks for the benefit of the organization (Millar, Considine & Garner, 2007). Although she highlighted the 'crucial steadying effect of emotional labor in structuring workplace interactions to maintain a type of civility', she pointed to the 'potential human costs of manufacturing emotion such as burnout and distress' (Hochschild, 1983, p. 187). These costs she related to the link between emotions and a sense of authentic self (Erickson & Wharton, 1997).

Much of the emotional labor literature has focused on frontline service jobs—e.g., checkout operators, waiters/waitresses, airline stewards and call center agents (Grandey et al., 2005; Korczynski, 2003; Shani, Uriely & Ginsburg, 2014)—and in that context, the emphasis on emotional displays has been explicitly driven by organizational concerns with providing better customer service encounters and thereby enhancing the bottom line. However, more recently, there has been a move to consider if professional roles have emotional labor requirements and work such as Harris (2002) on barristers, Ogbonna and Harris (2004) with lecturers, Cascón-Pereira and Hallier (2012) on medics and O'Brien and Linehan (2014) for human resource staff has shown the prevalence of emotional labor across many professional occupations. For example, Kosmala and Herrbach (2006) examined auditor's work and how competing aspects of professionalism can create conflicting emotions for these professionals, leading to a distancing attitude at work. O'Brien and Linehan (2014) outlined the types of emotional labor performed by HR professionals and indicated that as these workers attempt to negotiate the 'caring' (social) and 'control' (economic) requirements of their work that they needed to display many different kinds of emotion to effectively inhabit their roles.

Work in the emotional labor domain is useful to highlight the emotional requirements placed on workers in contemporary occupations and how they respond to such demands. It builds on contemporary perspectives on ideal professionals—as those workers who respond to implicit organizational norms and values to shape their construction of identities in such settings (e.g. Bailly & Léné, 2015; Reid, 2015). It develops such work by making explicit the emotional labor involved in producing appropriate performances or displays of 'feeling' at work, rather than assuming such displays are authentic expressions of self. Attending to these feeling rules gives us further insights into organizational requirements for enacting an ideal professional but by exploring the experiences, and drivers, of such performances in participants' accounts we can also explore the degree to which workers have agency in responding to, and sometimes deviating from, organizational requirements.

Method

The conceptual themes noted earlier are explored empirically as part of a broader qualitative exploration of human resource management professional's experiences of emotional labor. Fifteen human resource professionals were interviewed, 5 on 2 occasions, yielding 20 interviews in total. Each interview lasted 60–90 minutes and explored the nature of their role, if they engaged in emotion management as part of their role and the drivers, experiences and consequences of performing emotional labor. The sample was drawn from a range of industries and from varying types of HR roles (from general HR managers to specialist recruitment/training/compensation roles and at varying levels of experience and seniority). Six men and nine women were interviewed. Through diversity in the sample we sought to access experiences from a range of HR professionals. All interviews were recorded, transcribed and analyzed drawing on a grounded theory methodology (Strauss & Corbin, 1990; Pratt, 2006). The techniques of, for example, constant comparison within and across interviews was used to explore patterns of similarity and difference in participant's experiences. The overall analysis revealed the nature, extent and drivers of emotional labor in this occupational group. We draw from that analysis to consider when and how participants discussed what it means to be an HR professional and what emotional displays are required to live up to that ideal. We present those accounts and themes in the following section.

Findings

Performing as an Ideal Professional

Participants' accounts revealed that emotional labor was a consistent feature of what is required to inhabit and perform their work identities as professionals. Living up to an 'ideal professional' identity clearly drove many emotional labor performances—for example,

I think that sometimes there is huge drama here, but she would never get stressed about it; she would never scream at anybody, never raise her voice; she would never be rude to anybody; she would be very discreet, call someone into an office, just like I think somebody professional should behave.

(P13: Female, HR specialist, recruitment)

The ideal HR professional remains calm, neutral and discreet. This echoes discourses of professionalism for many white-collar workers where rational, objective, emotionally detached performances are required. For our participants, being 'professional' was code for being able to appropriately control one's emotion, which in turn was equated to competence:

My immediate reaction is to lift the phone when I'm feeling more emotional about the situation than I would approach it the following day when I've thought about it and that's coming with experience; I'm stepping back from the situation, and I'm saying look this is how I am now but I'll be able to approach it better in a more rational way the following day

(P3: Female, HR specialist—compensation and benefits)

Or this example:

People say to me, in terms of HR friends or colleagues say, "Look, people do relate to people being human", and you know maybe there is a function in expressing emotion, but it's the rules of the workplace are such that you can't; it's not appropriate to do that

(Female, HR director)

Professionalism also incorporated a separation of the 'work' and 'non-work' self, which it was believed enabled effective and competent role performance.

Leave your bit of baggage at the front door before you come in; it's very difficult to do, but you know people have to do that; you know because it's not fair on other people . . . if the baggage is with you every day or every second day or once or twice a week. . . . [shakes head to show it is not good].

(P15: Male, HR manager)

However, at times more variegated and subtle norms for professional behavior emerged from participants' accounts, and these involved requirements that went beyond merely displaying emotional detachment. A theme emerged from the data based on perceived professional norms around showing enthusiasm at work and sparking enthusiasm and positivity among others. To illustrate this theme, in the extract that follows, a participant describes the difficulties in keeping up the pretense of being 'happy smiley people'.

> I find it difficult to keep up the pretense; you couldn't let your guard down. HR are the happy smiley people; we are always happy and obliging and ready to help.
>
> (P5: Female, HR generalist)

Of course, required displays did not always involve the expression of neutral or positive emotions, sometimes more negative displays were required. Part of the HR role involves communicating and enforcing behavioral standards and at times this required displays of disapproval or reprimand. Here an HRP describes deliberately using an angrier tone in her interaction with a manager who had not followed an agreed upon script in an interaction with an employee during a disciplinary hearing.

> A manager was in the wrong, and you have to be seen to . . . let that manager know exactly that clearly what happened was unacceptable. I could display anger in my tone. . . . I would have been slightly more formal than previous meetings, and my tone would have been sharper, and the displeasure would have been noted . . . it was controlled.
>
> (P6: Female, HR manager)

We can see that the emotional labor HRPs engage in is done partly to meet generalized norms for professionals in work settings (being calm, objective and rational), but it extends beyond that to encompass displays of both positive and negative emotion to meet diverse role requirements. Since varied emotional displays are required to perform different aspects of the role, we would argue that this highlights that there are multiple identity options that professionals can, at least temporarily, align to depending on the interaction context. At times, they are cool, rational professionals; at others, they are rule enforcers displaying disapproval to enforce behavioral standards, and at times, they are 'cheerleaders' displaying and encouraging enthusiasm and positivity at work. All of which, in varying contexts, are what it takes to perform the 'ideal professional' identity in this role.

A pervasive question in the field of identity research is the degree to which actors have agency in identity construction (Alvesson, 2010). The data presented thus far suggests that participants' emotional displays, and the attendant identities performed, are largely done in the service of organizational, rather than personal, ends. On the question of the agency of individuals performing emotion and identity at work, some research (Collinson, 2003) situates worker agency largely in resistance to organizational requirements, or in distancing from organizationally required subjectivities. Gabriel (1999), however, points to opportunities for agency, not just in resistance or distance from corporate controls but also in the everyday struggles of 'obeying and disobeying, controlling and being controlled . . . defining and redefining control for itself and others'. By examining professional workers' accounts of balancing 'what is really me' (bearing in mind that this is, from a social constructionist perspective, an 'imaginary fantasy' of an authentic self (Costas & Fleming, 2009)) with 'who I need to be to be a professional at work', we sought to explore if they were distancing themselves from organizational requirements or seeking to align themselves and their emotions with such requirements to give us some insight into both the organizational requirements for ideal professionals and the degree to which such requirements colonized individuals subjectivities or were resisted by them.

Participants were clearly driven by impression management and a concern for how others viewed them, and engaged in emotional labor as a means of maintaining an image of professional competence. The following participant spoke of the reason why he manages his emotional displays:

> I want to protect my own image and ego to be seen to be a go-getter, maintain this notion I have of myself and the public perception of me
> (P2: Male, HR manager)

Note that though he acknowledges putting on displays of emotion to meet role requirements that he positions this performance as being done to meet both his own personal image of himself as a go-getter as much as meeting/shaping the public view of him. In a similar vein, Haber, Pollack and Humphrey (2014) explored the considerable efforts involved in impression management and termed it 'competency labor'. They argue that contemporary work features increasing demands for competence and that individuals exert considerable efforts to project an image of competency in the face of such demands. They also point to the need to conduct research on the experience of workers who fear a lack of, actual or perceived, competence at work. That fear of perceived incompetence in the eyes of others certainly emerged among our participants. For example, one participant spoke of the necessity of managing her own emotions and her emotional display during an emotional interaction with an employee and revealed the motives behind her behavior:

> I think your credibility as a person with the people you're in the room with, not just the employee but with the managers; they would be saying well hang on now if we have another situation here how is [role holder name] gonna react to it? Are we going to have her breaking down and getting very emotional, which we can't have.
> (P10: Female, HR manager)

Behind this role holder's performance was the desire to maintain credibility in the eyes of other managers as well as protect her future career progression. Such comments demonstrated that individuals may engage in emotion labor as a means to end. This end may be task related or for individual gain and sometimes both. Task and individual goals were not necessarily mutually exclusive as the achievement of one could also facilitate the achievement of the other. For example, both extracts that follow could be interpreted as being driven by maintaining professional credibility, both for the HRPs own reputation and for the HR role more generally—and in both cases to be seen to add value in the organization.

> So you have to be confident in what you say you have to be professional, because if you don't come across as confident and professional, people are going to say, you know they're not going to see you as credible.
>
> (P7: Female, HR manager)

> You are aware yourself that people are looking at you; they are making value judgments about you and your profession, particularly because HR isn't seen as the value-added entity; you are determined to prove that worth and that value of your profession.
>
> (P14: Female, HR manager)

The anxiety about their legitimacy, which has been ascribed to HR professionals, has been claimed by Collinson (2003) and Alvesson (2010) to be a common experience for many workers in contemporary organizations. Collinson (2003) argues that there is a 'broad-sweeping shift from ascriptions to achievement', prompting insecurities for workers as their reputations rest on the most recent success or failure of their endeavors and whether it has added value to the organization. Here we see such insecurities in the HRPs accounts where their concerns for 'value add' or in Collinson's (2003) terms 'achievements', affects their own sense of worth but also how credible and confirmed their professional legitimacy will be in the eyes of others. Alvesson (2010) represents this stream of work in identity research using the metaphor of 'self-doubters', driven by existential conditions of insecurity in work organizations. Whereby workers are not just holding or inhabiting a role and the status flowing from that—but focused on performance, achievements and proving time and again that you are a 'value adding' entity. Clearly, there is some choice/agency for the individual in constructing identity; however, it also needs to be a 'credible and confirmed' construction—that is, one that is accepted and legitimated by others in the organization. Focusing on the emotional displays required to convince oneself and others that you are a credible professional allows us to see (i) the insecurities of professional identities and (ii) the duality of both agentive and controlled shaping of identities—e.g., protecting one's own sense of self as a 'go-getter'—while that very sense of self is stimulated and constructed in response to organizational requirements to add value and simultaneously needs to be confirmed and legitimated by others to be secure.

Although display rules derived from wider normative expectations regarding 'professionalism' and HR occupational expectations, it was evident that these norms were adopted and incorporated into organizational rules and reinforced by organizational culture, talk and practice. In the quote that follows, for example, the role holder describes how he must have a 'professional attitude' because the company requires it.

> They [the company] do want me to have a professional attitude; they don't want to have a lunatic who is in control of salary information and accounts.
>
> (P2: Male, HR manager)

In another example that follows, the participant describes how despite her feelings of stress and overload, she is still very much aware of the need to provide an 'excellent service', and in this situation, she spoke of masking her own feelings in order to fulfill this job requirement. She went on to highlight how the customer service mantra 'customer is always right' overshadows all her interactions, and there was a general sense of frustration at having to meet this externally driven requirement.

> I have a lot on my plate and dealing with customers, and they are looking for stuff, and it's a juggling act; it's frustrating when you don't have enough hours in the day, and I think HR should give an excellent service, and if you give a time line, you should meet it, but sometimes it's not in your control to meet it and that reflects on your professionalism and my own professionalism, and I don't like it; it's not a good feeling.
>
> (P9: Female, HR generalist)

Professionalism here equates with giving 'excellent service' and managing high work demands—being seen to be in control and on top of things—even if such demands may be overwhelming. It is interesting that if she cannot give excellent service in a demanding context, rather than criticizing workload or staffing levels she feels that it 'reflects on "my own professionalism"'. This is evidence perhaps of the 'internalization' of contemporary work demands or the colonization of workers to feel personally responsible for delivering organizational targets.

Such findings have resonance with Alvesson and Robertson's (2006) exploration of 'elite' consultancy staff—where aligning with a professional identity prompted high standards of performance to be self-imposed. Self-categorization as a professional brings high expectations of performance which are reinforced by the need to maintain such behaviors in the eyes of others also—to be credible and confirmed by others as a professional.

> I felt annoyed and powerless as well, but I knew the decision had been made and there was nothing I could do about it . . . you've come to the crux of it; that's what upsets me because I don't agree with it. . . . I don't think it's very professional to show that, no I wouldn't show that.
>
> (P5: Female, HR generalist)

The expectation, as a professional, to align with role and organizational requirements can drive the need to suppress displays that show deviation from organizational actions/decisions, as in the example earlier. There were of course some instances where our professionals did not, or could not, meet requirements (deviance)—and our interest was in what kinds of situations did deviance arise, how did they account for this deviation and what were the personal and professional consequences of doing so.

Deviating From the Ideal

While the high level of work-role identification and desire to fulfill role requirements meant that compliance and success in living up to the rules of the role led to positive personal outcomes it also meant that deviance (i.e., not meeting display expectations) resulted in feelings of dissonance and negative personal outcomes. When participants met organizational display requirements they tended to feel a sense of personal accomplishment and self-efficacy. They talked about feeling "valued" and experiencing a sense of "worth and value", and "a sense of satisfaction" from being able to "put aside" 'inappropriate' emotion. This was particularly true when they received positive feedback from others and their credibility in the eyes of others was promoted. However, when they did not meet organizational requirements regarding emotional display participants tended to experience intense feelings of failure, which were further fuelled by a concern for their reputation as a 'professional' at work.

> One or two times in the early days, I said some things that I wish I hadn't said maybe letting the mask down by throwing my genuine feelings at it rather than the company piece.
>
> (P6: Male, HR director)

This in turn led to negative job consequences for the individual in terms of a lack of task achievement or inability to concentrate as well as negative personal consequences, such as feelings of shame, guilt and self-reproach. For example, the participant who follows described feeling annoyed with herself after inappropriately displaying her anger that an employee had made a complaint against her.

> My emotions were that it was personal against me; I took it personally . . . I shouldn't have displayed such an impulsive reaction; I could have done it much more calmly.
>
> (P4: HRD specialist)

This experience is in stark contrast to the rhetoric of 'just be yourself'/be authentic at work. Here a genuine display of emotion deviated from rules of professionalism—to remain calm and to not take things personally. This is an interesting paradox since the hallmark of many accounts of professionalism is the alignment of personal values with organizational requirements to 'be' a professional.

Another participant described the devastating personal consequences of deviating from the rules.

> I had a couple of managers in here one time in the recent past, and I couldn't believe I had done this, but I told them something I shouldn't have told them, and they knew I shouldn't have told them, and it was quite obvious from my demeanour. I was rigid. I was not breaking out into a cold sweat but next to it.
>
> I felt really stupid and unprofessional, and I felt that I had undermined my credibility not that it was hanging by a very fine wire or anything, but your ego takes a kicking. I felt such an idiot.
>
> During the situation I was flustered. I had stopped listening to what they were saying.
>
> Afterwards, I went out of my way to talk to them individually, not to refer to the incident but to re-establish the even keel of the relationship. I felt really, really bad, not for the person, but I felt bad for myself that I did something stupid.
>
> The feeling went home with me, but I felt so annoyed and embarrassed by it that I didn't tell my wife in case she would get annoyed and worried by it.
>
> (P2: Male, HR manager)

In this situation, the role holder failed to follow the confidentiality rules of his profession. This aroused feelings of intense panic and anxiety. His subsequent inability to successfully manage the aroused emotions in order to adhere to the emotional display rules of the situation (which required him to remain calm and to find a way out of the situation) further compounded his negative feelings and led to a sense of dissonance. His concern for the possible negative effects of his mistake on his credibility led him to take action to try and salvage the situation with his colleagues. The consequences of his inability to fulfill the emotion display requirements of his job reached beyond the workplace and into his home life, where he masked his emotions to protect himself from further embarrassment and his wife from worry.

Data presented suggests that the individual is active, rather than passive, in the emotional labor process and manages their emotional displays not only to achieve organizational goals but also to protect themselves and their reputation. Such findings highlight the point that emotional labor behavior while positioned in part by participants as being driven by external occupational and organizational norms/expectations can also emerge as the individual aligns his/her identity with that of the ideal professional. The latter point is exemplified by the following example in which a participant describes her frustration at the lack of enforcement of display rules in the organization in which she works. She described a situation in which one of the HR team lost her 'cool' when a foreign employee handed in his notice:

> This guy came up to us out of the office, and he was like, "I not work here anymore", and one of the [HR] girls stood up and she said, "You have to work here!" and started roaring at him, and I was like, she shouldn't be working in HR, and this is just a long list of examples, and this is never tackled. . . . That's the type of display that if I was HR manager, and she was reporting to me, I would absolutely annihilate her; that's just ignored. A lot of that behavior is allowed to pass here . . . I find that frustrating and really embarrassing for our department. I don't think it is good enough; it's not professional
> (P13: Female, HR generalist)

This example highlights the fact that rules for the display of emotion within the HR profession are not just created and prescribed by management or the organization but are derived from individual role holder's expectations, based on previous experience and their own standards of behavior.

Sometimes, participants felt that they had been deviant, even when their behavior complied with one aspect of the HR role because they felt that they had contravened the rules of another aspect. As mentioned earlier, success in the HR role is hard to ascertain because of the multiple and contradictory display rules at play. For instance, successfully meeting the display rules of the 'rule enforcer' and expressing disapproval often meant the display rules of the 'cheerleader', 'the happy-smiley HR people', were not met and vice versa. In such cases, participants felt deviant and a sense of failure at not living up to the multiple demands of the role.

The findings here support Bussing and Glaser (1999) who found deviant emotional displays (i.e., that do not comply with organizational requirements) to be positively related to emotional exhaustion and negatively related to job satisfaction. They also suggest that identifying with the role and a desire to live up to role requirements tends to exacerbate the dissonance experienced and to lead to feelings of failure when emotional displays are deemed deviant. This was particularly true when participants perceived that important others (i.e. supervisors) considered their behavior deviant. This is consistent with Reich and Rosenberg (2004) who suggest that when a person perceives congruence between the reflected self-image (i.e., image of ourselves in others' eyes) and self-standards he or she feels recognized, supported and legitimated as an actor in the role. Conversely, they suggest problems are created when the impression of self in the eyes of the audience does not correspond to his/her own self-standards. In this case, role identification meant that organizational/role standards were adopted as self-standards and participants were concerned about their credibility in the eyes of others when they deviated from display expectations.

Thus while identifying with the role may help offset the potential for negative consequences of performing emotional labor it is not sufficient and in fact may work against the individual when they perceived their emotion management efforts to be unsuccessful. The data suggested that to offset dissonance participants not only needed to identify with the role but to attain the skill and experience required to make emotion management efforts successful.

Discussion

The 'ideal' HR professional needs to be skilled at managing emotion (their own and others), but never actually become 'emotional' in the workplace. This chapter has shown that not only do HRPs engage in emotional labor but that a variety of emotion displays are required to perform as a professional in this role. This suggests that despite the apparent shift from an overly rational model of organizing, processes such as non-instrumentality, spontaneity or subjectivity (Ashforth & Humphrey, 1995) are still seen in a negative light and where emotionality may now feed into the image of the 'ideal' worker, only a limited range of the 'right' type of emotion and emotional expression are acceptable in this new ideal. So while rationality and emotionality may now be recognized as both having a role to play in determining behavior in organizations (Ashkanasy, 2002), we see the complexity/ambiguity that this visits on workers. 'Adding on' emotion has not only intensified the need for employees to understand emotions, attend to them and to manage them appropriately according to display rules but now they must reconcile this new discourse of emotionality with traditional notions of professionalism that emphasizes rationality, downgrades emotion and equates emotional detachment with rational competence. The new image of the ideal worker combining rationality and emotionality serves to intensify demands on workers, making attempts to understand and live up to the 'ideal' much more complex.

Requirements for differing kinds of emotional displays highlight the multiple, and at times conflicting, options for their professional identities. Clearly, there are some patterns across participants' accounts that shed light on what it means to be an ideal professional—for example, suppressing extremes of emotion, being seen to be rational, producing displays of neutrality and objectivity, modeling and encouraging positivity and enthusiasm and at times displaying disapproval and reprimand. Many of these displays are driven by concerns with professional competence, particularly around being seen to add value to the organization. In contrast to Reid (2015) who showed how professional service staff had to negotiate between expected (organizationally driven) and experienced (personal beliefs/values) professional identity here, we see a more variegated set of requirements that must be negotiated. For example, at times, there may be conflicting occupational and organizational norms around which display is appropriate in a given context. Clearly, not just employers, but also bodies which train or accredit (e.g., Chartered Institute of Personnel and Development (CIPD); Australian Human Resource Institute) human resource professionals play a role in shaping occupational norms. There are echoes of the CIPD 'Profession Map', which details key behaviors for HR professionals such as "showing enthusiasm", "remains calm", 'communicates in an authoritative, engaging and compelling way' (CIPD, 2018) across participants accounts. Indeed one of the eight key behaviors identified by CIPD is labeled being 'personally credible' and chimes with many participants concerns about creating and maintaining a sense of personal and professional credibility with stakeholders. Thus emotional labor requirements and norms for ideal professionals stem not just from employing organizations but also from educational and professional bodies shaping the occupation.

Our data shows the behind the scenes labor in producing an appropriate emotional display in professional work, driven by personal, occupational and organizational norms around what it means to be a professional worker. This raises questions of 'which' ideal do we mean when we speak of an ideal professional worker in contemporary work landscapes? There are different norms driving displays stemming from the personal, to the profession/occupation, to the organizational. It also gives us a more nuanced picture of what an 'ideal professional' might mean and how that might be enacted. Previous accounts (Acker, 1990; Reid, 2015) have focused on devotion to, and availability for, work as being the defining features of the professional 'ideal'. Yet here by exploring required emotion displays we see that norms and expectations about ideal workers go beyond demonstrating commitment and availability to exhibiting a range of emotional displays to inhabit the role, albeit most of which are focused on meeting organizational needs.

At times, as we have shown, participants did not or could not summon the appropriate emotional display. Such instances of deviating from norms/expectations for an ideal professional often resulted in negative emotional experiences for participants (shame, guilt) and stress at not living up to the role requirements. In some instances, this deviance stemmed from a lack of ability/experience to display required emotion, or a struggle with competing or conflicting display demands in a given context or less often but most impactful on participants—when they disagreed with the required display, e.g., when it did not seem right, or fair to participants or clashed with their values.

Turning to the question of agency in constructing professional identities both personal and organizational drivers and values were evident in participants' accounts. However, if one meets organizational requirements, in terms of giving what is deemed to be an appropriate display, does this necessarily indicate colonization? To assume so negates individual choice and agency in how participants interpret and behave with regard to professional norms of emotion display and attendant identities. The question is how to interpret these—is the HRP who feels personally responsible and committed to 'giving excellent service' an example of a completely colonized worker or by representing her as such are we further negating her agency if the provision of service is indeed of personal value to this individual. Or to examine the opposite scenario where, for example, the participant who speaks of a 'put on' mask or emotional display, in their own terms separating the 'real' me from the work requirements. Is this narration of a dichotomous identity any more or less commodified than the worker who attempts to align with organizational requirements? For example, Costas and Fleming (2009) argue that 'by protecting and/or constructing a back-stage preserve of 'authentic selfhood, actors establish a boundary between what is perceived to be genuine and what is counterfeit' a construction that may 'ironically integrate them into the rhythms of work more effectively given the impression of autonomy it engenders' (p. 354).

Costas and Fleming's (2009) point has resonance with the concept of emotional labor and its portrayal of performed versus authentic emotion—up to a point. In the emotional labor literature, the assumption of authentic emotion and the authentic selves it stems from is generally not questioned. However, by weaving in a performative and social constructionist view of identities, we attend not only to 'front-stage' construction of appropriate emotional and identity displays but also to how the back-stage self is being narrated and constructed. HRPs in this study clearly wished to align themselves with a professional identity and to the extent that the displays required of them fit with this image of self then it alleviated some of the negative consequences of performing emotional labor. However, it is perhaps the 'impression of autonomy' in their accounts that betrays a more subtle form of organizational control in contemporary work.

References

Acker, J. (1990). Hierarchies, jobs, bodies: A theory of gendered organizations. *Gender and Society*, 4(2): 139–158.

Alvesson, M. (2010). Self-doubters, strugglers, storytellers, surfers and others: Images of self-identities in organization studies. *Human Relations*, 63(2), 193–217.

Alvesson, M., & Robertson, M. (2006). The best and the brightest: The construction, significance and effects of elite identities in consulting firms. *Organization*, 13(2), 195–224.

Alvesson, M., & Willmott, H. (2002). Identity regulation as organizational control: Producing the appropriate individual. *Journal of Management Studies*, 39(5): 619–644.

Ashforth, B. E., & Humphrey, R. H. (1995). Emotion in the workplace: A reappraisal. *Human Relations*, 48(2), 97–125.

Ashkanasy, N. M., & Daus, C. S. (2002). Emotion in the workplace: The new challenge for managers. *Academy of Management Executive*, 16, 76–86.

Bailly, F., & Léné, A. (2015). What makes a good worker? Richard Edwards is still relevant. *Review of Radical Political Economics*, 47(2), 176–192.

Bardon, T., Brown, A. D., & Peze, S. (2017). Identity regulation, identity work and phronesis. *Human Relations*, 70(8) 940–965.

Bolton, S., & Boyd, C. (2003). Trolley dolly or skilled emotion manager? Moving on from Hochschild's managed heart. *Work, Employment and Society*, 17, 289–308.

Bussing, A., & Glaser, J. (1999). Work stressors in nursing in the course of redesign: Implications for burnout and interactional stress. *European Journal of Work and Organizational Psychology*, 8, 401–426.

Cascón-Pereira, R., & Hallier, J. (2012). Getting that certain feeling: The role of emotions in the meaning, construction and enactment of doctor managers' identities. *British Journal of Management*, 23, 130–144.

Chartered Institute for Personnel and Development (CIPD) (2018, February 8). Available from www.cipd.ie/learn/career/profession-map.

Collinson, D. (2003). Identities and insecurities: Selves at work. *Organization*, 10(3): 527–547.

Costas, J., & Fleming, P. (2009). Beyond dis-identification: A discursive approach to self-alienation in contemporary organizations. *Human Relations*, 62(3), 353–378.

Dumas, T., & Sanchez-Burks, J. (2015). The professional, the personal and the ideal worker: Pressures and objectives shaping the boundary between life domains. *The Academy of Management Annals*, 9, 803–843.

Edwards, R. (1979). *Contested Terrain: The Transformation of the Workplace in the Twentieth Century*. New York: Basic Books.

Erickson, R. J., & Wharton, A. S. (1997). Inauthenticity and depression: Assessing the consequences of interactive service work. *Work and Occupations*, 24, 188–213.

Fineman, S. E. (1993). *Emotion in Organizations*. Thousand Oaks, CA: Sage.

Fleming, P., & Sturdy, A. (2011). "Being yourself" in the electronic sweatshop: New forms of normative control. *Human Relations*, 64(2): 177–200.

Gabriel, Y. (1999). Beyond happy families: A critical reevaluation of the control-resistance-identity triangle. *Human Relations*, 52(2): 179–203.

Goffman, E. (1959). *The Presentation of Self in Everyday Life*. New York: Doubleday.

Grandey, A. A., Fisk, G. M., Mattila, A., Jansen, K. J., & Sideman, L. (2005). Is service with a smile enough? Authenticity of positive displays during service encounters. *Organizational Behavior and Human Decision Processes*, 96(1): 38–55.

Grandey, A. A., & Gabriel, A. (2015). Emotional labor at a crossroads: Where do we go from here? *Annual Review of Organizational Psychology and Organizational Behavior*, 2, 323–349.

Haber, J., Pollack, J. M., & Humphrey, R. M. (2014). Competency labor: A conceptual framework for examining individuals' effort and emotions in projecting an image of competence at work. In Chapter 12 in *Research on Emotion in Organizations* (Vol. 10, pp. 305–330). Emerald Group Publishing.

Harris, L.C. (2002). The emotional labor of barristers: An exploration of emotional labor by status professionals. *Journal of Management Studies*, 39, 553–584.

Hochschild, A. R. (1983). *The Managed Heart: Commercialization of Human Feeling*. Berkeley: University of California Press.

Hulsheger, U. R., & Schewe, A. F. (2011). On the costs and benefits of emotional labor: A meta-analysis of three decades of research. *Journal of Occupational Health Psychology*, 16(3), 361–389.

Korczynski, M. (2003). Communities of coping: Collective emotional labor in service roles. *Organization*, 10(1), 55–79.

Kosmala, K., & Herrbach, O. (2006). The ambivalence of professional identity: On cynicism and jouissance in audit firms. *Human Relations*, 59, 1393–1428.

Kreiner, G. E., Hollensbe, E. C., & Sheep, M. L. (2009). Balancing borders and bridges: Negotiating the work-home interface via boundary work tactics. *Academy of Management Journal*, 52(4), 704–730.

Lee, C. K. (1998). *Gender and the South China Miracle: Two Worlds of Factory Women*. Berkeley: University of California Press.

Lindebaum, D. (2012). I rebel—Therefore we exist: Emotional standardization in organizations and the emotionally intelligent individual. *Journal of Management Inquiry*, 21(3), 262–277.

Millar, K., Considine, J., & Garner, J. (2007). "Let me tell you about my job" Exploring the terrain of emotion in the workplace. *Management Communication Quarterly*, 20(3), 231–257.

Miscenko, D., & Day, D. (2016). Identity and identification at work. *Organizational Psychology Review*, 6(3):1–33.

Morgan, G. (1986). *Images of Organization*. Beverley Hills, CA: Sage.

O'Brien, E., & Linehan, C. (2014). A balancing act: Emotional challenges in the HR role. *Journal of Management Studies*, 51(8), 1257–1285.

Ogbonna, E., & Harris, L.C. (2004). Work intensification and emotional labor among UK university lecturers: An exploratory study. *Organization Studies*, 25, 1185–1203.

Pratt, M.G., Rockmann, K.W., & Kaufmann, J.B. (2006). Constructing professional identity: The role of work and identity learning cycles in the customization of identity among medical residents. *Academy of Management Journal*, 49(2), 235–262.

Qvotrup Jensen, S., & Prieur, A. (2016). The commodification of the personal: Labor market demands in the era of neoliberal postindustrialization. *Distinktion: Journal of Social Theory*, 17(1): 94–108.

Ramarajan, L., & Reid, E. (2013). Shattering the myth of separate worlds: Negotiating non-work identities at work. *Academy of Management Review*, 38(4), 621–644.

Reich, W. A., & Rosenberg, S. (2004). Reflected self-image and commitment to a career role. *Self and Identity*, 3, 115–123.

Reid, E. (2015). Embracing, passing, revealing, and the ideal worker image: How people navigate expected and experienced professional identities. *Organization Science*, 26(4), 997–1017.

Shani, A., Uriely, N., & Ginsburg, L. (2014). Emotional labor in the hospitality industry: The influence of contextual factors. *International Journal of Hospitality Management*, 37, 150–158.

Shrivastava, P., & Schneider, S. (1984). Organizational frames of reference. *Human Relations*, 37, 795–809.

Strauss, A. L., & Corbin, J. (1990). *Basics of Qualitative Research. Grounded Theory Procedures and Techniques*. Newbury Park, CA: Sage.

4 Working as an Independent Professional

Career Choice or the Only Option?

Tui McKeown

The recent growth of professionals working on a self-employed basis has been viewed as either a positive indicator of economic vitality or, alternatively, as a labor-market warning. These polarized views rest essentially on two opposing points of entry into self-employment—indicating either an 'entrepreneurial pull' or 'unemployment push.' There are also those who suggest that the sudden and rapid expansion of professional self-employment heralds that a new 'normal' is emerging in configuring work and career.

This chapter will offer both conceptual and empirical evidence to investigate the career intentions of self-employed professionals. Drawing on data from a range of Australian professionals working independently (hence the term independent professional or IPro that will be used throughout this chapter), the chapter will investigate notions of volition, satisfaction and career intentions. Prior research indicates that the generally highly positive results found for IPros in terms of volition and satisfaction become more revealing when broken down by these demographic variables—and that these nuances have important implications for the notion of an IPro career.

The chapter is organized into three sections. The first will provide a very brief overview of the recent debates within the literature on self-employment, as this is already well covered in prior chapters, to focus on the emerging discourse on the position on professional occupations. The second section will then present Australian data from a study of professionals working as independent contractors. The focus of the empirical section is on three key issues: the ways in which the IPros account for their move into this form of work, their satisfaction and the results of the move, and the extent to which they see this as a viable and sustainable career option. The concluding section goes to the theme of this book in offering a consideration as to how the roles of professionals, the organizations using their services and wider society in maintaining, retaining and sustaining what has become an increasingly vital component of the twenty-first-century workforce.

The Push and the Pull of Self-Employment

The last decade has seen marked shifts in the world of work. The changes are associated with powerful drivers, ranging from global competition and new technologies to the increasing fragmentation of work (Gratton, 2014; International Labour Organization, 2016). They are changes that are visibly reflected in aspects such as the increasing feminization of the workforce, or more subtle, such as the rising numbers working in non-traditional arrangements such as part time, casual, temporary and contract work.

Whether seen or unseen, they are changes which increasingly challenge traditional notions as to when, where and how work is performed and perhaps most fundamentally, transforming our notions as to what work actually 'looks' like. As Stone, Dagnino and Martínez (2017, p. vii) note, the changes occurring "follow different patterns in different countries, yet their dynamics are so interrelated that it is often hard, if not impossible, to distinguish the causal relationships among them." For example, a 2017 report by Manyika et al. from McKinsey suggests that

> independent workers (the term they use to capture everything from thee self-employed and temporary worker to uber drivers), accounts for 20–30 % of the working age population in the United States and in the EU. There are estimates that this will increase to 50% by 2030.
> (Pofeldt, 2016; Spera, 2017)

And with one researcher identifying over 130 different types of freelance careers so far (Shanbrom, 2017), the complexity and opacity associated with this area is likely to increase.

Narrowing the focus specifically to one of self-employment thus helps to reveal some of the tensions involved in these changes. While referring to the United Kingdom, Hatfield (2015) captures the wider issues well. She offers that the 40% rise in the British job market since 2010 attributed to self-employment has prompted

> a complex debate about the extent to which this should be celebrated. Some commentators have heralded it as a sign of entrepreneurial spirit, innovation and future economic growth, while others fear it is primarily indicative of a rise in precarious, insecure work.
> Ibid p. 3; Manyika et al., 2017; OECD, 2017)

Part of the explanation for such disparate views lies in the framing of self-employment as much of the discourse is within the context of contingent, atypical or non-standard work (ILO, 2016). While data on such arrangements are notoriously hard to aggregate, published statistics reveal that they capture over 20% of the American workforce (BLS, 2014) to almost 30% of the Australian labor market (ABS, 2016). The nub of the problem is that, as Cappelli and Keller (2013, p. 575) note, "alternatives to the archetypal model of full-time regular employment are now prevalent and wide ranging . . . yet most of our management and social science notions about economic work are based on the full-time employment model."

Many of the benefits that organizations derive from the use of workers, such as the self-employed, is precisely because they fall outside of the conventional provisions and protections often associated with employment (Blanpain Nakakubo & Araki, 2010). There is even a body of literature identifying the use of this workforce to purposefully circumvent obligations covering standard employees (Leighton & Wynn, 2011). However, the non-standard workforce can also be used to provide access to knowledge and expertise not available in-house (OECD, 2017; Taylor Marsh, Nicol & Broadbentl, 2017).

Added to the aforementioned, there is also evidence of individual preference for working as a non-employee, with many researchers agreeing with the sentiments expressed by Ashford George and Blatt (2007, p. 69), suggesting that the push from employers may be balanced by individual demand as people "take their careers into their own hands, construct their identities as professional and entrepreneurial, and view organizations in an increasingly negative light." This view is supported by the recent *Taylor Review* (Taylor et al., 2017) in the United Kingdom and research that reveals that those choosing non-employee status are often individuals who see themselves as multi-taskers, who have a holistic approach to work—who like to 'think outside the square' and 're-invent' themselves' so they can adapt to changing market requirements (Leighton & McKeown, 2015).

There are some for whom the move to self-employment may be in response to occupation or industry socially embedded norms and practices (Barley & Kunda, 2006; McKeown & Cochrane, 2017). For others, self-employment may provide a transition to re-enter the labor market after job loss or unemployment spells, involve periods of unemployment or be the result of limited work opportunities and options (Hyytinen & Rouvinen, 2008).

A key question that emerges is, is self-employment a career option—more specifically, is it a way of work that can be maintained and sustained within the concepts normally associated with that of having a career?

Career Theory and the Fit With Self-Employment?

Very much aligned with the disparate views on self-employment noted earlier, the body of literature explicitly exploring self-employment as a career option is not only relatively small but also largely limited to one of two polar extremes. On one side are studies which present self-employment as a fall back or default option for the marginalized and vulnerable—with migrants, ethnic minorities and women being the typical 'unit' of examination (see, for example, Granger, Stanworth & Stanworth's 1995 study of the "unemployment push in UK book publishing" or Cahill, Giandrea & Quinn's 2013 study of the "self-employment transitions among older Americans with career jobs"). Issues of choice and volition (or often the lack thereof) tend to characterize these studies. On the other side are those in positions of labor-market advantage—often presented as a high-tech elite (see, for example, futurologists, such as Bridges, 1994, writing about the 'end of the job' or Lozano, 1989 and the 'prima donna' workforce of the IT sector).

Given the wealth of detail on career theories in other chapters in this book, this section will narrow the discussions on these to focus on self-employed professionals as individuals who could reasonably be exemplars of the protean and boundaryless career theories in particular. The perspective will allow us to examine the implicit assumptions that still constrain how we think about careers. The notion of career is still typically embedded within the boundaries of the organization, where it is characterized by an ordered, predictable and upward trajectory of hierarchical progression—and where each step brings an associated increase in status and financial reward, as well as increased responsibility (a notion which dates back to Hall & Mirvis, 1995). While these constraints are now often located within the context of the changes noted in the earlier section, which have seen the careers become increasingly short-term, more mobile and flexible and even precarious (ILO, 2016; OECD, 2017), they still largely bounded by expectations of working within organizational contexts. For instance, in the notion of 'boundaryless' suggests that it is the permeability and mobility within and between organizations that is important and, while the protean career sees "the person, not the organization, is in charge" (Hall, 2004, p. 4), the organization still remains an essential element.

However, these changes occurring increasingly reveal the need for a more macro focus, as both organizational and individual expectations about work and career are situated within a larger context of society and the institutions associated with it. This sees an increasing realization as to the importance of factors, such as the laws surrounding labor and employment, through to the systems of welfare support and education they are embedded in are enacted through. These macro contextual factors also include cultural and economic dimensions, and they combine to provide the parameters that the boundaryless and protean career concepts often fail to acknowledge (Tams and Arthur, 2010; LaPointe, 2013). Indeed, there is a wealth of research into the implications of career theories that consistently identifies that precariousness is the key feature of protean and boundaryless work—and that such an arrangement operates to marginalize "lower skilled workers, women and minorities for whom boundarylessness simply means unemployment, insecurity and anxiety" (Inkson et al., 2012, p. 328).

Overall, the literature explicitly exploring self-employment as a career option is largely limited to examinations of it as a default option for the marginalized and vulnerable, or a position of labor-market advantage for an elite few; career theory appears to not only be relevant but also increasingly vital to apply to this work arrangement. Further, investigation of the growing body of professionals working as self-employed appears to offer the opportunity to reveal a view from individuals who could reasonably be expected to be part of this elite group.

Who Are Self-Employed Professionals?

A key feature within a world of work characterized by escalating change is the increasing number of individuals falling outside the once standard view of a worker as a male in a full-time stable job of an indefinite duration (Vorhauser-Smith & Cariss, 2017). Within this trend, the professional contractor workforce has been identified as a significant area of growth and covers occupations from high-level executives, accountants and information technology specialists through to educators, translators, scientists and attorneys (ILO, 2016; OECD, 2017). Note that while professions are variously defined, it is widely agreed that they are occupations distinguished by education and expertise, autonomy, values, identity and social ties (Adler & Kwon, 2013).

> Put into the context of the changes noted in the introduction to this chapter, professional work thus emerges as interwoven with the development of the 'knowledge economy' commonly seen as the foundation for the future prosperity of most nations (Yigitcanlar, 2010; OECD, 2016). In Australia, for example, professionals already account for approximately one in five workers, with their share of the workforce expected to increase further over coming years.
>
> (ABS, 2017)

Given the hyperbole surrounding the rise of the gig economy and the end of the traditional employer/employee basis of work, it is important to situate the independent self-employed professional (the IPro). While definitions remain contentious (Leighton & Wynn, 2011), the consensus is that IPro work attracts highly qualified individuals with unique human capital (Casale, 2011; Eurofound, 2017). IPros operate at the elite end of the non-employee spectrum with the premium attached to specialized skills seeing these individuals highly sought after by organizations requiring their expertise and abilities, and willing to pay generously (Bryant & McKeown, 2016).

As a subsector of non-standard work, IPros provide a rare opportunity to investigate what is happening at the 'high end' of this workforce. They account for over 32% of all non-standard workers in Australia in 2016 (ABS, 2017) and typically perform analytical, conceptual and creative tasks through the application of theoretical knowledge and experience in the fields of science, engineering, business and information, health, education, social welfare and the arts (ABS, 2013). The use of intellect and experience, rather than machinery and tools, for most professional occupations typically requires a level of skill commensurate with a bachelor's degree or higher qualification.

As already noted, combining professionals and self-employment generally yields the view of a privileged position within the changing world of work that remains relatively unquestioned. While studies of the growth in non-traditional work arrangements talk of marginalization and uncertainty, there is scant research addressing such issues within the context of the professional workforce. Indeed, the polarization between what Marler, Barringer and Milkovich (2002, p. 425) term the "boundaryless and the traditional contingent worker" highlights assumptions that professionals occupy a privileged labor-market position and possess a strong, well-developed sense of 'career.'

While studies of the growth in non-traditional work arrangements raise the important issues of marginalization and uncertainty, very little research addresses these within the context of the professional workforce. This is surprising given that a fundamental assertion of much of the theoretical literature on the future of work, with project work in particular being a feature of this future, is how suited professionals are to take advantage of it. There are even those who propose that the attributes that characterize such workers will, one day, become the way of work for the majority. Essentially, professionals are seen as being 'pulled' into non-standard work arrangements because of opportunity rather than being 'pushed' because of constraints such as redundancy and unemployment.

However, the reality is that we really know less about professions than we think. For instance, the privilege many associate with the medical profession quickly disappears when we find that many employed in the 'super clinics' that now pervade Western suburbia are actually contract employees—with responsibility for their own superannuation, sick and holiday pay, etc. (Jamrozik, Weller & Heller, 2004). The fact is that we know relatively little about how workforce arrangements affects the career aspirations of working in these arrangements—even within the university environment where much of push to research and academic writing is seeing teaching supplemented by increasing numbers of sessional staff employed on a part-time and casual basis such as universities' employment (Williams & Beovich, 2017).

Combining the notions of profession and career also provides a distinct aspect to the concept of career intent in terms of progression and planning. Decreasing tenure and increasing rate of 'job hopping' shorter organizational associations may in fact see very little difference in the career aspirations of traditional versus non-traditional workers. However, issues such as the portability of superannuation and access to organizational training opportunities still tend to elude the latter. Self-employment, while offering greater freedom and flexibility, also is commonly associated with greater financial insecurity and lack of access to traditional employment entitlements, such as superannuation, sick and holiday leave. As Leighton and Wynn (2011, p. 36) note,

> The orthodoxy has long been that the essence of the distinction between the employee and the self-employed is that of opportunity and risk. The genuine employee bears little financial and other risks; the self-employed carries far more risk, especially in terms of work instability and investment in materials, etc.

One result is a concern that countries, like the United Kingdom where the share of self-employment is rising, may need to look at job quality rather than just the standard indicator of quantity (Hatfield, 2015).

Framing the IPro Career

This third section of the chapter draws on both the wider academic literature, and presents data drawn from a seven-year (2009 to 2015) study of Australian IPros. The focus of the empirical contribution is on three key issues: the ways in which the IPros explain their move into this form of work, their satisfaction with this form of working and the extent to which they see this as a viable and sustainable career option.

Drawing on an online survey of professionals registered with one of Australia's leading contractor management companies, the IPros surveyed over this seven-year period provide for a diverse group in their personal and work-related characteristics. With between 200–400 responses each year and a response rate typically around 30%, the overall profile sees the majority of respondents as males (64%), Australian citizens (80%) and aged in their late 20s to mid-40s. Two-thirds of the respondents were educated to the bachelor degree or a higher level and work experience as an IPro ranged from less than 1 year to up to 45 years. The majority (61%) reported they had not had a previous work contract with their current client and three major industries dominated with information technology and telecommunication (42%), engineering and mining (18%) and accounting and finance professions (11%) making up over 70% of respondents. The results reported here are from two of the five sections used consistently for each of the seven years, while Section 6 on ingoing aspirations was added in 2013.

IPros may be faced with many challenges often associated with non-standard work arrangements, while at the same time, they are likely to begin new ventures in the future and provide key sources of innovation and job creation, which ultimately leads to economic growth and prosperity. Uncovering mechanisms that support and sustain IPro careers is of benefit at the individual, organization and national levels. The need to pursue a 'self-managed career' appears to be very much the reality for an increasing percentage of the workforce working outside of traditional organizational career structures. The question is how does this play out over the life course of the individual IPro? Are their career decisions made within the context of a wider institutional environment where perhaps labor and employment law constraints are circumvented by this form of work, and perhaps allow the individual to exercise greater control in his or her negotiations with client organizations?

The 'push' versus 'pull' theories of employment, with their origins in the classic economic theories of 'career' (Knight, 1933) versus 'default' (Schumpeter, 1934) are clearly appropriate to this workforce. The decision for the professional is essentially a self-employment/paid-employment choice based on the individual identifying the opportunities and constraints associated with each. While the voluntary versus involuntary nature of this decision is explicit within most studies of self-employment, it is often treated as being of little relevance to the professional.

The push and pull of self-employment takes on a very specific focus when applied to the careers of IPros. They present a group that aligns well with the assertion by Ashford, George and Blatt (2007, p. 69) that there is an increasing move of those who "take their careers into their own hands, construct their identities as professional and entrepreneurial, and view organisations in an increasingly negative light." Ardichvili and Kuchinke (2009, p. 155) go further to suggest that career management now "includes preparation for living as independent contractors and consultants with rapid changes in terms of the meaning of working and the issues this raises for of talent management and employee engagement."

Mention must also be made of the body of literature devoted to IT, construction, engineering, the creative industries and architecture where IPros have long been an industry and professional norm (see, for example, Hyytinen & Rouvinen, 2008; Lee, Wong & Tong, 2014)

Career Drivers

Applying the notion of push and pull forces to career decisions also implies the concept of agency—that to be 'successful' in a career means making choices and then, as Bandura (1997, p. 2) suggested, "to intentionally make things happen by one's actions." IPros appear to capture both individuals who have made an active and positive career choice and operate at the 'high end' of the peripheral or non-standard labor market. This aligns well with both protean and boundaryless career notions of 'taking charge' of one's own career.

The notion of an agentic pathway into the investigation of the IPro career provides some interesting suggestions. For instance, in writing about the protean career, De Vos and Soens (2008) offer that an individual must be able to develop a capacity for understanding and managing the self, as this is what allows them to convert attitude into career success outcomes, such as ongoing employability and career satisfaction. Taking this wider perspective, the motives for entering into an IPro work arrangement are important factors in determining career outcomes, a view which resonates De Vos and van Heijden's (2015) work on career sustainability.

Further, placing the notion of the IPro career within the organizational context also identifies another aspect of the potential drivers for an individuals' move to this way of working. For instance, Lozano (1989) offers a 'prima donna and grunt' theory of the workforce. Here, skilled professionals equate to an uncontrollable and aberrant workforce assigned to the organization's periphery and subject to a different set of HRM rules, a notion supported by writers such as Koene and Riemsdijk (2005) and Hall (2006). Contrary to common perceptions of professionals operating from a position of advantage, Lozano's suggestion of prima donna and grunt workforces sees IPros operating in organizations where social isolation and separation are likely and, for the organization at least, even desirable. In such situations, the worker is disadvantaged.

An Australian IPro Perspective

This section presents the results of data gathered over seven years of surveying IPros in Australia to provide some insight into just what does motivate, retain and sustain this form of work as a career. As Figure 4.1 shows, while pull factors dominate, the notion of the IPro career is much more complex than an explanation of being driven by either a simple push or pull factor.

Figure 4.1 identifies the top-six factors selected by participants to explain why they were currently working as an IPro. The results reveal consistent patterns across the seven years, with the lack of push factors (that they were not being driven by difficulty in finding permanent work, not the result of job loss and not the result of a tight labor market), rating as important to very important for over 50% of respondents nearly every year. Given the dynamic and even turbulent nature of the changes discussed in the opening to this chapter, the lack of push factors identified by IPros is interesting and indicates that volition is a key feature of this arrangement. Individuals are either working this way by choice, not as a default option, or because they feel pushed.

Looking at this result another way, these 'non-push' factors are also consistently rated significantly higher than the drivers traditionally cited in self-employment research as part of the pull into this form of work,

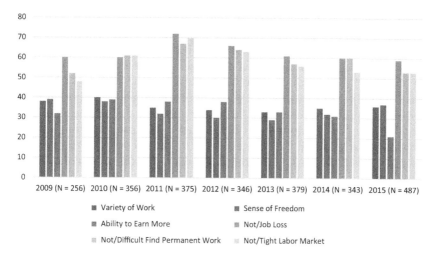

Figure 4.1 Push and Pull of Working as an IPro

such as the importance of a variety of work, the ability to earn more and a sense of freedom. This is not to say that IPros do not experience insecurity, marginalization or vulnerability. What it does suggest is that the IPro career seems to be one that is actively chosen and that it is a choice associated with increased job quality. This result resonates strongly with the 'free agents' quadrant noted in the EU and US results of independent workers reported by Manyika, Chui, Madgavkar and Lund for McKinsey in 2017.

A second key aspect from career literature discussed earlier is the notion of satisfaction. As Hatfield (2015) notes, a key feature of self-employed work is that individuals enjoy the benefits of being their own boss—the greater freedom and flexibility over their own work reflected in Figure 4.1. The self-employed also typically report very high levels of satisfaction with their work. The European Social Survey (EWCS, 2010) reveals evidence that supports this: in 2010, 37% of self-employed workers in Europe rated their job satisfaction as a 9 or 10, on a scale of 0 to 10. This compares with just 26% of those in employee jobs. Further, the high levels of IPro satisfaction also resonate with the results of the 'free agent' segment of the 2017 McKinsey study of independent workers.

Figure 4.2 provides two perspectives from Australian IPros, offering views of satisfaction with working as an IPro as well as with the work they actually do. The distinction between the two is consistent across the seven-year period, with high to very high satisfaction with working as an IPro for around the 68% to 75% of all IPros. Satisfaction with the actual work that they do is even higher and varies from a high in 2009 when

88% of surveyed IPros were highly to very highly satisfied with their work, down to a steady rate of around 70–72% for most other years.

Prior research has noted that it is the nature of the work itself that emerges as the most important facet in job satisfaction, and that while it is predictive of performance, this is strongest for professional jobs (Judge et al., 2001). The distinction between working as an IPro and the work they actually perform allows separation of the larger notion of an IPro career from the day-to-day realities of the job. What is surprising in this separation is that it appears to be the latter that provides the greatest source of satisfaction. This result seems to accord with the suggestion from De Vos and Soens (2008) that individuals must be able to develop a capacity for understanding and managing the self, as this is what allows them to convert attitude into career success outcomes—such as ongoing employability as well as career satisfaction. However, they also suggest that this relationship is linked to perceptions of the opportunities available. This suggestion was examined with Australian IPros in two ways; first is the intent to remain working as an IPro and the second is perceptions of the ability to find either similar or better work.

Lack of individual attachment to one specific work arrangement is frequently cited as a key feature of the changing world of work and provides a useful counterpoint to the discussion earlier. While it seems that IPros should have a long-term desire to continue working this way, there is a growing body of literature questioning whether contracting is a bridge to a sustainable lifestyle or an inescapable trap (De Vos & Van der Heijden, 2015; Xhauflair, Huybrechts & Pichault, 2017). The results presented in Figure 4.3

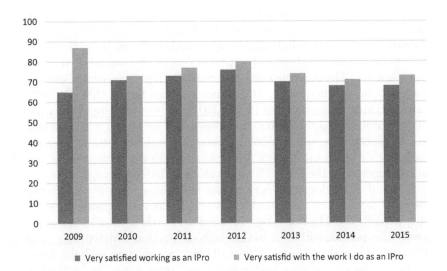

Figure 4.2 Satisfaction as an IPro

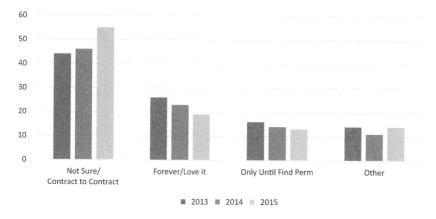

Figure 4.3 Intentions to Remain Working as an IPro

summarize intent to the questions as to the individual's intent to remain or to leave in the next (note that this question was only used from 2013 on).

The results provide a startlingly different perspective on the career of the IPro. Rather than an ongoing dedication and commitment to this way of work, the consistent theme across the three years is that it is very much a contingent way of work. It is taken on by between 43% (in 2013) to over 55% (in 2015) on a 'contract to contract' basis. This increase is concomitant with a decreasing trend for the next most popular response, which does cover the dedicated IPros we had expected to dominate, those who see themselves as 'doing it forever because I love it.' This was at a high of 27% in 2013 but has decreased to around 19% just two years later. This rather surprising finding is tempered with the slight decline in preference for permanent work as well as the quite consistent result for 'other.' Free text comments accompanying this latter category identified labor market exit options, such as retirement, maternity and childcare, as well as migration as key explanations.

These explanations do align with the recent model developed by Tomlinson et al. (2018), which presents a life course perspective that takes into account key transition points and life stages. While writing specifically about flexible careers rather than specifically about IPros, many of the insights seem very relevant. For instance, they suggest that

> as a whole, the organizational level is at the nexus of the employment relationship where workers experience and, sometimes, negotiate their working conditions, their schedules and the degree of flexibility in their jobs. It is a key site of action and a contextual factor in constructing or inhibiting flexible careers.
>
> (Tomlinson et al., 2018, p. 14)

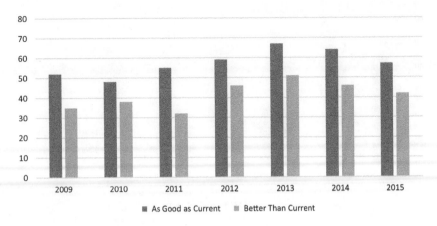

Figure 4.4 Finding Work as an IPro

This assertion provides another way of examining the empirical results presented in Figure 4.3, as it suggests that the organizational context that an IPro is currently working in may be a key source of the lack of certainty about continuing to work as an IPro. The individual may simply not be confident of finding more work—a result reflected in the 'free agent' to 'casual earner' segments found in Manyika et al. (2017), where choice and financial income provide the two key dimensions. However, as Figure 4.4 shows, the reality seems to be rather more complex than this.

Adding the dimension of certainty to the choice option provides another perspective. Here, the question centered on the degree of certainty in the ability to find another job as good as the one they currently have hit a low in 2010 (to be just under 40%), but a high level of confidence is generally at least 50% and better. Note here that if a more general level of confidence is applied (from mildly to highly confident), then the rates would be at 70+ each year. Finding something better sees the levels of confidence fall but also suggests that IPros keep an active eye on the marketplace and are aware of their employability.

Placing these results within the wider literature, IPros emerge here as essentially high-skill professional workers who do not wish to be employees and who have rejected the hierarchies, and, as they see it, much of the negativity of contemporary organizational human resource management practices (McKeown, 2016; Xhauflair et al., 2017). Overall, trying to accommodate IPros within a career framework does not appear an easy task. Despite the widely cited 'elite' position of the professional, contracting for the professional has elements ranging from being

- a career trap for some where it may well be associated with job insecurity, low earnings and where entry was and continues to be a defensive move against unemployment to being. This matches the 'reluctant' and even 'financially strapped' segments of Manyika et al. report for McKinsey (2017).
- for others, a transitional career is only a part of a pathway to traditional, permanent employment arrangements (akin to the 'casual earners' of Manyika et al., 2017); and
- being a successful career option for a dedicated and satisfied few who see it as the only way to work (the 'free agent' of Manyika et al., 2017).

These options highlight the disparate and varying views held by the IPro workforce and challenge the homogenous view often presented in the literature of a privileged elite.

In sum, the profile that emerges of the IPro career confirms an attachment to contracting but, contrary to common assumptions of it being an ongoing way of work, the empirical data presented suggests that this affiliation is seen as relatively short-term for the vast majority of IPros. While these results challenge perceptions of professionals in contract employment as a comfortable, privileged elite with well-developed career trajectories, they do offer opportunity for organizations—that those who provide a supportive work environment in terms of for their IPro workforce could achieve immediate benefits and influence their future ability to access talented IPros in a competitive labor market. Breitsohl and Ruhle (2013) contend as individual careers increasingly span across a greater number of organizations, individuals may experience residual affective commitment and remain affectively committed to an organization after departure.

IPros have emerged generally as individuals willingly accepting being in charge of their own careers. It is a finding that does much to mediate the traditional legal and human resource management concerns, such as sham contracting (Tomlinson et al., 2018), which often operate to discourage organizations from career discussions with their contract workforce. This suggests that greater organizational knowledge about IPro careers—why individuals work as contractors, why and how they move into and out of contract arrangements—may also provide those wishing to use their services with greater insight into how to attract, retain and sustain the on- and in-demand workforce.

Conclusion

This necessarily brief and selective overview of IPro careers has explored some established academic discourses that appear of relevance and found that they fail to reach any clear conclusions. In part, this is because of the limited research in this area to date. With this in mind, a selection of some of the empirical data from a seven-year study of IPros in Australia has been able to supplement some of this lack.

IPros have stepped outside of the bounds of traditional work, and they face ongoing change from the challenges of redundancy, dynamic labor markets and altered expectations of work. This appears to create new opportunities where some individuals adapt, and flourish, and others do not. The notion that professional contractors undertake careers where they are somehow more adept and proficient at negotiating their way within the changing world of work is unsupported by either the literature or the empirical evidence offered here. Instead, professionals are as much in need of assistance, especially in terms of protection from income fluctuation and the overwork/underwork dichotomy, as any other non-standard worker. For organizations, the opportunities provided by contracted professionals, such as restraining costs, need to be balanced with longer-term issues of loyalty and commitment while effectively accessing the knowledge that typifies this particular workforce. Note must also be made of the fact that these considerations are part of a much wider debate about non-standard employment. This is seen for instance in Crimmins et al. (2016) examination of the tensions between quality assurance of teaching and assessment in higher education, and the need to support casual academics' professional development.

In conclusion, this chapter suggests that there is an opportunity for employers to provide career services more traditionally associated with employees to their contracted professional workforce in order to maintain and retain such workers or simply just to be able to attract such workers. The challenges for the employing organization are identical to those that they face with any other worker: first, finding individuals who meet their needs, and second, retaining and maintaining their services for the length of time they are required.

Understanding the heterogeneous nature of professional contract arrangements, particularly in terms of the motivators for an individual in entering such arrangements, will also better inform institutional and organizational decision makers. It will also contribute to the ongoing debate as to the balance between individual and organizational career management factors in the career literature (see, for example, Baruch & Vardi, 2016; Tomlinson et al., 2018). This chapter moves the focus from career management for the self-employed being almost solely one of individual (and often vocationally oriented) responsibility to one where organizational managers and institutions play a vital role.

The contingent nature of the attachment to an IPro career is a last and important finding of our empirical investigation. This has important implications for individuals pursuing this form of work as the results from the study presented here suggest that careers are still largely seen as something that they do not control. The notion of an 'IPro career' largely remains more one of opportunity than of something that can be predictably planned and methodically worked through, as most standard employee work plans are. While the demise of a 'job for life' is well known with the employee/employer relationship, it seems that employment still offers a degree of support for the notion of an individual career plan that working outside of this relationship cannot. As Tomlinson et al. (2018, p. 17) advocate, there is the need to "help researchers and practitioners see how individuals would be able to self-manage their careers and to achieve success by flexibly adjusting to both their organizational support environments and their own aging." Tools, such as the McKinsey report by Manyika et al., (2017) where the segmentation of the independent workforce specifically identifies the heterogeneity of this group as a way for then tailoring more individualized responses to career drivers and needs.

Consideration of the IPro career clearly needs to take into account the broader institutional context. Labor and employment law in particular have historically been key constraints in organizations have interacted with the non-standard workforce in general and contractors in particular. Further, the role of self-employment as a viable way of working is not generally presented as a vocational option within either the educational or the labor-market institutions. Both of these factors make it difficult to present a coherent and compelling argument for the IPro career.

Despite this, the advent of the 'gig' economy and hyperbole surrounding it in the popular press present debatable but powerful force for change. Career models, such as that offered by Tomlinson et al. (2018), which provide explicit links between institutions, organizations and individuals, offer the potential to not only understand the history behind how and why careers have developed but to also offer alternatives into how they may develop. This can only be good for groups, such as the IPro, previously excluded from any considerations of career options.

References

ABS (2013). ANZSCO—Australian and New Zealand Standard Classification of Occupations, 2013, Version 1.2. Cat No 1220.0

ABS (2016). Characteristics of Employment, Cat No 6333.0, Australia, August 2016.

ABS (2017). *Forms of Employment* 2016 Cat. No. 6359.0. Australian Bureau of Statistics. AGPS, Canberra.

Adler, P. S., & Kwon, S. W. (2013). The mutation of professionalism as a contested diffusion process: Clinical guidelines as carriers of institutional change in medicine. *Journal of Management Studies*, 50(5), 930–962.

Ardichvili, A., & Kuchinke, K. P. (2009). International perspectives on the meanings of work and working: Current research and theory. *Advances in Developing Human Resources*, 11(2), 155–167.

Ashford, S.J., George, E., & Blatt, R. (2007). Old assumptions, new work: The opportunities and challenges of research on nonstandard employment. *The Academy of Management Annals, 1*(1), 65–117.

Bandura, A. (1997). *Self-efficacy: The Exercise of Control.* New York: Freeman.

Barley, S. R., & Kunda, G. (2006). Contracting: A new form of professional practice. *Academy of Management Perspectives, 20,* 45–66.

Baruch, Y., & Vardi, Y. (2016). A fresh look at the dark side of contemporary careers: Toward a realistic discourse. *British Journal of Management, 27*(2), 355–372.

Blanpain, R., Nakakubo, H., & Araki, T. (2010). *Regulation of Fixed-term Employment Contracts.* The Netherlands: Kluwer Law International BV.

BLS (2014). Self-employment: What to know to be your own boss. Available from www.bls.gov/careeroutlook/2014/article/self-employment-what-to-know-to-be-your-own-boss.htm

Breitsohl, H., & Ruhle, S. (2013). Residual affective commitment to organizations: Concept, causes and consequences. *Human Resource Management Review, 23*(2), 161–173.

Bridges,W. (1994). *Jobshift: How to Prosper in a Workplace without Jobs.* Reading, MA: Addison-Wesley.

Bryant, M., & McKeown, T. (2016). Experts, outsiders or strangers? The self-positioning of highly skilled contractors. *Journal of Management & Organization, 22*(3), 388–403.

Cahill, K. E., Giandrea, M. D., & Quinn, J. F. (2013). New evidence on self-employment transitions among older Americans with career jobs (No. 463).

Cappelli, P., & Keller, J. R. (2013). Classifying work in the new economy. *Academy of Management Review, 38*(4), 575–596.

Casale, G. (Ed.) (2011). *The Employment Relationship: A Comparative Overview.* Geneva: Hart Publishing.

Crimmins, G., Nash, G. Oprescu, F., Alla, J., Brock, G., Hickson-Jamieson, B., & Noakes, C. (2016). Can a systematic assessment moderation process assure the quality and integrity of assessment practice while supporting the professional development of casual academics? *Assessment & Evaluation in Higher Education, 41*(3), 427–441.

De Vos, A., & Soens, N. (2008). Protean attitude and career success: The mediating role of self-management. *Journal of Vocational Behavior, 73*(3), 449–456

De Vos, A., & Van der Heijden, B.I.J.M. (Eds.) (2015). *Handbook of Research on Sustainable Careers.* Cheltenham: Edward Elgar Publishing.

Eurofound (2017). Aspects of nonstandard employment in Europe. *Eurofound,* Dublin. Available from http://cite.gov.pt/pt/destaques/complementosDestqs2/Employment_europe_eurofound.pdf

EWCS (2010). European Working Conditions Surveys. Available from www.eurofound.europa.eu/ewco/surveys/index.htm

Granger, B., Stanworth, J., & Stanworth, C. (1995). Self-employment career dynamics: The case of unemployment push in UK book publishing. *Work, Employment and Society, 9*(3), 499–516.

Gratton, L. (2014). *The Shift.* London: HarperCollins UK.

Hall, D. T. (2004). The protean career: A quarter-century journey. *Journal of Vocational Behavior, 65*(1), 1–13.

Hall, D. T., & Mirvis, P. H. (1995). The new career contract: Developing the whole person at midlife and beyond. *Journal of Vocational Behavior, 47*(3), 269–289.

Hall, R. (2006). Temporary agency work and HRM in Australia "Cooperation, specialisation and satisfaction for the good of all?" *Personnel Review, 35*(2), 158–174.

Hatfield, I. (2015). *Self-employment in Europe.* London, England: Institute of Public Policy Research.

Hyytinen, A., & Rouvinen, P. (2008). The labour market consequences of self-employment spells: European evidence. *Labour Economics, 15*(2), 246–271.

Inkson, K., Gunz, H., Ganesh, S., & Roper, J. (2012). Boundaryless careers: Bringing back boundaries. *Organization Studies, 33*(3), 323–340.

International Labour Organization (ILO) (2016). International Labour Conference, 95th Session, Report V (1). The employment relationship, ILO, Geneva.

Jamrozik, K., Weller, D. P., & Heller, R. F. (2004). Research assessment: There must be an easier way. *Medical Journal of Australia, 180*(11), 553.

Judge, T. A., Thoresen, D. J., Bono, J. E., & Patton, G. K. (2001). The job satisfaction-job performance relationship: A qualitative and quantitative review. *Psychological Bulletin, 127*(3), 376–407.

Knight, F. (1933). *The Economic Organization: With an Article, Notes on Cost and Utility.* Chicago: University of Chicago Press

Koene, B., & van Riemsdijk, M. (2005). Managing temporary workers: Work identity, diversity and operational HR choices. *Human Resource Management Journal, 15*(1), 76–92.

LaPointe, K. (2013). Heroic career changers? Gendered identity work in career transitions. *Gender, Work and Organization, 20*(2), 133–146

Lee, W., Wong, A., & Tong, C. (2014). A qualitative study of the Software Adoption of building information modelling technology in the Hong Kong construction industry. *Business and Economic Research, 4*(2), 222–236.

Leighton, P., & Wynn, M. (2011). Classifying employment relationships: More sliding doors or a better regulatory framework? *Industrial Law Journal, 40*(1), 5–44.

Leighton, P., & McKeown, T. (2015). The rise of independent professionals: Their challenge for management. *Small Enterprise Research, 22*(2–3), 119–130.

Lozano, B. (1989). *The Invisible Workforce.* New York: The Free Press.

Manyika, J., Chui, M., Madgavkar, A., & Lund, S. (2017). *Technology, Jobs, and the Future of Work.* San Francisco, CA: McKinsey Global Institute.

Marler, J. H., Barringer, M., & Milkovich, G. T. (2002). Boundaryless and traditional contingent employees: Worlds apart. *Journal of Organizational Behavior, 23*(4), 425–453.

McKeown, T. (2016). A consilience framework: Revealing hidden features of the independent contractor. *Journal of Management & Organization, 22*(6), 779–796.

McKeown, T., & Cochrane, R. (2017). Independent professionals and the potential for HRM innovation. *Personnel Review, 46*(7), 1414–1433.

OECD (2010). *SMEs, Entrepreneurship and Innovation.* France: Organisation for Economic Co-operation and Development.

OECD (2016). OECD Science, Technology and Innovation Outlook 2016, France Organisation for Economic Co-operation and Development.

OECD (2017). *Economic Outlook*. France: Organisation for Economic Co-operation and Development.

Pofeldt, E. (2016). Gig economy workforce is bigger than official data shows. *Forbes*, October 10.

Schumpeter, J.A. (1934). *Theory of Economic Development*. Cambridge, MA: Harvard University Press.

Shanbrom, B. (2017). How many different freelance careers do you know of? Available from http://nation1099.com/freelance-careers-types-freelance-jobs/

Spera (2017). Freelancing Report 2016. Available from https://spera.io/ebooks/freelancing-a-new-frontier/

Stone, K., Dagnino, E., & Martínez, S. F. (Eds.) (2017). *Labour in the 21st Century: Insights into a Changing World of Work*. Cambridge: Cambridge Scholars Publishing.

Tams, S., & Arthur, M. B. (2010). New directions for boundaryless careers: Agency and interdependence in a changing world. *Journal of Organizational Behavior, 31*, 629–646.

Taylor, M., Marsh, G., Nicol, D., & Broadbent, P. (2017). *Good Work: The Taylor Review of Modern Working Practices*. London, England.

Tomlinson, J., Baird, M., Berg, P., & Cooper, R. (2018). Flexible careers across the life course: Advancing theory, research and practice. *Human Relations, 7*(1), 4–22.

Vorhauser-Smith, S., & Cariss, K. (2017). *Cliffhanger: HR on the Precipice in the Future of Work*. Melbourne, Australia: PageUp People Limited.

Williams, B., & Beovich, B. (2017). Experiences of sessional educators within an Australian undergraduate paramedic program. *Journal of University Teaching & Learning Practice, 14*(1).

Yigitcanlar, T. (2010). Making space and place for the knowledge economy: Knowledge-based development of Australian cities. *European Planning Studies, 18*(11), 1769–1786.

Xhauflair, V., Huybrechts, B., & Pichault, F. (2017). How can new players establish themselves in highly institutionalized labour markets? A Belgian case study in the area of project-based work. *British Journal of Industrial Relations, 56*(2), 370–394.

Part II

Making the Most of Flexible Work Practices

The Need for Spatial Job Crafting and Boundary Management

5 Reflecting on and Proactively Making Use of Flexible Working Practices Makes All the Difference

The Role of Spatial Job Crafting

Christina Wessels and Michaéla Schippers

This chapter adds to our understanding of how employees and companies can profit from flexible working practices, and offers organizations and scholars a new direction to investigate flexible working practices. Some studies show positive effects, other studies negative or null effects, and it seems that experiences on the shop floor indeed reflect these findings. Consider the following example:

> Peter and Mary both work for a telecommunications company that allows their employees to adjust working hours and work locations in a flexible manner. They both make use of the flexible working policy, but experience the usage of the policy in a completely different way. Mary is quite enthusiastic about working flexibly and carefully thinks about the different work locations she has available to choose from. For instance, on a Monday morning, she decides to start working from home because this seems to be the best option as she needs to finish a presentation for the next day, which is best done in silence. At lunch time, she also has a doctor´s appointment, which is close to her home. Mary communicates to her team at work that she will come to the office afterward for the planned meeting. Her team accepts her working flexibly, and she feels quite happy and productive. In contrast, Peter is confused about the flexible working policy and feels that it has been hyped-up rather than being something necessary. He does not know what to make of it, and even though he does work from home now and then, he feels working from home does not offer him great benefits.

The examples of Peter and Mary depict two common situations in flexible organizations. On the one hand, there are employees who regard flexible working as something beneficial for their work. They feel that they are more productive and happier with the flexibility offered by their employer. On the other hand, there are also employees who are confused about the increase in flexibility. They do not think it is something valuable that helps them in managing their working day and in accomplishing their working tasks. This presumably means that simply having flexibility is not enough to increase employee well-being and productivity; rather, it is the way in which employees use this flexibility that may make all the difference.

Even though flexible working practices—having discretion over where and when to work (Hill et al., 2008)—are popular in many organizations across Europe and the USA, after 40 years of research, no clear case can be made regarding the actual benefits of these practices for employee outcomes (De Menezes & Kelliher, 2011). In their review, De Menezes & Kelliher (2011) concluded that flexible working practices can lead to both positive, negative, and null effects for employee outcomes, and hence those mixed outcomes make it hard to argue for a compelling business case.

This raises the question of what does make a difference, or in our case, what does Mary do, in contrast to Peter, that enables her to reap the benefits of flexibility? Not only does Mary have a more positive attitude than Peter regarding flexible working practices, but Mary also seems to deal with the flexibility on offer in a different way. She is able to profit from flexible working because, in contrast to Peter, she proactively shapes her own working day. She carefully chooses the locations from where to work so that they fit to working tasks and private demands. In short, she engages in *spatial job crafting* (Wessels, 2017).

General job crafting behavior has been understood as a strategy that employees use to proactively modify aspects of their jobs, such as the quantity of working tasks, the frequency of social interactions (Wrzesniewski & Dutton, 2001), or job demands and job resources (Tims, Bakker & Derks, 2012). As an extension, to encompass both the spatial and temporal aspects of work, Wessels (2017) and Wessels et al., (2016, 2018) introduced the idea of time-spatial job crafting. With time-spatial job crafting, employees proactively alter work locations and working hours to stay engaged and productive when working flexibly. By so doing, the authors suggest that employees are able to reap the benefits of flexibility.

The central aim of this chapter is to test how *spatial job crafting* can help employees to stay engaged, productive, and innovative when flexibility is available. In both the scientific and practitioner literatures, there is a lack of attention to how companies and employees can exploit the benefits from flexible working practices. This is quite unfortunate considering the heavy uptake of this practice. In this chapter, we aim to demonstrate that employees need to actively shape their working day by engaging in spatial job crafting, in order to derive engagement and innovation benefits. On top of that, we aim to show that one's own attitude toward flexible working practices, as well as the acceptance of the practice inside the organization are key in shaping the experience of flexible working. We define attitudes towards flexible working practices in terms of the cognitive dimension (Ajizen, 1984) and adopt the definition given by Eagly and Chaiken (1998, p. 27) as "beliefs express positive or negative evaluation of greater or lesser extremity, and occasionally are exactly neutral in their evaluative content." Hence, cognitive attitudes are understood as favorable or unfavorable judgments and beliefs regarding objects, people, or events (Robbins & Judge, 2014). A positive attitude toward flexible working practices represents employees' favorable judgments about the practice.

In this chapter, we first briefly review the current status of flexibility research and its inadequacy with respect to dealing with the mixed outcomes. Second, we elaborate on the idea of (time-) spatial job crafting, embed it in the existing job crafting landscape and offer it as a potential solution to the mixed outcomes. After briefly providing information about our data and measures, we empirically demonstrate how spatial job crafting can be used as a tool by employees to derive benefits for work outcomes and show how one's own attitude and acceptance of the practices functions as an antecedent. We also elaborate on the mediational role of spatial job crafting. Please refer to Figure 5.1.

This chapter draws upon empirical data from a telecommunications company that introduced flexible working practices into their organization. The results of this chapter are interesting for both practitioners and scientists. For practitioners, demonstrating the positive effects of spatial job crafting provides support for a behavioral tool that organizations can use to derive positive effects from flexibility. Organizations are advised to invest in training to increase awareness of spatial job crafting. For researchers, the results of this chapter are important as they shed light on the question of when flexibility leads to positive effects. Thereby, our results do not only add to the literature on flexibility, but we also add to and extend the job crafting literature. The central question that guides this research is how employees can profit from flexible working practices.

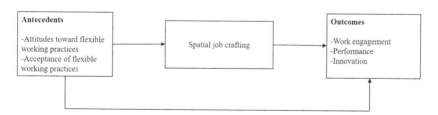

Figure 5.1 Research Model

Theoretical Background

Flexible Working Practices—What Do We Know and What Do We Not Know?

Flexible working practices—having discretion of where and when to work—(Hill et al., 2008) have become a central HR policy in many organizations across Europe and the USA. Factors such as increased competition, the war for talent, the aging workforce, and women participating in the labor market have resulted in an uptake of flexible working practices (European Commission, 2010). Discretion over when to work is also known as temporal flexibility; flexibility in the location of work is also referred to as teleworking (Nilles, 1998). An increasing number of European countries have introduced laws to reinforce the usage of flexible working practices, such as in the Netherlands or the United Kingdom. Despite this popularity, and claims for better performance, well-being, and work-life balance, a real business case for flexible working cannot be made yet (De Menezes & Kelliher, 2011). An ample amount of studies have investigated the effects of flexible working practices on various outcomes variables and found mixed results. On the one hand, there are studies that found positive effects on performance and well-being (e.g., Gajendran & Harrison, 2007; Kelliher & Anderson, 2008); on the other hand, there are also studies that found negative effects (e.g., Kelliher & Anderson, 2008; ten Brummelhuis et al., 2012), or even no effects (e.g., Staples, 2001). Extensive reviews of flexible working practices are available elsewhere, and we do not aim to repeat them here (e.g., De Menezes & Kelliher, 2011; Gajendran & Harrison, 2007). Hence, despite 40 years of flexibility research, it is still not possible to make a real claim for flexible working practices. This results in a lack of understanding of how employers and employees can profit from flexibility.

How Can Employees Profit From Flexible Working Practices? The Concept of Time-Spatial Job Crafting

Part of the problem of the mixed results in flexibility research stems from a lack of incorporating mediators, moderators, and the notion of time in flexibility research (De Menezes & Kelliher, 2011). To account for this, Wessels (2017) and Wessels et al. (2016, 2018) developed a model of time-spatial job crafting that helps in explaining the mixed outcomes.

In the job crafting literature, employees are regarded as active agents of their own work and this understanding has extended the traditional top-down approach of work design (Morgeson & Humphrey, 2008). Popular bottom-up approaches of work design are idiosyncratic deals, or job crafting. Whereas early research on job crafting has defined it in terms of making changes to the quantity of working tasks and frequency of social interactions (Wrzesniewski & Dutton, 2001), subsequent work has focused on defining job crafting in terms of altering job demands and job resources (Tims et al., 2012). Wrzesniewski and Dutton (2001) argue that employees engage in job crafting because they want to exercise some form of control over their work, to produce a positive self-image of themselves in their work, and to build and manage their social relations at work. Tims, Bakker, and Derks (2012) argue that employees proactively increase structural job resources, social job resources, and challenging job demands and decrease hindering job demands.

To include the time and spatial dimensions of work, Wessels (2017) and Wessels et al. (2016, 2018) have recently extended the notion of job crafting calling it "*time-spatial job crafting.*" The time dimension of time-spatial job crafting refers to job crafting related to working hours; the space dimension to job crafting related to work locations. Time-spatial job crafting is defined as a "context-specific type of job crafting in which employees (a) reflect on specific work tasks and private demands; (b) select workplaces, work locations, and working hours that fit those tasks and private demands; and (c) possibly adapt either their place/location of work and working hours or tasks and private demands to ensure that these still fit each other (. . .)" (Wessels, 2017, p. 28). In their theoretical model of time-spatial job crafting, the authors discuss the antecedents of time-spatial job crafting and explain how time-spatial job crafting is related to positive work outcomes through time/spatial-demands fit. Hence, they propose time-spatial job crafting as a tool that helps employees to benefit from time-spatial flexibility by optimizing a time/spatial-demands fit (for the full model, please see Wessels et al., 2018).

The focus of this chapter is only on the *spatial* dimension; hence, we adapt the definition of time-spatial job crafting. In this chapter, *spatial job crafting* is understood as

> a context-specific type of job crafting in which employees (a) reflect on specific work tasks (. . .) (b) select work locations that fit those tasks (. . .); and (c) possibly adapt their location of work or tasks (. . .) to ensure that these still fit with each other.
>
> (cf. Wessels, 2017, p. 28)

In defining the original time-spatial job crafting concept, the authors drew from reflexivity research. Reflexivity is conceptualized as a self-regulatory concept at the team level that consists of three elements: reflection, planning, and action (Swift & West, 1998; for reviews, see Konradt et al., 2015; Moreland & McMinn, 2010; Schippers, Edmondson & West, 2014; Schippers, West & Edmondson, 2017; Widmer, Schippers & West, 2009). Those three elements are intertwined as an iterative cycle of reflection, planning, and action (Schippers et al., 2017). Analogous to this cycle, the original time-spatial job crafting concept consists of a reflection component, a selection component, and an adaptation element. Whereas reflecting about working tasks and work locations represents the cognitive part, the actual selection of work locations and the potential adaptation are regarded as the behavioral element. For spatial job crafting this means that reflection represents a conscious act of thinking about working tasks and work locations, where employees first think about the tasks to be carried out during a working day and then select the work location(s) accordingly. Examples of reflection are as follows: What are my working tasks today? (e.g., I have two meetings, I have to prepare a presentation). Which work locations are available today? (e.g., home, train, office). Once employees have that clear, they can engage in selection. For example, an employee decides to work from home since he or she needs to work in silence to finish a presentation. Hence, selection represents the actual choice of the work location, which stems from scrutiny of the different alternatives (cf. Vohs et al., 2008). Needless to say, choosing where to work does not occur in isolation (e.g., decision may also depend on colleagues), but for the sake of this chapter, we only consider spatial choices related to work tasks (Wessels et al., 2016, 2018). The final element, adaptation, is understood as "performing adaptive behaviors that address changing conditions" (Hirschi, Herrmann & Keller, 2015, p. 1) and Wessels et al. (2016, 2018) argue that adaptation of work locations may, for instance, occur because of a suboptimal work location decision in the first place. Together, these three elements represent a chain in which reflection leads to selection, which is likely to lead to adaptation.

A critical assumption of the overall time-spatial job crafting model is that employees need to take an active role if they want to reap the benefits from flexible working practices. The main idea is that the three components of time-spatial job crafting allow for this active role. The underlying idea with regard to spatial job crafting is that, once employees consciously choose a work location, they are able to fit the work location to their own preferences, which is likely to foster engagement, innovation, and productivity. When employees are able to seek out work locations that fit with their task needs, they are more likely to use their capabilities at work. This should consequently energize them and should make them more productive. Hence, by altering spatial aspects of the work so that these fit with employee's own task preferences, we expect that employees are able to increase their engagement at work and performance. Even though innovation is not part of the original model proposed by Wessels and colleagues, we argue that spatial job crafting can also lead to feelings of higher innovation. By consciously choosing work locations, employees are most likely to perform their work tasks in a work environment that fits with their own needs. Hence, the work environment can also become a source of inspiration, which is likely to foster innovation.

Proactively crafting the spatial dimension of work resonates with the idea that spaces are seen as dynamic. According to Beyes and Steyaert (2011, p. 47), a space is "processual and performative, open-ended and multiple, practiced and of the everyday." Viewing spaces as dynamic, Richardson and McKenna (2014) showed in their case study that employees, who worked flexibly, reordered their private lives. For instance, they report the case of a manager who opts to stop working at 5 pm to spend time with her child and restarts work after normal office hours. They deemed this behavior to be one of a successful flexworker and contested that "flexworkers have to assume more responsibility for managing themselves and their whole lives" (Richardson & McKenna, 2014, p. 734). To emphasize the fact that flexible workers need to take action themselves to successfully work flexibly, in the following chapter, we apply job crafting literature to empirically test and explain how employees can do this.

Consequently, we tested the idea of spatial job crafting and what the consequences are for work engagement, productivity, and innovation. Specifically, we expect that employees, who engage in spatial job crafting, are more likely to be productive, innovative, and engaged with their work. Wessels et al. (2018) introduced a number of antecedents of time-spatial job crafting to explain what might prompt employees to engage in time-spatial job crafting. In line with the reasoning of Wessels et al. (2018), we expect that employees are more likely to engage in spatial job crafting if they have a positive attitude toward flexible working and if the organization accepts them working flexibly. We understand cognitive attitudes as favorable or unfavorable judgments and beliefs regarding objects, people, or events (Robbins & Judge, 2014), and hence a positive attitude toward flexible working practices represents employees' favorable evaluations about the practice. This, for instance, comprises seeing the value of flexible working practices. From flexibility research at Microsoft Netherlands, it became evident that only if the entire organization supports flexible working practices, and it is accepted throughout the organization, can flexible working become a success in the organization (see van Heck et al., 2012). Fursman and Zodgekar (2009) sustain this line of thought by revealing that one barrier, which prevents the usage of flexible working practices, is a non-supporting organization. Hence, we expect that attitudes toward flexibility, as well as acceptance of flexibility, will have positive effects on work engagement, productivity, and innovation, and lead to spatial job crafting.

Example Data

For illustrative purposes, we will use data from a cross-sectional study of 292 employees working in a telecommunications company in the Netherlands from 2011. In 2010, the company under investigation introduced the concept of flexible working practices throughout its organization. Data were collected by means of an online questionnaire, which was distributed by the HR department. The survey was developed to measure employees' opinions and experience with flexible working practices after the first year of its introduction. The online survey was available for completion for a period of two and a half weeks. From the 674 employees working at the company, a total of 292 respondents filled out the survey, corresponding to a response rate of 43.26%. From the 292 respondents, 216 were male, representing 74% of the surveyed workforce, and 76 were female (26%). This highly unequal allocation is not uncommon for the organization as 80% of the total workforce is male and only 20% is female. This can be attributed to the technical orientation of the company. The mean age of the respondents was 42.72 years.

Measures

All variables were measured on a 5-point Likert scale ranging from one (strongly disagree) to five (strongly agree). The following control variables were taken into account: Age, gender, tenure, education, and how many days employees come to the office.

Work Engagement

Work engagement was assessed with the English version of the Utrecht Work Engagement Scale (Schaufeli et al., 2002). For the purpose of this research, we used an overall engagement measure (Schaufeli, Bakker & Salanova, 2006) with six items. Example items are as follows: "When I get up in the morning, I feel like going to work"; "I am enthusiastic about my job"; "I feel happy when I am working intensively" ($\alpha = 0.84$).

Innovation

Innovation was measured using four adapted items of the attitude toward innovation scale (e.g., adoption of innovation or ease of implementation) developed by Ettlie and O'Keefe (1982). Example items are as follows: "I try to use new ideas and approaches to problems"; "People can rely on me to find a new use for existing methods or existing equipment" ($\alpha = 0.77$).

Attitude and Acceptance

Attitude toward and acceptance of flexible working practices were measured with five and three items, respectively, that were developed by the authors themselves. Example items for attitude are as follows: "Flexible working is easily compatible with most aspects of my work"; "In my opinion, flexible working is useful within my work" (α = 0.77). Example items for acceptance are as follows: "Flexible working is accepted within the organization"; "Within the organization, flexible working is regarded as normal" (α = 0.78).

Spatial Job Crafting

Spatial job crafting was measured with the items developed by Wessels (2017) for the time-spatial job crafting model. Since we were only interested in the spatial aspect of time-spatial job crafting, only items of the spatial dimensions were used. Example items are as follows: "I try to match my tasks to my work location"; "When I notice that a work location is not suited to a specific task that I am performing, I will select a different work location" (α = 0.69).

Productivity

Productivity was measured with 13 items using a mixture of items from Staples, Hulland, and Higgins (1999) and Ramírez and Nembhard (2004). Example items are as follows: "I believe that I am an effective employee," "My activities and/or the projects in which I am involved are generally very profitable for the organization" (α = 0.86).

Results

Spatial Job Crafting as a Tool That Helps to Reap Benefits for Engagement and Innovation

Results of the hierarchical regression analyses are demonstrated in Table 5.1. In order to test our expectations, three regressions were run to examine the suggested effects of spatial job crafting on productivity, work engagement, and innovation. On top of that, we also examined the direct effects of attitude and acceptance on our three main outcome variables. In each regression, control variables were entered in a first step, the main effects of attitude and acceptance were entered in a second step, and spatial job crafting was entered in a third step to test for potential mediation as well.

For the main effects of attitude and acceptance, our results show that only attitude toward flexible working practices had a significant and positive effect on spatial job crafting (β = 0.30 p < 0.001); acceptance of flexible working practices inside the organization did not show a significant effect (β = 0.07, *ns.*). Hence, only attitude toward flexible working practices can act as a potential mediator and will be taken into account in subsequent mediation analyses.

Table 5.1 Hierarchical Regression Analyses

Variable	Spatial Job Crafting		Work Engagement			Performance			Innovation		
	M1	M2	M1	M2	M3	M1	M2	M3	M1	M2	M3
Constant	3.60	3.61	3.61	3.62	3.61	3.66	3.66	3.66	3.80	3.80	3.80
Control Variables											
Gender	0.15	0.13	0.10	0.08	0.06	−0.06	−0.08	−0.08	−0.18*	−0.18*	−0.20**
Age	−0.00	−0.01	0.11	0.10	0.10	0.01	0.01	0.01	−0.02	−0.02	−0.01
Education	0.14*	0.12	0.10	0.08	0.07	0.11	0.10	0.09	0.10	0.09	0.07
Employment	0.16*	0.14*	0.22**	0.20**	0.17*	0.07	0.05	0.05	0.13	0.13	0.11
Days at the Office	0.05	0.08	−0.026	0.00	−0.011	−0.08	−0.06	−0.07	−0.04	−0.02	−0.03
Main Effects											
Attitude		0.30***		0.19**	0.15*		0.23***	0.21***		0.21***	0.17**
Acceptance		0.07		0.15**	0.14*		0.06	0.05		−0.04	−0.05
Mediation											
Spatial Job Crafting					0.15*			0.05			0.15*
R²	0.04	0.14	0.06	0.14	0.16	0.03	0.09	0.09	0.09	0.13	0.15
R² adjusted	0.02	0.12	0.04	0.12	0.13	0.01	0.07	0.07	0.07	0.11	0.12
Δ in R² adjusted		0.08		0.08	0.01		0.06	0.00		0.04	0.01
F	2.19	6.13***	3.40**	5.88***	5.92***	1.82	3.78***	3.36***	5.14***	5.57***	5.65***
Δ in F		3.94		2.48	0.04		1.96	0.42		0.43	0.08

Note: N = 292, values in table are standardized β coefficients.
*p ≤ 0.05, **p ≤ 0.01, ***p ≤ 0.001.

Our results further revealed that, both acceptance of flexible working ($\beta = 0.15$ p < 0.05) and attitude toward flexible working ($\beta = 0.19$ p < 0.01) were positively related to work engagement. It seems that in flexible organizations, it is important that employees themselves see the value of flexible working and that the organization accepts that employees work flexibly so that they are able to feel engaged with their work. Our main variable of interest, spatial job crafting, also showed a positive significant relationship with work engagement, implying that employees who spatially job craft are more engaged with their work in organizations that offer flexible working practices ($\beta = 0.15$ p < 0.05). Since the β of attitude toward flexible working declined, but was still significant when spatial job crafting was entered into the model (change in β from $\beta = 0.19$ p < 0.01 to $\beta = 0.15$ p < 0.05), we further tested for partial mediation by means of a Sobel test. Results of the Sobel test produced a p value of 0.04 (p < 0.05) with a corresponding t-statistic of 2.10 and a standard error of 0.02; thus, the decrease of the beta value for attitude was significant and hence spatial job crafting partially mediated the relation between attitude and work engagement. Consequently, part of the relation between attitude and work engagement can be explained by spatial job crafting.

For productivity, different patterns emerged. The results from the hierarchical regression analyses revealed that acceptance of flexible working ($\beta = 0.056$, *ns.*) was not significant, but attitude toward flexible working showed a highly significant relationship with productivity ($\beta = 0.23$ p < 0.001). Hence, for productivity it seems that an individual's attitude toward flexible working practices is more important to feel productive than a supporting organization. Further, results demonstrated that spatial job crafting was not significantly positively related to productivity ($\beta = 0.046$, *ns.*). Hence, proactively changing work locations seems not to be related to higher perceived productivity for employees.

For innovation, our results are partly in line with the results for productivity. While attitude toward flexible working had a significant positive relation with innovation ($\beta = 0.21$ p < 0.001), acceptance did not show a significant positive relation ($\beta = -0.037$, *ns.*). Hence, if people think positively about flexible working in general, they also feel more innovative in a flexible organization. In contrast to performance, spatial job crafting did show a significant and positive relation with innovation ($\beta = 0.15$ p < 0.05). This implies that employees feel more innovative if they actively think about and adapt the locations from which they work. Similar to work engagement, once spatial job crafting was entered into the model, the β of attitude of flexible working declined but was still significant (change in β from $\beta = 0.21$ p < 0.001 to $\beta = 0.17$ p < 0.01); thus, we further tested for partial mediation by means of a Sobel test. The decrease of the beta value is significant with a corresponding p value of 0.02 (p < 0.05) and a corresponding t-statistic of 2.35 and a standard error of 0.01; hence, spatial job crafting also partially mediated the relation between attitude toward flexible working practices and innovation. Therefore, part of the relation between attitude and innovation can be explained by spatial job crafting. In the following section, these results will be discussed.

Discussion

The aim of this chapter was to empirically test the idea of spatial job crafting. Time-spatial job crafting has been recently introduced as an extension to the traditional conceptualization of job crafting (Wessels, 2017; Wessels et al., 2016, 2018). In an effort to integrate the temporal and spatial aspects of work to the job crafting literature, time-spatial job crafting has been defined as a context-specific type of job crafting, where employees have flexibility in terms of where and when to work. So far, scholars and practitioners have been left behind with a lack of understanding of how flexibility can lead to positive work outcomes. Many studies about the effects of flexibility have led to mixed outcomes, some studies found positive effects, some studies found negative effects and no clear case for flexible working can be made yet (De Menezes & Kelliher, 2011). The results of this chapter are crucial because they shed light on the understanding of how employer and employees can profit from flexible working practices in flexible organizations.

In this chapter, we focused only on the spatial aspect of time-spatial job crafting and linked spatial job crafting to innovation, work engagement, and productivity. In line with the time-spatial job crafting model by Wessels et al. (2018), we also tested whether one's attitude toward flexible working practices and acceptance of flexible working inside the organization serve as antecedents to spatial job crafting.

Our analysis has shown that if employees engage in spatial job crafting, they are able to be engaged and innovative. However, spatial job crafting did not increase feelings of perceived productivity. Hence, by reflecting and proactively choosing work locations, employees are able to reap the benefits from flexibility, but only for work engagement and innovation. Our analysis also gives insights into what triggers employees to engage in spatial job crafting. In particular, we have shown that if employees have a positive attitude toward flexible working practices and feel that it is accepted within the organization, they are more likely to engage in spatial job crafting. This positive attitude toward flexibility seems also to be vital to derive benefits for work outcomes as our results have shown that especially one's attitude is also positively related to work engagement, productivity, and innovation. Our analysis further demonstrated that part of this relationship can be explained by spatial job crafting. Spatial job crafting partially mediated the relation between attitude toward flexible working practices and two of the outcome variables, namely work engagement and innovation.

In the following, theoretical and practical implications, as well as limitations of this study and avenues for future research are discussed.

Theoretical and Practical Implications

Our results are important for existing flexibility research and the literature on job crafting. By demonstrating the value of spatial job crafting in the context of flexible working practices, we were able to create a bridge between flexibility and job crafting, and thereby, develop theory in both arenas. Spatial job crafting is offered as a tool that leads to higher engagement and innovation. The results of this study thereby highlight the importance of bottom-up approaches to work design when working flexibly. Previous literature has shown that flexibility can have both a positive and a negative effect at the cross-sectional level (for reviews, see Baltes et al., 1999; De Menezes & Kelliher, 2011; Gajendran & Harrison, 2007). Through spatial job crafting, we explained when flexibility will be favorable for innovation and work engagement at the cross-sectional level. Hence, the idea of employees as active agents of their own working day, in the context of flexible working practices, should be incorporated when studying the effects of flexibility on work outcomes. However, as shown by our analysis, to our surprise, spatial job crafting did not result in higher perceptions of productivity. Hence, it seems that proactively shaping work locations does not make employees more productive at the cross-sectional level. It might be that productivity effects of flexibility cannot be observed in the short-term and thus for employees to profit from spatial job crafting for productivity, a long-term perspective should be taken. This is indeed what Wessels (2017) found in her study on the long-term effects of flexibility.

On top of that, we also add to the job crafting literature by substantiating the extension of job crafting to the spatial aspects of work. Spatial elements have so far been neglected in job crafting research, even though they are important considering the uptake of flexible working practices. Hence, spatial job crafting seems to be a timely addition to the general job crafting literature. The results of this chapter are in line with prior studies on job crafting. Job crafting has proven to be beneficial for employees, especially for work engagement (Tims et al., 2013; for a review, see Demerouti & Bakker, 2014).

Furthermore, we also demonstrated the importance of attitudes in the context of flexible working practices and thereby add to literature on attitudes (Ajizen, 1984). Our results have shown that especially an individual's own judgment turns out favorable for work outcomes in the context of flexible working practices and triggers spatial job crafting behavior. In addition, the outcome of our analysis also revealed the importance of a supporting organization. We thereby confirm the conceptual assumptions made by Wessels et al. (2016, 2018).

Our reflection/proactivity lens on flexibility gave first insights into how employees and their organizations are able to profit from flexibility, especially for innovation and work engagement. This seemed to be crucial considering that organizations struggle with the successful implementation of flexible working practices. The results of our chapter suggest a behavioral tool that organizations can use to benefit from the positive effects of flexibility. By promoting spatial job crafting inside the organization, flexible organizations are able to show employees how they can profit from flexible working practices. In this regard, it is suggested that organizations should offer trainings to increase awareness for spatial job crafting among employees. The importance of one's attitude with regard to flexible working practices also represents an interesting finding for flexible organizations, as well as the notion that acceptance of flexible working inside the organization leads to higher engagement and fosters spatial job crafting. Since attitudes are an important determinant of behavior and can be influenced (Eagly & Chaiken, 1998), organizations play an important role in framing employees' attitudes toward flexible working practices. Hence, this could, for instance, be done with the aid of a promotion program about flexible working practices.

Limitations and Future Research

While we believe that our research has added valuable knowledge about how employees are able to profit from flexible working practices, there are a number of limitations that should be acknowledged. First, we were only able to gather self-reported data for our outcome variables. Hence, common method bias cannot be excluded. Future research is therefore directed to obtain data from multiple sources. A second related limitation concerns the cross-sectional design of our study. Such a design does not allow causal relationships to be established. Therefore, future research is advised to use data from multiple waves. Third, since the concept of time-spatial job crafting is new, the scale of spatial job crafting was not previously validated. Hence, this might compromise the interpretation of our results to a certain extent.

Given that this study was the first empirical one to test the idea of spatial job crafting, we hope to have stimulated further interest in this concept. In particular, fruitful avenues for future research lie in the following. Future research on flexibility is advised to incorporate spatial job crafting as a potential moderator into analyses, as reflecting and proactively choosing work locations has been shown to be linked to positive outcomes. This would reveal when flexibility effects will be more positive and when negative. Furthermore, an intervention study might also be an interesting design to get more insights into the concept of spatial job crafting.

Conclusion

One of the greatest challenges in flexibility research lies in explaining the mixed results for work outcomes. In this chapter, we empirically tested the idea of spatial job crafting and offer this as a potential explanation for the mixed outcomes. Spatial job crafting—a context-specific form of job crafting that entails reflection on the work location—has been introduced as an extension to the traditional conceptualization of job crafting. The results of this chapter have demonstrated that spatial job crafting can be seen as a strategy to foster work engagement and innovation when working flexibly. Accordingly, our findings add to the understanding of how employees can profit from flexible working and offer organizations and scholars a new direction to investigate flexible working practices.

References

Ajizen, I. (1984). Attitudes. In R. J. Corsini (Ed.), *Wiley Encyclopedia of Psychology* (pp. 99–100). New York: Wiley.

Baltes, B., Briggs, T., Huff, J., Wright, J., & Neumann, G. (1999). Flexible and compressed workweek schedules: A meta-analysis of their effects on work-related criteria. *Journal of Applied Psychology, 84*, 496–513.

Beyes, T., & Steyaert, C. (2011). Spacing organization: Non-representational theory and performing organizational space. *Organization, 19*, 45–61.

De Menezes, L. M., & Kelliher, C. (2011). Flexible working and performance: A systematic review of the evidence for a business case. *International Journal of Management Reviews, 13*, 452–474.

Demerouti, E., & Bakker, A. B. (2014). Job Crafting. In M. C. W. Peeters, J. de Jonge, & T. Taris (Eds.), *An Introduction to Contemporary Work Psychology* (pp. 414–433). Chichester, UK: Wiley-Blackwell.

Eagly, A. H., & Chaiken, S. (1998). Attitude structure and function. In D. T. Gilbert, S. T. Fiske, & G. Lindsey (Eds.), *Handbook of Social Psychology* (2nd ed., pp. 269–322). Boston: McGraw-Hill.

Ettlie, J. E., & O'Keefe, R. D. (1982). Innovative attitudes, values and intentions in organizations. *Journal of Management Studies, 19*, 163–183.

European Commission. (2010). Flexible working time arrangements and gender equality. Retrieved November 27th, 2017, from ec.europa.eu/social/BlobServlet?docId=6473.

Fursman, L., & Zodgekar, N. (2009). New Zealand families and their experiences with flexible work. *Family Matters, 81*, 25–36.

Gajendran, R. S., & Harrison, D. (2007). The good, the bad, and the unknown about telecommuting: Meta-analysis of psychological mediators and individual consequences. *Journal of Applied Psychology, 92*, 1524–1541.

Hill, E. J., Grzywacz, J. G., Allen, S., Blanchard, V. L., Matz-costa, C., Shulkin, S., & Pitt-Catsouphes, M. (2008). Defining and conceptualizing workplace flexibility. *Community, Work & Family, 11*, 149–163.

Hirschi, A., Herrmann, A., & Keller, A. C. (2015). Career adaptivity, adaptability, and adapting: A conceptual and empirical investigation. *Journal of Vocational Behavior, 87*, 1–10.

Kelliher, C., & Anderson, D. (2008). For better or for worse? An analysis of how flexible working practices influence employees' perceptions of job quality. *International Journal of Human Resource Management, 19*, 421–433.

Konradt, U., Otte, K.-P., Schippers, M. C., & Steenfatt, C. (2015). Reflexivity in teams: A review and new perspectives. *The Journal of Psychology, 0*(0), 1–34.

Moreland, R. L., & McMinn, J. G. (2010). Group reflexivity and performance. *Advances in Group Processes, 27*, 63–95.

Morgeson, F. P., & Humphrey, S. E. (2008). Job and team design: Toward a more integrative conceptualization of work design. *Research in Personnel and Human Resources Management, 27*, 39–91.

Nilles, J. (1998). *Managing Telework: Strategies for Managing the Virtual Workforce*. New York: Wiley and Sons.

Ramírez, Y. W., & Nembhard, D. A. (2004). Measuring knowledge worker productivity. *Journal of Intellectual Capital, 5*, 602–628.

Richardson, J., & McKenna, S. (2014). Reordering spatial and social relations: A case study of professional and managerial flexworkers. *British Journal of Management, 25*, 724–736.

Robbins, S., & Judge, T. (2014). *Organizational Behavior* (16th ed.). Upper Saddle River, NJ: Person Education.

Schaufeli, W., Bakker, A. B., & Salanova, M. (2006). The measurement of work engagement with a short questionnaire: A cross-national study. *Educational and Psychological Measurement, 66*, 701–716.

Schaufeli, W. B., Salanova, M., González-Romá, V., & Bakker, A. B. (2002). The measurement of engagement and burnout: A two sample confirmatory factor analytic approach. *Journal of Happiness Studies, 3*, 71–92.

Schippers, M. C., Edmondson, A. C., & West, M. A. (2014). Team reflexivity as an antidote to team information processing failures. *Small Group Research, 45*, 731–769.

Schippers, M. C., West, M. A., & Edmondson, A. C. (2017). Team reflexivity and innovation. In E. Salas, R. Rico & J. Passmore (Eds.), *The Wiley Blackwell Handbook of the Psychology of Teamwork and Collaborative Processes*. Chichester, UK: Wiley-Blackwell.

Staples, D. S. (2001). A study of remote workers and their differences from non-remote workers. *Journal of Organizational and End User Computing, 13*(2), 3–14.

Staples, D. S., Hulland, J. S., & Higgins, C. A. (1999). A self-efficacy theory explanation for the management of remote workers in virtual organizations. *Organization Science, 10*, 758–776.

Swift, T. A., & West, M. A. (1998). *Reflexivity and Group Processes: Research and Practice*. Sheffield: The ESRC Centre for Organization and Innovation.

ten Brummelhuis, L. L., Bakker, A. B., Hetland, J., & Keulemans, L. (2012). Do new ways of working foster work engagement? *Psicothema, 24*, 113–20.

Tims, M., Bakker, A. B., & Derks, D. (2012). Development and validation of the job crafting scale. *Journal of Vocational Behavior, 80*, 173–186.

Tims, M., Bakker, A. B., Derks, D., & van Rhenen, W. (2013). Job Crafting at the Team and Individual Level: Implications for Work Engagement and Performance. *Group & Organization Management, 38*, 427–454.

van Heck, E., van Baalen, P., van der Meulen, N., & van Oosterhout, M. (2012). Achieving high perfomance in a mobile and green workplace: Lessons from Microsoft Netherlands. *MIS Quarterly Executive, 10*(2), 115–117.

Vohs, K. D., Baumeister, R. F., Schmeichel, B. J., Twenge, J. M., Nelson, N. M., & Tice, D. M. (2008). Making choices impairs subsequent self-control: A limited-resource account of decision making, self-regulation, and active initiative. *Journal of Personality and Social Psychology, 94,* 883–898.

Wessels, C. (2017). Flexible working practices: How employees can reap the benefits for engagement and performance. Available from http://hdl.handle.net/1765/99312

Wessels, C., Schippers, M. C., Stegmann, S., Bakker, A. B., Van Baalen, P. J., & Proper, K. I. (2018). How to Cope with Flexibility in the New World of Work: A Model of Time-Spatial Job Crafting. Manuscript Submitted for Publicaton.

Wessels. C., Schippers, M. C., van Baalen, P. J., & Proper, K. I. (2016). Proactively coping with flexible work practices: Testing a context-specific model of job crafting. In *Proceedings of the Annual Meeting of the Academy of Management, (AOM 2016),* August 5–9, 2016, Anaheim, USA.

Widmer, P., Schippers, M. C., & West, M. A. (2009). Recent developments in reflexivity research: A review. *Psychology of Everyday Activity, 2,* 2–11.

Wrzesniewski, A., & Dutton, J. E. (2001). Crafting a job: Revisioning employees as active crafters of their work. *The Academy of Management Review, 26,* 179–201.

6 "Bounded Flexibility"

The Influence of Time-Spatial Flexibility and Boundary-Management Strategies on Women's Work-Home Interference

Pascale Peters and Beatrice Van der Heijden

Introduction

In many countries, time-spatial flexibility is an increasingly popular working practice that organizations may introduce under the broader heading of 'New Ways of Working' (Kelliher & Richardson, 2012; Peters, 2011). It can also be viewed to be one of the drivers of the increase in solo-self-employment (cf. Álvarez & Sinde-Cantorna, 2014). Time-spatial flexibility entails sovereignty for individual workers about both the timing and location of their work-related activities (Ala-Mursula et al., 2002; Spreitzer, Cameron & Garrett, 2017). Typical examples of HR practices that are associated with time-spatial flexibility comprise having a say over when to start and end working and tele(home)working (cf. Peters, Den Dulk & Van der Lippe, 2009; Peters et al., 2014). Researchers and practitioners alike have presented time-spatial flexibility as a possible 'multiple-gain' strategy that can be used to generate positive outcomes for society, organizations and individuals (Peters, 2011).

At the individual level, the focus of attention in this chapter, time-spatial flexibility can foster individuals' career, work, and life satisfaction (cf. Crompton, 2002), which may be reflected in the experience of a better balance between their work and home domains. Although we acknowledge that not all individuals have a cohabiting partner and/or children and may have to deal with multiple other roles in their daily lives besides work and family roles (i.e., they may also be involved in leisure pursuits, community activities, religious or volunteering activities, supporting extended family members, neighbors, and friends, *et cetera*) (Eby et al., 2005), this chapter explicitly focuses on how individuals experience the balance between roles in their work and home domains. Valcour (2007) refers to 'work-family balance' in this regard which she defines as "an overall level of contentment resulting from an assessment of one's degree of success at meeting work and personal role demands" (p. 1512). In this chapter, however, we use the concept of work-home balance to refer to a worker's experience of negative interference and/or positive interference between their roles in the work and home domains, respectively (cf. Friedman & Greenhaus, 2000; Greenhaus & Beutell, 1985; Greenhaus & Powell, 2006). More specifically, negative work-home interference, or work-home conflict, implies that a worker experiences the role enactment in her work and non-work domains to be conflicting in terms of a lack of time and energy resources available to adequately fulfill her work and non-work roles (Tausig & Fenwick, 2001). In the literature, three types of work-home conflict are distinguished (Greenhaus & Beutell, 1985). 'Time-based conflict' (e.g., schedule conflict) develops when time devoted to obligations in the one domain (e.g., work) makes it difficult to fulfil requirements in the other domain (e.g., home). 'Strain-based conflict' (e.g., work-role overload) refers to the extent to which strain developed in the one domain (e.g., work) hampers functioning in the other domain (e.g., home). 'Behavior-based conflict' (e.g., psychological strain) occurs when behavior required in the one role (e.g., work) makes it difficult to fulfill requirements in the other role (e.g., home). Our focus will be on time-based and strain-based conflict, as these are particularly associated with work-home conflict (Allen et al., 2000). Positive work-home interference relates to whether a worker perceives that her participation in the one role or domain generates resources that enhance the functioning and satisfaction in the other role or domain (cf. Bakker & Geurts, 2004; Geurts et al., 2005; Greenhaus & Powell, 2006; Rastogi, Rangnekar & Rastogi, 2016).

The dominant 'work-home balance discourse' suggests that it is critical for workers to develop so-called boundary-management strategies to deal optimally with time-spatial flexibility (Dumas & Sanchez-Burks, 2015; Friedman & Greenhaus, 2000; Kossek et al., 2012; Kreiner, 2006; Kreiner, Hollensbe & Sheep, 2009). In particular, in order to understand how workers experience the combination of their daily work and home roles, 'boundary theory' looks into how workers create, maintain, and frequently transition across work-home role boundaries (Ashforth, Kreiner & Fugate, 2000; Nippert-Eng, 1996). In practice, individuals may differ both in how they would like to manage their work-home boundaries (i.e., their 'preferred boundary-management strategies') and how they actually enact this (i.e., their 'enacted boundary-management strategies') (Kossek et al., 2012; Nippert-Eng, 1996). In theory, workers may construct their preferred and enacted work-home boundaries, respectively, along a continuum, ranging from highly segmented to highly integrated. Examples of boundary-management strategies that are high on segmentation are 'having a separate entrance to a home office' and 'having a home and work telephone', or 'hiring a babysitter while working' (Mirchandani, 2000).

With regard to how boundaries are managed, a distinction can be made between the degree of 'flexibility of a certain role boundary' (i.e., the degree to which a worker's roles are bound to spatial and temporal work-nonwork boundaries); the degree of 'permeability of a certain role boundary' (i.e., the degree to which a worker can be physically located in one role domain, but psychologically and/or behaviorally involved in another role domain), and the degree of 'contrast in role identities' (i.e., the degree to which norms, values, beliefs, goals, and characteristics of a worker's work and home role identities differ or overlap) (Ashforth et al., 2000). Hence, whereas the dimension 'time-spatial flexibility' of a worker's enacted boundary-management strategy focusses on whether she uses the flexibility that may be provided by her work environment to enact work and home-role-related activities at different times and locations, the dimension 'boundary permeability' focusses on whether she integrates a role activity in one domain (e.g., engaging in a virtual business meeting) into activities in the other domain (e.g., activities with her family). Moreover, role-identity contrast refers to whether the attributes (skills, opinions, values) she reveals in the one role (e.g., the degree of friendliness and understanding or exercising authority in the work role) differs or overlaps with those in the other role (e.g., that of being a parent). Whilst we acknowledge that a worker's preferred boundary-management strategy can deviate from the enacted principles used by the worker to organize her role demands and expectations into specific realms of home and work (Kreiner et al., 2009), the focus in this study will be on the *enacted* boundary-management strategy. In line with the scholarly literature in this field, we will distinguish two directions of enacted 'cross-role interruption behaviors': work-into-home-interruptions and home-into-work-interruptions (Kossek & Lautsch, 2008; Kossek et al., 2012).

Both in the boundary-management literature and in management practice, the relationships between a worker's enacted boundary-management strategies and negative and positive outcomes in the work and home domains have been debated. On the one hand, top managers have started to advocate the idea of workers 'bringing their whole authentic self to work', as this form of role-identity integration may enhance individual and organizational performance in the work domain (Dumas & Sanchez-Burks, 2015). For example, when the home domain provides salient skills that can be useful in the work domain or when perceived time scarcity hinders a worker's organizational commitment, it is argued that integration of home and work-role attributes could lead to better performance at work. Also, when a worker's personal attributes match organizational values, this could be useful as it allows her to better manage her identity and relationships at work (Dumas & Sanchez-Burks, 2015).

On the other hand, however, some top managers have become increasingly resistant to allow integration (via time-spatial flexibility and permeability of work and non-work boundaries), as they believe this may negatively affect performance at work. For example, in 2013, Yahoo's CEO Marissa Mayer decided to eliminate (full-time) tele(home)work practices in her organization in view of a perceived loss of productivity caused by virtual working, as this may affect collaboration and communication, and would stimulate workers' opportunistic and untruthful work behaviors (Webwereld, 2013). Conversely, however, a leading consumer and business analyst company (Mindmetre, 2012) presented a study performed among 16,000 managers around the globe that revealed that tele(home)work has the potential to improve productivity and that a large proportion of the managers attributed this to its motivating potential. Both claims, however, call for more substantiation by academic research. Moreover, no insight was given into whether time-spatial flexibility can have motivational potential which may lead to more or less work-home interference, which may possibly underlie work outcomes, such as productivity (cf. Hoornweg, Peters & Van der Heijden, 2016).

The current chapter, therefore, combines the Job Demands-Resources model (JD-R model) (Demerouti et al., 2001) and boundary theory (Kossek et al., 2012) to examine both negative (time-based and strain-based) and positive work-home interference experienced by employed and self-employed women workers in the Dutch labor market context, which can be characterized as a 'part-time economy' (i.e., the majority of women in the Netherlands work reduced hours, whereas men work mostly full-time). As women, for the larger part, are still mainly responsible for meeting home demands, having access to time-spatial flexibility to balance their work and home obligations may be more salient to them in comparison to men. In a similar vein, women may be more subject to negative and positive work-home interference than men (Beham et al., 2017; Franks, Schurink & Fourie, 2006; Geurts et al., 2005; Marais et al., 2014; Straub, Beham & Islam, 2017).

Although negative and positive work-home interference can be regarded as bidirectional concepts (Geurts et al., 2005; Greenhaus, Parasuraman & Collins, 2001), we will look into the interference of work with home, as empirical research has consistently shown that work is far more likely to interfere (negatively) with home than *vice versa* (Bakker & Geurts, 2004). More specifically, we will examine how women workers' access to time-spatial flexibility and their enactment of boundary-management segmentation (work-to-home and home-to-work segmentation, respectively) impacts their perceptions of (negative and positive) work-home interference (Crompton, 2002; Kossek et al., 2006). In addition, we will analyze whether segmentation can be used as an individual boundary-management strategy that may affect the alleged effects of time-spatial flexibility on negative and positive work-home interference. The model to be tested in this study is presented in Figure 6.1.

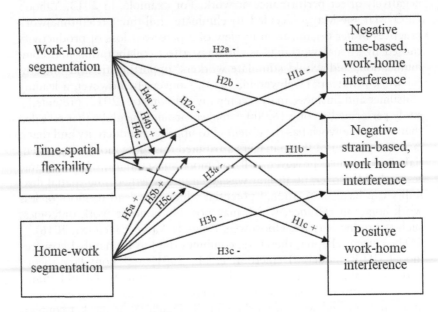

Figure 6.1 Conceptual Model

Theoretical Lens and Hypotheses

The Job Demands-Resources Model

The Job Demands-Resources (JD-R) model distinguishes between job demands and job resources, and defines job demands as aspects of individuals' work roles that "require sustained physical and/or psychological effort or skills and are therefore associated with certain physiological and/or psychological costs" (Bakker, Demerouti & Verbeke, 2004, p. 86). In a related vein, job resources can be defined as those physical, psychological, social, or organizational aspects of the job that are (1) functional in achieving work and home goals, (2) reduce job and home demands and the associated physiological and psychological costs; or (3) stimulate personal growth and development (Bakker et al., 2004, p. 86).

The JD-R model also describes two psychological processes that play a role in the development of strain and motivation, respectively, affecting individual outcomes (Bakker & Demerouti, 2007), such as work-home balance. The first one comprises a so-called health-impairment process, a process wherein high job demands exhaust workers' mental and physical resources, and may therefore lead to a depletion of energy, exhaustion, health problems, and eventually premature withdrawal from their profession. The second underlying process is motivational in nature and comprises job resources that have either intrinsic (because they foster growth, learning and development) or extrinsic (because they are instrumental in achieving work goals) motivational potential and may lead to positive work outcomes, such as work engagement and high job performance. In line with Bakker and Geurts (2004), we argue that the health-impairment process is associated with negative work-home interference and the motivational process with positive work-home interference.

Time-Spatial Flexibility, Boundary Permeability, and Work-Home Interference

Time-spatial flexibility can be viewed as a job resource (Ala-Mursula et al., 2002; Geurts et al., 2005; Peters & Van der Lippe, 2007; Peters & Wildenbeest, 2012; Powell & Greenhaus, 2006) that can enable work-home balance (Friedman & Greenhaus, 2000; Rastogi et al., 2016). First, it has the potential to counteract the health-impairment process and thereby to decrease both time- and strain-based conflicts. Time pressure can be reduced when workers use their sovereignty over when and where they work to optimize their work schedule (Peters & Van der Lippe, 2007). They can do this, for example, by adjusting their working hours to meet the obligations they have in their home domain (Madsen, 2003), thereby reducing temporal and physical barriers to combine work and home obligations. Time-spatial flexibility can increase perceived control over time and place of work, which allows workers to be available for both work and home roles when necessary, thereby reducing negative spillover of strain across domains. As a result, workers may experience their jobs as less demanding. In addition, since the behavioral and emotional availability in the family role is protected as a result of the decreased job demands, it is expected that less negative load effects would spill over from work to the home domain and that it therefore becomes easier to combine work and home (Friedman & Greenhaus, 2000). Based on the account earlier, the following hypotheses were formulated:

Hypothesis 1a/b: Time-spatial flexibility is associated with lower levels of negative time-based (H1a) and negative strain-based, work-home interference (H1b).

Second, viewed as a job resource, time-spatial flexibility may also have motivational potential. That is, resources gained by time-spatial flexibility at work can possibly be directly employed in the home domain ('the instrumental way'). Alternatively, positive affect gained by time-spatial flexibility may spill over to, and improve performance in, the home domain ('the affective way') (Powell & Greenhaus, 2006). For example, workers who can work from home may be better able to focus on doing their jobs, which may evoke positive experiences (Lambert, 2000; Peters & Wildenbeest, 2012). They may also work more efficiently and achieve more (Friedman & Greenhaus, 2000). The resultant positive experiences, in turn, may develop positive load effects that can spill over from the work role into the family role, because workers may enhance their own emotional gratification and attain personal fulfillment at work (Friedman & Greenhaus, 2000; Greenhaus & Powell, 2006). Therefore, the following hypothesis was formulated:

Hypothesis 1c: Time-spatial flexibility is associated with higher levels of positive work-home interference (H1c).

Besides having more say in where and when to work, in some cases, time-spatial flexibility may also imply more individual control regarding setting work-home boundaries (Kossek et al., 2012). Boundary control allows workers to choose an individual strategy to construct the boundaries between the work and home domains, so that these fit their preferences regarding how to organize their social environment and to meet the often competing job and home demands (Kossek, Noe & DeMarr, 1999; Nippert-Eng, 1996). Using meaningful boundary-management strategies in both directions of cross-role interruption behaviors [work-into-home interruptions and home-into-work interruptions (Kossek et al., 2012)] is expected to decrease negative work-home interference and to increase positive work-home interference. The chosen boundary-management strategy can enable workers to concentrate more on the domain that is, at any point in time, in most urgent need of their attention (Ashforth et al., 2000). That is, it can help to make workers physically and psychologically available to the domain that matters most. More specifically, an integration strategy allows individuals to shift from one frame of mind to another if needed and to act in a way that is appropriate to the role they want, or need to be in at a certain moment in time (Kossek et al., 2006), and may hence be accompanied by multiple role switches. Generally, however, an expanded number of role switches and, consequently, higher levels of multi-tasking and distractions by other domain activities can consume extra energy (Kossek, 2009). This implies that it is also possible that performance in a particular domain does not improve as a result of greater integration, and that more negative and less positive work-home interferences are developed. In the literature, therefore, enacting segmentation is viewed as a boundary-management strategy that can reduce the number of role switches and, in turn, can reduce negative work-home interference (Dumas & Sanchez-Burks, 2015). This may be important particularly in view of ever more demanding work contexts and the growing use of technological devices that facilitate boundary crossings (Kelliher & Anderson, 2010; Kossek, Lautsch & Eaton, 2006; Peters et al., 2017). In the case of higher levels of boundary permeability, it is easier to continue working for longer hours, which may increase work stress and work overload (Hill et al., 1998; Peters et al., 2009), and allows workers to ponder over work at moments that used to be assigned to family engagement, resulting into work-related stress spilling over into the home domain (Bakker & Geurts, 2004; Kossek et al., 2006).

In some cases, however, a strategy high on integration may be used to enhance performance in the work and home domains (cf. Derks et al., 2016). Enacting segmentation may, therefore, limit positive work-home interference that could result from the instrumental and affective boundary-crossing mechanisms as described by Greenhaus and Powell (2006). In other words, under conditions of segmentation, resources, and positive affect gained in the work domain may less easily be transferred into the home domain (Dumas & Sanchez-Burks, 2015).

Based on the line of reasoning earlier, the following hypotheses were formulated:

> **Hypothesis 2a/b/c:** Enacting stricter work-home segmentation is *negatively* associated with: negative time-based (H2a) and negative strain-based, work-home interference (H2b), and with positive work-home interference (H2c).
>
> **Hypothesis 3a/b/c:** Enacting stricter home-work segmentation is *negatively* associated with: negative time-based (H3a) and negative strain-based, work-home interference (H3b), and with positive work-home interference (H3c).

In conclusion, in view of the trend toward increasingly blurred work-home boundaries and the expectations of others for higher availability in the work and home domains (Peters et al., 2017), getting (back) in control is deemed important for work-home balance (Kossek et al., 2006, 2012). However, protecting one's work-home balance becomes problematic when the two domains become too mixed for boundaries to be effectively controlled (*ibid.*). Due to enhanced access to time-spatial flexibility in the work domain, work activities may be less tied to specific places and times. Consequently, the borders between work and home domains can become (too) permeable; roles can become (too) weakly differentiated, allowing (too) frequent cross-role interruptions (Ashforth et al., 2000; Kreiner et al., 2009). In line with boundary theory (Dumas & Sanchez-Burks, 2015; Kossek et al., 2006; Nippert-Eng, 1996), we assume that workers who experience both higher levels of time-spatial flexibility and simultaneously enact a segmentation strategy have better chances to counteract any possible negative work-home interference. However, when time-spatial flexibility is accompanied by a segmentation strategy, positive spillover from resources and affect gained in the work domain into the home domain may also be limited (Dumas & Sanchez-Burks, 2015).

Therefore, the following hypotheses were formulated:

Hypothesis 4a/b/c: The relationship between time-spatial flexibility and work-home interference is moderated by workers' boundary-management strategies, such that more work-home segmentation enhances the alleged negative effects of time-spatial flexibility on negative time-based (H4a) and negative strain-based, work-home interference (H4b), but reduces the alleged positive effect of time-spatial flexibility on positive work-home interference (H4c).

Hypothesis 5a/b/c: The relationship between time-spatial flexibility and work-home interference is moderated by workers' boundary-management strategies, such that more home-work segmentation enhances the alleged negative effects of time-spatial flexibility on negative time-based (H5a) and negative strain-based, work-home interference (H5b), but reduces the alleged positive effect of time-spatial flexibility on positive work-home interference (H5c).

Methodology

Participants and Procedure

The data used in this study were collected via an e-questionnaire among women workers registered at a Dutch work agency for virtual work in the business service sector. All (unemployed, employed, or self-employed) persons registered at the agency's data base (N = 7,700) were approached via email with the work agency's permission and recommendation letter. After 3 reminders, 583 registered persons filled in the e-questionnaire (response rate 8%), and in total, 448 usable data points of women workers were obtained after elimination of respondents that had not been working in the past 3 months.

Measures

Negative Work-Home Interference (Negative WHI) and Positive Work-Home Interference (Positive WHI) were measured using the thoroughly validated subscales from the Dutch SWING questionnaire (Geurts et al.,

2005). All scale anchors ranged from 1 to 4, with 1 indicating that "the work/non-work domain does not have much influence on the respondent's non-work/work domain" and 4 indicating that "the work/non-work domain has a lot of influence on the respondent's non-work/work domain". Negative time-based WHI consisted of four items, negative strain-based WHI of four items, and positive WHI of five items (Geurts et al., 2005) (scale reliabilities are presented in Table 6.1). An example item of negative strain-based WHI is, "How often does it happen that . . . you are irritable at home because your work is demanding?" An example item of negative time-based WHI is, "How often does it happen that . . . your work takes up time that you would have liked to spend with your spouse/family/friends?" An example item of positive WHI is, "How often does it happen that . . . you fulfil your domestic obligations better because of the things you have learned on your job?"

Enacted segmentation was measured by a selection of items derived from Kossek and Lautsch's measure (2008). The selection was based on Kossek et al.'s (2012) later study in which the directions of the permeability of the work-home interface [the enacted degree of work-to-home (WH) and home-to-work interruptions (HW), respectively] were taken into account. The original items were designed in the English language, but were translated by the authors into the Dutch language and back-translated in order to check the quality of the translation. Enacted WH interruptions (recoded such that higher scores imply more WH segmentation) were measured by means of three items. An example item is as follows: I almost never work over time outside my normal working hours. Enacted HW interruptions (recoded such that higher scores imply more HW segmentation) were measured by means of five items. An example item is as follows: I only deal with my personal and family affairs at work during (lunch) breaks, unless it is urgent.

Time-spatial flexibility was measured by means of seven items inspired by the scale on temporal flexibility by Ala-Mursula et al. (2002) that is worded in English. For the purpose of this study, however, our own developed Dutch version refers to time-spatial flexibility: the respondent's perceived freedom of action in both deciding where and when to complete their working tasks. Respondents were asked whether they agreed with the following propositions: I am flexible in my temporal work planning; I can choose the time when I start working during the day; I can choose the time when I stop working during the day; I can chose the days that I do my work; I can work from home when there is an emergency at home; I can take a day off when there is an emergency at home; I can work at least one day per week from home. Scale anchors ranged from 1 to 5 (1 = 'I do not agree at all'; and 5 'I do fully agree') (scale reliability presented in Table 6.1).

Table 6.1 Descriptive Statistics, Reliability Coefficients (Cronbach's Alpha on the Diagonal), and Correlations Between the Study Variables, N = 448

Variables	Min	Max	Mean	SD	1	2	3	4	5	6
1. Time-Based, Work-Home Interference	1.00	3.75	1.70	0.52	0.77					
2. Strain-Based, Work-Home Interference	1.00	3.50	1.66	0.48	0.66***	0.76				
3. Positive Work-Home Interference	1.00	4.00	2.19	0.62	0.15***	0.08	0.79			
4. Time-Spatial Flexibility	1.00	5.00	3.43	1.06	−0.03	−0.11*	0.12*	0.90		
5. Work-Home Segmentation	1.00	5.00	2.49	0.93	−0.16***	−0.13*	−0.13**	−0.34***	0.76	
6. Home-Work Segmentation	1.00	5.00	3.26	0.80	−0.14**	−0.06	−0.06	−0.21***	0.37***	0.77

* $p < 0.05$ level.
** $p < 0.01$ level.
*** $p < 0.001$.

Control Variables

The multiple regression analyses conducted were controlled for some demographics as they were expected to have a significant influence on the women respondents' work-home balance.

1. A dummy variable was used to measure the respondent's highest educational level attained (1 = highest level of vocational or academic training = 60%; 0 = lower educated). Because higher educated workers probably have jobs with more accountability, this variable was expected to correlate positively with strain-based negative WHI (Peters & Van der Lippe, 2007);
2. Young children especially demand more time and energy from their parents (*ibid.*). Therefore, two dummy variables (1 = youngest child in that particular age bracket) were calculated to control for *age of the youngest child*: 'Youngest child under 4' (9.6%); 'Youngest child aged 4–12' (33.3%);
3. The respondent's weekly working hours (M = 26.97; SD = 11.65) was used as a control variable since longer hours can be expected to lead to more negative WHI (Peters & Van der Lippe, 2007);
4. A dummy was created distinguishing self-employed women workers (1 = 45%) from employed women (0) because it was expected that self-employed workers would experience more strain-based negative WHI, as they carry more responsibilities and do not have the social security that is offered by a regular job;
5. A dummy variable was created to distinguish between partnered [1 = partnered (79%)] and single (0) women.

Analyses

Descriptives for all variables in the model (see Table 6.1) were calculated and bivariate correlation analyses were conducted to test the relationships between the predictors, dependents, and moderators in our study. To test our hypotheses, multiple regression analyses were conducted (Baron & Kenny, 1986) (see Table 6.2). To try to combat possible problems associated with multi-collinearity, all independent variables, except for the dummies, were centered. Subsequently, two interaction terms (flexibility * work-home segmentation; and flexibility * home-work segmentation) were calculated. In a first step, the controls were included in the analysis model. In a second step, the hypothesized main effects were added. In a third step, the two interaction terms were added to test for moderation. Since the interaction effects were not significant, and the significance levels of the effects of the predictor variables did not change when adding the controls, for the sake of the power size of the analyses, Table 6.2 presents the effects of the main effects only.

Results

Descriptives

Preliminary analyses (Table 6.1) indicated that the average scores for negative time-based and strain-based WHI were not very high. In general, the respondents experienced more positive WHI (M = 2.19; SD = 0.62) in comparison with negative time-based and strain-based WHI [M = 1.70 (SD = 0.52) and 1.66 (SD = 0.48), respectively]. Moreover, both types of negative WHI correlated quite strongly with one another (r = 0.66***). In addition, both the average score and the standard deviation for time-spatial flexibility were quite high (M = 3.43; SD = 1.06), which implies that, in general, a large group of women in our sample had access to time-spatial flexibility, but that the within-group differences are large. Contrary to our expectations, time-spatial flexibility did not correlate significantly with negative time-based WHI (r = –0.03) and only weakly positively with negative strain-based WHI (r = –0.11*), and with positive WHI (r = 12*).

Although clearly interrelated (r = 0.37***), the average score for WH segmentation (M = 2.49; SD = 0.93) was shown to be much lower than the score for HW segmentation (M = 3.26; SD = 0.80), indicating that the respondents' boundaries between the work and home domains are relatively more permeable than the ones between the home and work domains. Moreover, both types of segmentation were negatively correlated with both negative time-based WHI (WH segmentation: r = –0.16***; HW segmentation: r = –0.14**) and negative strain-based negative WHI (WH segmentation: r = –0.09*; HW segmentation: r= –0.12*).

However, HW segmentation was not significantly correlated with positive WHI (r = –0.06), while, unexpectedly, WH segmentation correlated negatively with positive WHI (r = –0.13**). Interestingly, both WH and HW segmentation correlated negatively with time-spatial flexibility (r = –0.34*** and r = –0.214***), indicating that those who have more access to time-spatial flexibility have more blurring boundaries between the work and home domains.

Hypotheses Testing

Negative Time-Based WHI

In line with Hypothesis 1a, higher levels of time-spatial flexibility were associated with less negative time-based WHI (β = –0.16***) (see Table 6.2, Model 1). Hypothesis 2a, stating that stricter WH segmentation is associated with lower levels of negative time-based WHI, was confirmed as well (β = –0.14**). However, this did not hold true regarding the hypothesis on HW segmentation (H3a) (β = –0.07). The moderation Hypotheses

4a and 5a stating that WH and HW segmentation would strengthen the negative effect of time-spatial flexibility on negative time-based WHI was not confirmed either (therefore, not reported in Table 6.2). In addition, the control variables 'working hours' ($\beta = 0.14^{**}$) and 'self-employment' ($\beta = 0.13^{**}$) were associated with more negative time-based WHI. The multiple regression model appeared to be significant [$F(df = 6) = 5.317^{***}$], with all variables together explaining a reasonable amount of variance ($R^2 = 10.5\%$; Adjusted $R^2 = 8.2\%$).

Negative Strain-Based WHI

In line with Hypothesis 1b, respondents reporting higher levels of time-spatial flexibility experienced less negative strain-based WHI

Table 6.2 Standardized Regression Coefficients (Beta) Explaining Time-Based, Strain-Based, and Positive Work-Home Interference by Time-Spatial Flexibility and Work-Home Segmentation and Home-Work Segmentation (N = 448).

	Model 1 Time-Based, Work-Home Interference	Model 2 Strain-Based, Work-Home Interference	Model 3 Positive Work-Home Interference
	Beta	Beta	Beta
Highest Level of Vocational Training or Academic Level: YES	0.07	0.18***	0.02
Dummy: Youngest Child [0–3]	–0.06	–0.07	–0.04
Dummy: Youngest Child [4–12]	0.07	0.03	0.09*
Respondent's Weekly Working Hours	0.14**	0.09*	0.05
Dummy: Self-Employed: Yes	0.13**	0.06	–0.07
Dummy: Partnered: Yes	–0.04	0.02	0.07
Time-Spatial Flexibility	–0.16***	–0.22***	0.10*
Work-Home Segmentation	–0.14**	–0.09*	–0.09
Home-Work Segmentation	–0.07	–0.08*	0.00
R^2 in %	10.5%	9.7%	4.3%
Adjusted R^2 in %	8.2%	8.0%	2.4%

* $p < 0.05$ level.
** $p < 0.01$ level.
*** $p < 0.001$ level.
Hypotheses were tested one-tailed.

Note that interactions between time-spatial flexibility and, respectively, work-home and home-work segmentation on negative or positive work-home interference were not significant and, therefore, not reported.

($\beta = -0.22^{***}$; Table 6.2, Model 2). As regards Hypotheses 2b and 3b, respondents setting both stricter WH and HW boundaries appeared to experience less negative strain-based WHI ($\beta = -0.09^*$ and $\beta = -0.08^*$, respectively) indeed. However, Hypotheses 4b and 5b, assuming moderation effects of the two distinguished segmentation strategies on the relationship between time-spatial flexibility and negative strain-based WHI, were not supported (therefore, not reported in Table 6.2). In addition to these findings, both the control variables 'working hours' ($\beta = 0.09^*$) and 'higher education' ($\beta = 0.18^{***}$) appeared to be linked with more negative strain-based WHI. The regression model showed a significant outcome [$F(df = 6) = 5.199^{***}$], with all variables together explaining a significant amount of variance ($R^2 = 9.7\%$; Adjusted $R^2 = 8.0\%$).

Positive WHI

In line with Hypothesis 1c, time-spatial flexibility was associated with higher levels of positive WHI ($\beta = 0.10^*$). Contrary to Hypotheses 2c and 3c, no significant effects of WH segmentation and HW segmentation were found ($\beta = -0.009$ and $\beta = 0.00$, respectively). Also Hypotheses 4c and 5c, assuming moderation effects of the two distinguished boundary-management strategies on the relationship between time-spatial flexibility and positive WHI, were not confirmed (therefore, not reported in Table 6.2). 'Age of the youngest child [4–12]' ($\beta = 0.09^*$) was the only control variable that appeared to be significant in explaining effects in positive WHI. The regression model outcome was significant [$F(df = 6) = 2.20^*$], with all variables together explaining some variance in positive WHI ($R^2 = 4.3\%$; adjusted $R^2 = 2.4\%$).

Discussion and Conclusion

First, as time-spatial flexibility appeared to be associated with, on the one hand, less negative time-based and strain-based WHI, and, on the other hand, with more positive WHI, we argue that time-spatial flexibility can be seen as a job resource that has the potential to improve work-home balance. From our study, we may conclude that women workers who can use sovereignty over when and where to work are indeed better able to gain optimal work and family schedules, probably because time and energy are less depleted (Greenhaus & Beutell, 1985; Tietze & Musson, 2005). As a result, they appear to be better able to make their lives less demanding and counteract the so-called health-impairment process associated with working life (combined with home obligations) (Bakker & Demerouti, 2007). Also as a result of time-spatial flexibility, negative load effects from work to the home domain are prevented, thereby protecting women's behavioral and emotional availability regarding their roles in the home domain (cf. Friedman & Greenhaus, 2000), possibly improving their home performance (Greenhaus & Powell, 2006).

This chapter has also added to the scarce (and often contradictory) literature on the relationship between time-spatial flexibility and positive WHI (Friedman & Greenhaus, 2000; Greenhaus & Powell, 2006; Kossek, 2009; Kossek et al., 2006; Lambert, 2000). Concrete, time-spatial flexibility was shown to stimulate spillover of positive load effects from work into the home domain, thereby enhancing the so-called motivational process. In particular, positive experiences, such as personal development (e.g., decision latitude, family support), may possibly be generated in the case of time-spatial flexibility.

Second, this chapter has elaborated on the so-called boundary theory (Kossek et al., 2006; Kossek & Lautsch, 2008; Nippert-Eng, 1996) by examining the effects of two types of segmentation strategies (cf. Kossek et al., 2012) on working women's WHI. More specifically, our outcomes showed that both WH- and HW-segmentation strategies have the potential to affect WHI. Particularly WH segmentation appeared to be beneficial, as it was shown to reduce both feelings of time famine in the home domain and to prevent negative emotions and behaviors from spilling over from work into the home domain. In our study, setting stricter boundaries—i.e., reducing the permeability between the two domains of work and home seemed to make it easier for women workers to concentrate on the particular role that was most demanding to them at a particular moment (cf. Ashforth et al., 2000; Kossek et al., 2006). Stricter work-home segmentation strategies, however, were not shown to either reduce, or enhance the women's degree of positive WHI.

In addition, this chapter has examined the possible moderation effects of WH- and HW segmentation strategies on the relationships between time-spatial flexibility, on the one hand, and negative and positive WHI, on the other hand. Contrary to our expectations, we did not find any empirical support for our moderation hypotheses stating that more segmentation would enhance the negative effects of time-spatial flexibility on, respectively, negative time-based and strain-based WHI, and reduce the positive effect on positive WHI. Instead, our results imply that all our respondents, regardless of their degree of access to time-spatial flexibility, may gain from WH and HW segmentation, possibly being a counter strategy to juggle effectively the, often opposing, demands of work and home in women's lives.

Limitations and Recommendations for Future Research

First, we believe that although our diverse sample of women workers was very interesting in the context of our research problem, it was not representative for the whole (Dutch) working (women) population as it mostly comprised women that were highly educated. Moreover, many women in our sample appeared to have access to time-spatial flexibility and experienced low average levels of negative WHI. The typical Dutch national context, characterized by high levels of women (and men) working reduced hours (Keuzenkamp et al., 2009), may also account for the relatively low amount of explained variance in our work-home balance outcome indicators. Working reduced hours probably also enabled the women in our study to cope with the demands of home and work (Peters et al., 2009).

However, in comparison with their male counterparts, women's work-home balance may benefit relatively more from time-spatial flexibility (*ibid.*), as women still tend to do more unpaid work in the domestic sphere that can conflict with paid work, such as taking children to/from school, or taking part into leisure activities with them. In order to shed more light on possible gender differences, future research could examine men's boundary-management strategies, in relation to time-spatial flexibility and positive and negative WHI. More scholarly work is also needed to better understand these relationships across various national and organizational contexts (Beham et al., 2017).

Second, the present study focused on enacted boundary-management strategies, starting from the theoretical assumption that segmentation is (overall) the best strategy to enhance work-home balance (Dumas & Sanchez-Burks, 2015). Of course, we acknowledge that enacting integration can lead to better work-home outcomes as well, particularly when it is congruent with one's preferences (cf. Derks et al., 2016; Kreiner et al., 2009). Moreover, it should also be acknowledged that contextual factors, such as national culture, gender ideology, or workplace-related factors, such as work overload and the need to be on call for colleagues, customers, or family members (Peters et al., 2017), may lead to incongruence between one's enacted and preferred boundary-management strategies (Kreiner et al., 2009). Future research could focus on how (gendered) preferred and enacted boundary-management strategies are shaped by contextual factors and how this may possibly lead to incongruence and work-home interference (cf. Kossek & Lautsch, 2008; Kreiner et al., 2009).

Practical Implications

This chapter has practical importance, both for individual (women) workers and for the organizations and businesses they work in, particularly since flexible working is an emergent form of organizing (Kelliher & Richardson, 2012; Peters, 2011; Peters et al., 2009; Spreitzer et al., 2017; Tietze & Musson, 2005). In fact, the scholarly literature in this domain suggests that when room for flexibility is not offered, many women are frustrated by a demanding and inflexible working environment (Hewlett, 2002) and may decide to become self-employed (Thompson, Jones-Evans & Kwong, 2009), herewith resulting in a significant loss for companies, especially since the latter often applies to women with substantial work experience (Bruni, Gherardi & Poggio, 2004).

From the perspective that time-spatial flexibility can also be imposed on workers (Kossek et al., 2006), the latter need to find ways to deal with it and have to develop strategies and tactics to stay in control (Kreiner et al., 2009). However, we advocate that setting boundaries is also important for workers who deliberately choose to work flexibly, for example, for workers that request an individual telework arrangement, or for those who opt for self-employment. The present study suggests that, in general, all (women) workers may benefit from boundary segmentation as a counter strategy to 'get back in control' and to be able to juggle effectively the demands of work and home.

Time-spatial flexibility and being able to exercise some control over work (job autonomy) are key factors persuading, especially women, to extend their labor-market hours (Keuzenkamp et al., 2009) and/or to (be able to) work overtime (Kelliher & Anderson, 2010; Peters et al., 2009), being beneficial for other parties in work organizations as well. Due to the possible decrease of negative WHI, flexible workers may remain more committed and productive (Greenhaus & Parasuraman, 1997). All this may stimulate women to further develop their employability (career potential) and upward mobility, and may allow employers to make optimal use of women's human capital in the workforce (Van der Heijden, Peters & Kelliher, 2015). By offering flexible work arrangements, women may be less likely to leave their organization and become self-employed in order to gain more flexibility (Álvarez & Sinde-Cantorna, 2014). Yet, in order to achieve this, a shift towards a culture that places less importance on hours of attendance in the workplace and moves toward a more results-oriented approach is needed at all organizational levels (Bleijenbergh, Gremmen & Peters, 2016).

Conclusion

The study presented in this chapter demonstrates the usefulness of time-spatial flexibility to improve work-home balance (in terms of decreased work-home conflicts and enhanced positive spillover between the work and non-work domains). Moreover, it elaborated on the notion of the boundary theory by studying the influence of two different directions of permeability characterizing individuals' boundary-management strategies (Kossek et al., 2012), particularly focusing on working women's work-home balance. Moreover, we revealed the importance of setting stricter boundaries (i.e., segmentation) between the work and home domains in order to decrease work-home conflict. However, we also discovered that setting stricter boundaries neither improves nor hampers the functioning and satisfaction of individual workers and their households (that is their perceived positive WHI).

References

Ala-Mursula, L., Vahtera, J., Kivimaki, M., Kevin, M. V., & Pentti, J. (2002). Employee control over working times: Associations with subjective health and sickness absences. *Epidemiol Community Health*, 56, 272–278.

Allen, T. D., Herst, D. E. L., Bruck, C. S., & Sutton, M. (2000). Consequences associated with work-to-family conflict: A review and agenda for future Research. *Journal of Occupational Health Psychology*, 5, 278–308.

Álvarez, G., & Sinde-Cantorna, A. I. (2014). Self-employment and job satisfaction: An empirical analysis. *International Journal of Manpower*, 35(5), 688–702.

Ashforth, B. E., Kreiner, G. E., & Fugate, M. (2000). All in a day's work: Boundaries and micro role transitions. *The Academy of Management Review*, 25, 472–491.

Bakker, A. B., & Demerouti, E. (2007). The job demands-resources model: State of the art. *Journal of Managerial Psychology*, 22, 309–328.

Bakker, A. B., Demerouti, E., & Verbeke, W. (2004). Using the job demands-resources model to predict burnout and performance. *Human Resource Management*, 43, 83–104.

Bakker, A. B., & Geurts, S. A. E. (2004). Toward a dual-process model of work-home interference. *Work and Occupations*, 31, 345–366.

Baron, R. M., & Kenny, D. A. (1986). The moderator-mediator variable distinction in Social Psychological research: Conceptual, strategic, and statistical considerations. *Journal of Personality and Social Psychology*, 51, 1173–1182.

Beham, B., Drobnič, S., Präg, P., Baierl, A., & Lewis, S. (2017). Work-to-family enrichment and gender inequalities in eight European countries. *The International Journal of Human Resource Management*, DOI: 10.1080/09585192.2017.1355837

Bleijenbergh, I. L., Gremmen, C. C. M., & Peters, P. (2016). Timing ambition: How organisational actors engage with the institutionalised norms that affect the career development of part-time workers. *Scandinavian Journal of Management*, 32(4), 179–188. DOI: 10.1016/j.scaman.2016.08.004

Bruni, A., Gherardi, S., & Poggio, B. (2004). Doing gender, doing entrepreneurship: An ethnographic account of intertwined practices. *Work and Organization*, 11, 406–429.

Crompton, R. (2002). Employment, flexible working and the family. *British Journal of Sociology*, 53, 537–558.

Demerouti, E., Bakker, A. B., Nachreiner, F., & Schaufeli, W. B. (2001). The job demands-resources model of burnout. *Journal of Applied Psychology*, 86, 499–512.

Derks, D., Bakker, A. B, Peters, P., & Van Wingerden, P. (2016). Work-related smartphone use, work–family conflict and family role performance: The role of segmentation preference. *Human Relations*, 69(5), 1045–1068.

Dumas, T. L., & Sanchez-Burks, J. (2015). The professional, the personal, and the ideal worker: Pressures and objectives shaping the boundary between life domains. *The Academy of Management Annals*, 9(1), 803–843.

Eby, L. T., Casper, W. J., Lockwood, A., Bordeaux, C., & Brinley, A. (2005). Work and family research in IO/OB: Content analysis and review of the literature (1980–2002). *Journal of Vocational Behavior*, 66(1), 124–197.

Franks, K., Schurink, W., & Fourie, L. (2006). Exploring the social construction of life roles of career-oriented women. *South African Journal of Industrial Psychology, 32*(1), 17–24.

Friedman, S. D., & Greenhaus, J. H. (2000). *Work and Family: Allies or Enemies? What Happens When Business Professionals Confront Life Choices.* New York: Oxford University Press.

Geurts, S. A. E., Taris, T. W., Kompier, M. A. J., Dikkers, J. S. E., Van Hooff, M. L. M., & Kinnunen, U. (2005). Work-home interaction from a work psychological perspective: Development and Validation of a New Questionnaire, the SWING. *Work and Stress, 19*, 319–339.

Greenhaus, J. H., & Beutell, N. J. (1985). Sources of conflict between work and family roles. *The Academy of Management Review, 10*, 76–88.

Greenhaus, J. H., & Parasuraman, S. (1997). The integration of work and family life: Barriers and solutions. In S. Parasuraman & J. Greenhaus (Eds.), *Integrating Work and Family: Challenges and Choices for a Changing World* (pp. 232–240). London: Quorum Books.

Greenhaus, J. H., Parasuraman, S., & Collins, K. M. (2001). Career involvement and family involvement as moderators of relationships between work–family conflict and withdrawal from a profession. *Journal of Occupational Health Psychology, 6*, 91–100.

Greenhaus, J. H., & Powell, G. N. (2006). When work and family are allies: A theory of work-family enrichment. *Academy of Management Review, 31*, 72–92.

Hewlett, S. A. (2002). *Creating a Life: Professional Women and the Quest for Children.* New York: Talk Miramax Books.

Hill, E. J., Miller, B. C., Weiner, S. P., & Colihan, J. (1998). Influences of the virtual office on aspects of work and work/life balance. *Personnel Psychology, 51*, 667–683.

Hoornweg, N., Peters, P., & Van der Heijden, B. (2016). Finding the optimal mix between telework and office hours to enhance employee productivity: A study into the relationship between telework intensity and individual productivity, with mediation of intrinsic motivation and moderation of office hours. In J. De Leede (Ed.), *New Ways of Working Practices: Antecedents and Outcomes* (pp. 1–28). Bingley, UK: Emerald Group Publishing.

Kelliher, C., & Anderson, D. (2010). Doing more with less? Flexible working practices and the intensification of work. *Human Relations, 63*(1), 83–106.

Kelliher, C., & Richardson, J. (Eds.) (2012). *New Ways of Organizing Work: Developments, Perspectives and Experiences.* New York, NY: Routledge.

Keuzenkamp, S., Hillebrink, C., Portegijs, W., & Pouwels, B. (2009). *Deeltijd (g)een probleem. Mogelijkheden om de arbeidsduur van vrouwen met een kleine deeltijdbaan te vergroten.* Den Haag: SCP.

Kossek, E. E. (2009). *Portable Work: Why Flexibility Access is Not Enough to Improve Your Life.* Ann Arbor, MI: Center for the Education of Women, University of Michigan.

Kossek, E., & Lautsch, B. (2008). *CEO of Me: Creating a life that Works in the Flexible Job Age.* New Jersey: Pearson Education.

Kossek, E. E., Lautsch, B. A., & Eaton, S. C. (2006). Telecommuting, control and boundary management: Correlates of policy use and practice, job control, and work-family effectiveness. *Journal of Vocational Behavior, 68*(2), 347–367.

Kossek, E. E., Noe, R. A., & DeMarr, B. J. (1999). Work-family role synthesis: Individual and organizational determinants. *The International Journal of Conflict Management, 10,* 102–129.

Kossek, E. E., Ruderman, M. N., Braddy, P. W., & Hannum, K. M. (2012). Work-non-work boundary management profiles: A person-centered approach. *Journal of Vocational Behavior, 81*(1), 112–128.

Kreiner, G. E. (2006). Consequences of work-home segmentation or integration: A person-environment fit perspective. *Journal of Organizational Behavior, 27*(4), 485–507.

Kreiner, G. E., Hollensbe, E. C., & Sheep, M. L. (2009). Balancing borders and bridges: Negotiating the work-home interface via boundary work tactics. *Academy of Management Journal, 52*(4), 704–730.

Lambert, S. (2000). Added benefits: The link between work-life benefits and organizational citizenship behavior. *Academy of Management Journal, 43,* 801–815.

Madsen, S. R. (2003). The effects of home-based teleworking on work-family conflict. *Human Resource Development Quarterly, 14,* 35–58.

Marais, E., De Klerk, M., Nel, J. A., & De Beer, L. (2014). The antecedents and outcomes of work-family enrichment amongst female workers: Original research. *SA Journal of Industrial Psychology, 40*(1), 1–14.

Mindmetre (2012). *Flexibel werken leidt tot hogere productiviteit* [Flexible working leads to higher productivity]. Available from www.vkbanen.nl/

Mirchandani, K. (2000). "The Best of Both Worlds" and "Cutting My Own Throat": Contradictory images of home-based work. *Qualitative Sociology, 23,* 159–182.

Nippert-Eng, C. (1996). Calendars and keys: The classification of "home" and "work". *Sociological Forum, 11,* 563–582.

Peters, P. (2011). New Forms of Work-Flexible working time arrangements in Netherlands: Exchange of good practice. Expert Report for European Commission. 24–25 October, The Hague. Available from http://ec.europa.eu/justice/gender-equality/files/exchange_of_good_practice_nl.

Peters, P., Blomme, R., Van Heertum, A., & Derks, D. (2017). Exploring the "Boundary Control Paradox" and how to cope with it: A social theoretical perspective on managing work-life boundaries and work-life balance in the late modern workplace. In S. De Groof (Ed.), *Work-life Balance in the Modern Workplace: Interdisciplinary Perspectives From Work-family Research, Law and Policy on the Blurring of Boundaries between Work and Private Life* (pp. 261–284). The Bulletin of Comparative Labour Relations. Alphen aan den Rijn, the Netherlands: Kluwer Law International.

Peters, P., Den Dulk, L., & Van der Lippe, T. (2009). The effects of time-spatial flexibility and new working conditions on employees' work-life balance: The Dutch Case. *Community, Work & Family, 12,* 279–298.

Peters, P., Poutsma, F., Van der Heijden, B. I. J. M., Bakker, A. B., & De Bruin, T. (2014). Enjoying new ways to work: An HRM process approach to study flow. *Human Resource Management, 53*(2), 271–290.

Peters, P., & Van der Lippe, T. (2007). The time-pressure reducing potential of telehomeworking: The Dutch Case. *International Journal of Human Resource Management, 18,* 430–447.

Peters, P., & Wildenbeest, M. (2012). Telecommuters: Creative or exhausted workers? A study into the conditions under which telecommuters experience flow and exhaustion. In C. Kelliher & J. Richardson (Eds.), *New Ways of Organizing Work: Developments, Perspectives and Experiences* (pp. 122–139). New York/London: Routledge.

Powell, G. N., & Greenhaus, J. H. (2006). Is the opposite of positive negative? Untangling the complex relationship between work-family enrichment and conflict. *Career Development International, 11*, 650–659.

Rastogi, M., Rangnekar, S., & Rastogi, R. (2016). Flexibility as a predictor of work–family enrichment. *Global Journal of Flexible Systems Management, 17*(1), 5–14.

Spreitzer, G.M., Cameron, L., & Garrett, L. (2017). Alternative work arrangements: Two images of the New World of work. *The Annual Review of Organizational Psychology and Organizational Behavior, 4*, 473–99.

Straub, C., Beham, B., & Islam, G. (2017). Crossing boundaries: Integrative effects of supervision, gender and boundary control on work engagement and work to-family positive spill over. *The International Journal of Human Resource Management.* Available from http://dx.doi.org/10.1080/09585192. 2017.1340324

Tausig, M., & Fenwick, R. (2001). Unbinding time: Alternate work schedules and work-life balance. *Journal of Family and Economic Issues, 22*, 101–119.

Tietze, S., & Musson, G. (2005). Recasting the home-work relationship: A case of mutual adjustment? *Organization Studies, 26*, 1331–1352.

Thompson, P., Jones-Evans, D., & Kwong, C. (2009). Women and home-based entrepreneurship: Evidence from the United Kingdom. *International Small Business Journal, 27*, 227–239.

Valcour, M. (2007). Work-based resources as moderators of the relationship between work hours and satisfaction with work-family balance. *Journal of Applied Psychology, 92*(6), 1512–1523.

Van der Heijden, B. I. J. M., Peters, P., & Kelliher, C. (2015). New ways of working and employability. Towards an agenda for HRD. In R. F. Poell, T. S. Rocco & G. L. Roth (Eds.), *The Routledge Companion to Human Resource Development* (pp. 542–551). London, UK: Routledge.

Webwereld (2013). *Baas Yahoo! Verbiedt thuiswerken.* Available from http://webwereld.nl/mobility/59488-baas-yahoo-verbiedt-thuiswerken

Part III

Professionalization in the Service Industry

Cicerones and Baristas

7 Craft Beer, Cicerones and Changing Identities in Beer Serving

Daniel Clarke, David Weir and Holly Patrick

Introduction

> When I meet new people and tell them 'I work in a bar' it's as if they look at me, thinking: well, you are young and educated, so why are you wasting your time working in a bar?! [. . .] Yeah, there is still a lot of stigma surrounding bar work. Stigma is a real problem.
>
> (Eve, certified beer server level 1)

The nature of bar work is changing. Today, if you walk into a pub in Dundee, York or Edinburgh in the UK you may not only enjoy a pint of locally brewed craft beer but also expect your server to inform you of where the hops are grown, what tastes you can expect to experience and what food best matches your choice of beer.

To begin our conversation about contemporary bar work, we asked a server in a craft beer bar in Dundee, *What is it like serving beer?* It was through speaking with Eve that we alighted upon the Cicerone certification program, which went live in 2008. Cicerone is designed for people who sell and serve beer, and covers a number of areas: (1) keeping and serving beer, (2) beer styles, (3) beer flavor and evaluation, (4) beer ingredients and brewing processes and (5) food pairing (Sheahan, 2018). Where wine has sommeliers, beer now has Cicerones (Prichep, 2013).

Changes in the beer industry are driving shifts in the nature of work in pubs and bars across the UK so in our opening epigraph we have served up some of what Eve said because it speaks, in part, to some of the 'work' that programs such as Cicerone are 'doing' in the world. Changes are afoot in the beer industry and as of mid-December 2017, with over 94,000 certified beer servers—just like Eve—across the world (Sheahan, 2018), Cicerone is driving shifts in the nature of work in pubs/bars the world over. This is a UK study drawing on organization, management and marketing literatures on craft, prosumption and professionalization to analyze the relationship between craft consumerism and beer servers' experiences of work.

In the UK, beer consumption has been historically associated with the special venue of the public house now typically perceived as in a stage of decline (Guardian, 2016a; Andrews and Turner, 2012). There has been a shift from public consumption in bars, pubs and restaurants to consumption at home (Guardian, 2016b). New offerings of 'craft beer' and 'real ale' are promising opportunities to arrest this decline in the UK and elsewhere, for example, as in Australia (see Argent, 2017) and craft beer is a large existing market in other countries, such as the United States. Government funding (e.g. Scottish Enterprise, 2017) and strategic plans (e.g. Scotland, a Land of Food & Drink, 2017a, 2017b) further enhance the contribution of food and drink to economic development in Scotland, encouraging growth in the sale of craft beer (Beercast, 2017). There has been a revival of traditional beer in the UK (Thurnell-Reed, 2014), and the craft beer market is becoming more and more competitive (Cabras & Higgins, 2016; Guardian, 2017), while domination of on-sale trade and intensity of competition in British brewing has long been observed (Lewis, 2001).

Writing about the sale of Premium Bottled Ale in the UK, Scotland Food & Drink (2013, p. 13) note, "Anything that brings a little more theatre to the category is welcome in order to increase browsing time". While increasing browsing time is important for attracting new customers, taste is key to developing a craft beer drinker (Avery, 2011). Since beer enthusiasts are ever more discerning (Wickens, 2010), driving a more sophisticated demand among beer drinkers (Cabras & Bamforth, 2016), a whole industry has emerged around flavor training (see www. cicerone.org/), ensuring that beer has its own language and beer servers are not at a loss as to how best to match drinker to beer (Prichep, 2013).

This chapter is a qualitative inquiry, organized by three guiding theoretical concepts (craft, prosumption and professionalization). In each section of the chapter, we provide some theoretical background to the topic and insights regarding the nature of beer service work. Empirical material created through auto-ethnographic consumer research (Hackley, 2007) and online materials from industry alliances and the media (Levy, 2015) systematically illustrate our theoretical proposals. We drew inspiration from symbolic interactionism and in particular from Levy's (2015) intègraphic approach, which places the researcher at the heart of the inquiry and makes use of diverse approaches to selecting materials through exposure to media, everyday naturally occurring interactions and netnography to examine a given situation. According to Levy (2015), "Olio" encompasses

> the familiar activities called ethnography, netnography and symbolic analysis, as well as participant observation and use of the media, the purpose is to integrate information, data, findings and examples from a variety of sources in the environment that bear on topics of

interest and to explicate what they mean to members of the culture, including the subjects, the researchers, and the audience.

(p. 133)

We use insights derived from our *olio* of data to illustrate our theoretical contentions, rather than as a form of proof. Our study focusses on craft beer servers in the UK where craft beer is traditionally produced and distributed on a local scale; yet the emergence of globalized certification programs, such as Cicerone, mean that there may be implications within our discussion for the same kind of phenomenon happening elsewhere.

The Craft in Craft Beer

"The Lyf so short the craft so long to lerne" (Chaucer, 1382) is one of the favorite quotes in the English language. A typical dictionary definition of "craft" is, "an activity involving skill in making things by hand" (Oxford English Dictionary [OED], 2017a) and the etymology relates to the Old English cræft, 'strength, skill', of Germanic origin. A less positive aspect of "craft" is a "Skill used in deceiving others" (OED, 2017a). Conceivably, most of these definitions could appear in descriptions of the craft aspects of beer dispensing.

"Craft" is one of the most established terms in the study of work often implying pre-industrial roots with implications for a postulated pre-modern type of production, (Ogilvie, 2007; Shanks & McGuire, 1996). It also has a special relevance to the field of beer production and consumption, differentiating a specific type of beer production with consequences for marketing, consumption and cultures of beer (Clemons et al., 2006) and for identities of participants in these performances of serving beer (Thurnell-Read, 2014), tourism (Murray & Kline, 2015) and space marketing (Hede & Watne, 2013).

If there is a re-emergence of craftwork and craft consumption in Western societies as a possible antidote to some of the alienating features of work in modern capitalist societies (Thurnell-Read, 2014), there is not necessarily a common understanding of whether these craft factors are the same in all sectors or through what processes it is organized.

Cabras and Bamforth (2016) describe three waves of micro-brewery development. The first of these occurred between late 1970s and mid-1980s after CAMRA (Campaign for Real Ale) stimulated interest in 'real ale' lobbying for the return of cask-conditioned beer products. The entry of new players, often without previous experience of the sector was encouraged by the Beer Orders that forced larger beer companies to free most of their pubs from the tied status. The third wave dates from the early 2000s, evidenced by "a further and sharper increase in the number of micro-breweries" based on "cheaper, more compact and easier to install" equipment (Cabras & Higgins, 2016, p. 633).

Experts in the trade are divided on what craft brewing is, but BrewDog founders and owners James Watt and Martin Dickie note the dimensions of **size** (less than 500,000 HL annually), **authenticity** (brews all their beers at original gravity and does not use rice, corn or any other adjuncts to lessen flavor and reduce costs), **honesty** (all ingredients clearly listed on the label of all of their beers and the place of brewing clearly listed on all of their beers) and **independence** defined as "no more than 20% owned by a brewing company which operates any brewery which is not a craft brewery" (Watt & Dickie, 2017). This complex definition happens to cover the BrewDog way of producing craft beer rather precisely.

There may be a "globalized social movement around craft beer and local food production" (Kjeldgaard et al., 2017, p. 54). In Britain, since the 1970s, CAMRA has fought for cask ale, arguing that **all cask is craft** (Cask-Marque, 2017). Macnaught (2014) notes, "There is no one single definition in the UK as to what is a craft beer, but this usually indicates they have more intense flavor and contain more premium ingredients". The cask versus keg debate continues. *The Cask Report* (Cask-Marque, 2017) states that "56% of craft drinkers say cask is a craft beer", whereas only "8% of craft drinkers believe keg is craft beer" (p. 16). On this, the beer drinker is now "not free to merely consume a beer, but must deal with the contention of what a beer is and should be" but craft beer has long relied on "contentiousness" to "alter field logics" (Kjeldgaard et al., 2017, p. 66). To use Hartmann's (2016, p. 14) vocabulary, whereas brewers like BrewDog may be described as "gearheads" interested in what flavors can be created using the latest gear; brewers furthering CAMRA's cause are "purists" interested in preserving traditional methods of dispensing beer using handpull methods or letting gravity deliver beer to the glass.

Chapman (2015) applies the production of culture model (Peterson & Anand, 2004) to the emergence of craft breweries in the United States proposing the recognition of consumers who engage in 'craft consumption'. "The term 'craft' is used to refer to consumption activity in which the 'product' concerned is both "made and designed by the same person" and to which the consumer typically brings skill, knowledge, judgement and passion while being motivated by a desire for self-expression" (Campbell, 2005, p. 23). This use of 'craft' differs from other tropes like those of personalization and customization but may apply to other crafts like teaching where the capacity of reflectiveness central to the emergence of the craftful teacher is rooted in the learned experience of dealing with the essential materiality of the context (Brookfield, 2015; Tremmel, 1993; Pirsig, 1999).

Greer (2014) adds "craftivism" in which the other dimensions of craft are powered by political activism. But a central trope of *authenticity* is tacitly implicit in these characterizations of the craft beer scene. The craft beer capital of the world, Portland, Oregon, is in a special kind of urban domain where this authenticity can be realized but can be lost as quickly by the commodification of memory, the rise in rents and capitalization of space, which undermines the potential of small-scale processes of creation and exchange, increasing precarity and monetarization that compromises the identity of the city (London, 2014, p. 1).

The *Oxford English Dictionary* (2017b) definition of craft beer, "a beer made in a traditional or non-mechanized way by a small brewery" clearly identifies the place and type of production as a prime source of what is special about craft as in craft beer. However, this definition ignores the essential distinctions in the service encounter that imbue 'craft' beer with its special status. So we will now shift the focus to the point of intersection with the consumer—to the bar/pub where the product is served to the consumer.

Although the decline of the traditional pub is well attested, some observers claim that "these are often replaced by locales for craft ale, which are typically smaller than traditional pubs and fueled by an interest in the taste, flavor, quality and variety of the beer" (Austin-Clarke, 2017). Knowledge of hopping recipes and the relative merits of, for example, Cascade versus Citra or Chinook now also forms part of this curriculum of the new crafty beer-pullers (HomebrewTalk, 2008; Cicerone, 2017).

Consumers often find it difficult to articulate precisely what it is about the craft beer experience that attracts them and keeps them hooked (Fehribach, 2017). When beer enthusiasts describe their consumption patterns as 'independent' or involving 'revolution', they find it hard to define from what dependence they are escaping and against what they are revolting. Nonetheless, it may be

> the status symbolism that craft beer provides, contrasting the craft beer drinkers' 'enlightened consumption' against the perceived ignorance and indifference of drinkers of non-craft 'shit beer', craft beer drinkers often relate that, while craft beer is typically much more expensive, its ineffable superiority is 'worth it'.
>
> (Di Mario, 2013, pp. 20–1)

Issues of spatiality and materiality are relevant to the locales and spaces in which the product becomes available to the would-be consumer via its mediating personnel: the bar staff (Dale, 2007; Orlikowski, 2007; Carlile et al., 2013; Gibson, 2016). In a study of the downtown craft beer bar scene in Rio de Janeiro, Gioia and Chaves (2016, p. 11) show how specific values evolve within a particular urban milieu to frame "Rio culture", noting that

> Some craft brewers' communication actions showcase craft beer as the complete opposite of mass-produced beer, thus positioning their

products as more refined, sophisticated and civilized. Behind these concepts lie the value of knowledge, both the value of fully appreciating beer's sensory features and the value of understanding the brewing process.

The spatial organization of the places where decisions are taken in complex organizations frame the modalities of the decision processes themselves (Van Marrewijk, 2009; Weir, 2008b; Weir, 2010), and these intermediary events in spaces can also be characterized as in some sense "sacred" co-creations in collaborative space (Weir, 2008a). In the craft bar experience, this may be the creation of a "community", which results from targeting specific "crowds" of patrons whose identification with the "specific bar atmosphere" by symbolic signals, including visual, auditory and sensory features (Hou, 2015), are supported by the reinforcing tactics of the bar owners (Hartshorn, 2014). These symbolic appreciations create encounters within "aestheticized" market situations involving "refined notions of beauty, originality and superiority" (Figueiredo, 2015, p. 6). If such milieu can be understood, they may also be planned, and Reynolds (2010), in his account of "experiencing inebriation in place", asks "Why architecture is not valued through our sensibilities? Or a better question, how can architecture be valued through our sensibilities?" and answers his question by implicating emotions. "Our emotions", Reynolds (2010: abstract) writes, "are developed through our experiences. The movement through the pub, my actions within the space, and the senses being formed from my surroundings helped my understanding of why I enjoyed the pub". We, therefore, focus on the locales of interaction and consider what are the craft aspects of the dispensing of craft beer, and what are the knowledge bases and experiences in which these are rooted?

Now "craft bartending is starting to be recognized as a viable—and even admirable—career choice in some places around the world" (Abarabove, 2017) with a putative career ladder (see Figure 7.1).

But instead of precision, this advice consists of tired platitudes and nostrums that have been around since Samuel Smiles and can be found on any airport newsstand best seller:

> It's all about the Attitude. You can always train someone to make great cocktails, but you can't train someone to have a good attitude. Being a barback is hard—sometimes grueling—work. But the difficulty of the job can be a great way to see someone's real personality shine through, quickly. Do your job with a smile on your face. Pay attention to what's happening around you and show that you're interested in learning and growing. If they offer training, ask to join, even if it's intended for bartenders only. If you can show initiative in everything you do while keeping a positive attitude, it'll be a giant step towards getting your name on the bartending schedule.
>
> (Abarabove, 2017)

The Bar Career

For the right person, there is nothing better than a hospitality role in a great bar. But what if you're looking ahead at your career and aren't sure what's next? Here is an overview of the "typical" bar career and some common non-bar jobs that you can branch off to along the way

Behind the Bar   **Outside the Bar**

YEAR 1

Barback
Like the bartender's assistant and a great stepping stone to your first bar job

YEAR 2

Bartender
Know the menu. know the drinks and be a great host

Private Events
Bar catering/events companies and consulting

Lead Bartender
The bartender who designs the seasonal cocktail menu and may help with staff training

Sales
Start working for spirits brands, helping them sell to bars and restaurants

YEAR 5

Bar Manager
Run the bar program, watch the numbers and manage the staff

Brand Ambassadorship
Our team gathers all relevant materials for the project

YEAR 10

General Manager
Final execution of the approved idea

Bar Consulting
Our team gathers all relevant materials for the project

Bar Owner
Done! Time to party and celebrate!

YEAR 20

ABarAbove.com

Figure 7.1 The Bar Career

Other job adverts seek to attract "amazing people" without over-precise definition of these amazing attributes or of how their "passionate" qualities are displayed in the work itself (Tap Taverns, 2017).

It's OK, of course, to be "fun and friendly", but what are you expected to *know* or to have to learn about beer and what are the skills, knowledge and craft you will be expected to display in your performance? The urban ethnographer Richard Ocejo has tried to answer these questions in respect of cocktail bar work by defining their cultural repertoires and the philosophical underpinnings of their weltanschauungen (Ocejo, 2010, 2017). His conclusion harks back to the classic bartenders' expertise in "mixology" (Regan, 2004), thus he states that "cocktail bartenders add creativity to the manual labor of bartending by engaging in 'craft production' that is based on the historical principles of 'mixology'". (Ocejo, 2010: abstract; Gioia & Chaves, 2016). Ocejo finds that it is this knowledge that adds the dimensions of craft and creativity to produce the bartender expertise. Associated with the increasing professionalization of the bar staff is the increasing sophistication of the client, creating a new feature in this workplace environment: that of *prosumption*.

Prosumption

We can also draw on the lens of prosumption—a portmanteau combing the activities of production and consumption—to understand these changes in the craft beer serving landscape. Producers are typically those who create content and cultural objects, whereas consumers are the audience/purchasers of those services/objects. Occupying a middle ground in this debate is prosumption. Here, "consumers take over . . . activities traditionally performed by commercial producers . . . and consumers produce their own products and services as opposed to buying them" (Hartmann, 2016, p. 5). For example, Build-A-Bear (www.buildabear.co.uk/) provides the components but consumers assemble the bear in-store themselves. Similarly, as illustrated in the following vignette (Innis & Gunn, 2017), which is an advertisement Daniel spotted on the *Innis & Gunn Beer Kitchen Dundee* Facebook page, prosumption is also happening in contemporary beer culture.

Like the blurring of the boundary between production/consumption, there is also a blurring between the professional (hobbyist)/consumer. Beer enthusiasts have become increasingly dedicated to the pursuit of their hobby, sometimes elevating their quest for flavor, passion and knowledge to the point of commanding certain skills on par with those of a professional. The professional slant of this "prosumer" is visible in Innis & Gunn's (2017) offering to "brew your own". While this attracts some beer enthusiasts because it presents the opportunity to use new gear (e.g., the Grain Father), for others, it may simply represent a good day

Dundee Brew School. 23rd December 2017.

Impress your pals with a pint of your very own beer and learn how to recreate some of your favorite beer styles at home. Using our favorite new bit of brewing kit, the Grain Father, we'll coach you through the basics behind a great brew, unravel styles and flavor profiles and teach you all the know how you need. As if that wasn't enough, you'll also get a 5-liter mini keg of your own beer to take away.

The day involves the following:

- Bacon rolls and coffee on arrival with welcome from the host.
- Discussion on what will be covered and the raw ingredients used to make beer.
- Start adding ingredients.
- Lunch served. Though no rest for the wicked! You'll be adding the hops during this time.
- Finish off the brew.

£55 per person

Why not include an Innis & Gunn sampling session to round off your day for an extra £10 per person?

What you get—A fun day brewing up your very own beer, lots of tasty beery samples and a 5-liter mini keg of your own brew each to take away. All guests must be aged 18 or over.

For more information, or to book your place now, email us or call *01382 20 20 70.*

Payment is required in advance to confirm your booking.

Figure 7.2 Dundee Brew School

out. To obtain the recipes, coaching and to pick up "all the know-how you need" to brew your own however, you need not go to Dundee Brew School; you can go to the blogosphere.

In the publishing industry, a Read Only (RO) culture occurs where authors create content and consumers read, alternatively in a Read/Write (RW) culture fanfiction is celebrated and encouraged. Likewise, in a RO beer culture dominated by "homogenized taste structures" (Kjeldgaard et al., 2017, p. 66), standardized and mass-produced beers reign supreme, but within a RW beer culture where traditional recipes are shared freely, there is opportunity to modify or create a derivative and even make money from the sale of such beers (see www.freebeer.org). As the website states, "FREE BEER is beer which is free in the sense of *freedom*, not in the sense of *free beer*". Originally conceived in Copenhagen by students and an arts collective, the project applies open source methods, publishing the recipe and branding under a Creative Commons license. This means that anybody can use the recipe and is free to make money from FREE BEER "but they must publish the recipe under the same license and credit our work".

So the ripping and mixing (Press et al., 2011) of recipes by prosumers—thanks to open source methods—constitutes **participatory culture**. This term was popularized by Jenkins (1992) who identified the key characteristics of these cultures, noting that they offer psychic rewards for participation, there are low barriers to participation, there is strong support for sharing and informal mentorship, thus creating members who feel that their contributions matter and who care about the participation of others. On this, consumers sometimes act roles as quasi-producers. Hartmann (2016) observes how, over the years, people have come to gardening and guitar playing in much the same way, noting that the same can also be said about professional consumers who post DIY solutions online and photographers who blog about the way they work.

Navigating the Serving Landscape

Due, in part, to greater involvement and new opportunities to dabble in production processes, craft beer drinkers are becoming more discerning. In their quest for flavor, craft beer drinkers take their identities and voices to the bar, placing expectations on servers, anticipating that they 'know their stuff'. *The Cask Report* (Cask-Marque, 2017, p. 25) states that "86% of cask drinkers expect bar staff to have received some training in beer", stating that, "As customers grow increasingly aware and interested in the products they consume, their thirst for new knowledge is putting more pressure on pubs to **engage** and enthuse drinkers" (p. 25). Engaging drinkers implies entering into conversations about, for example, taste profiles, craftwork, history, innovation and agentic properties of different shaped glasses. Beer servers might also be expected to offer advice on food pairing. There is a view which holds, then, that the ability to engage in the craft conversation leads to better service quality and increased patronage.

If bar staff are unable to 'speak beer' it may impact negatively upon their credibility and professional respectability, so giving pub owners/managers the tools to train their servers "is crucial" and "accredited programmes . . . help provide vital skills to enhance quality" (Cask-Marque, 2017, p. 25). The report continues, "To build on the positive contribution of these schemes, a new training platform, the Beer Education Alliance [BEA] is launching in 2018". *The Cask Report* argues that enabling servers to lead 'cask conversations' with consumers means that 74% of cask drinkers return to the pub, 45% stay for another drink and 71% recommend that pub. Programs such as the BEA are not however new. Cicerone certified beer serving qualifications have been around since 2008 although few people in the UK had heard of them until April 2013 when BrewDog brought Ray Daniels, the founder of Cicerone, over from USA to hold the first certified Cicerone exams in the UK. Eight members of the team passed and Brewdog rewarded those studying for certification by offering "a [pay] rise" (BrewDog, 2013).

The rewards for getting the serving right for the pub and beer industry are obvious and well documented. But what's in it for the server? In view of the BEA program launch and the fact that more than 94,000 people in 10 years have already passed through the Cicerone ranks (Sheahan, 2018), where is all this leading for those with and without certification?

From Serving Standardized Beer to Co-producing Tasteful Moments

Beer hasn't always been about an "alternative logic of craft and diversity" (Kjeldgaard et al., 2017, p. 64) or authenticity of craft (Hatch & Schultz, 2017). At a typical bar in a pub in the UK that is organized around a dominant logic of commerce and standardization "reflecting a homogenized taste structure" (Kjeldgaard et al., 2017, p. 66), a server-consumer conversation might unfold as follows:

SERVER: Who is next? What can I get you?
BEER DRINKER: I'll have a pint of [Carlsberg/Tenants/Worthington] please.
SERVER: That'll be £2.87 please.
BEER DRINKER: Thanks

Contrasted with the conversation Daniel had with a server (see the following), this interaction is merely transaction based: it is not about knowledge, passion and wonder, and it certainly is not curiosity-driven.

Although, phenomenologically, taste is in the mouth, in the body and in the world, through server-consumer dialogue, taste can also be in words. In pubs dispensing craft beer up and down the country, it is not uncommon to hear, "Can I please try some of the. . .?" Indeed, beer **tasting** is becoming a common form of socialization within beer culture, and since craft beer is all about the promotion of diversity and craft (Kjeldgaard et al., 2017), **TRY BEFORE YOU BUY** has become a popular institutional arrangement (Lok et al., 2017) beer drinkers have come to expect from purveyors of craft beer. This practice is one that matters to beer enthusiasts (Cask-Marque, 2017, p. 15), making their lives more meaningful and can "prime how they think and feel" (Lok et al., 2017, p. 593).

During a visit to Drygate Brewery, Bar + Kitchen, in Glasgow, Scotland, on Saturday 2nd December 2017; Daniel had the following conversation with a server:

SERVER: Do you know what you want?
DWC: I don't, no. This is all very exciting for me. It's my first time here. . . [eye-balling the handpull options at the bar and a row of keg beer on tap against the back wall]
SERVER: What have you been drinking lately?
DWC: I have been enjoying porters recently. Speak to me about what you have on. . .

SERVER: Have you tried the Black Ball Stout by Williams Brothers?

DWC: I haven't. . .

SERVER: Here! [Pouring a taster] See what you think. . .

DWC: [Tasting. . .] It's very light. Not much creaminess. . .

SERVER: Yeah. . ., have you tried our own Orinoco? It's a breakfast stout. . . [pouring another taster]

DWC: I have been enjoying Cairngorm's *Black Gold* of late. . . . That's a milk stout, right?! What's all that about?

SERVER: That'll be the lactose giving the smoothness that you like. . . . The Orinoco is made with Lactose Sugar, so you might get that. . . [serving yet another taster], you might like this more than the Black Ball?!? Its fuller bodied, sweeter, a bit stronger and with coffee notes . . . a bit chocolatey. . .

DWC: Oh! I like that one! Can definitely taste the coffee. Let's go for that then. . .

Hartmann (2016, p. 11) highlights a basic premise of Latourian thought, that "objects carry agentic properties" and "can be understood as non-human actors". On this, it might be argued that recipes producing flavorsome beers carry affective intensities capable of impacting customer experiences during the moment of truth, at the bar, when tasting and discussing flavors with servers. Recipes, appearances, aromas, flavors and mouthfeels, for example, therefore have the capacity to affect and be affected through a multitude of encounters with bodies, objects and words.

While servers produce beer in that they deliver it from the cellar (via lines and faucets), the immediate product in the consumption of craft beer is taste, and flavor is one of the logics along which the field works: beer drinking is all about taste (Avery, 2011). Although it is the handpull handles/keg taps and lines which dispense beer, it is the hands and words of the server that produces tasters, producing what Hartmann (2016, p. 8) describes as "a **productive moment** along the way" to deciding which beer to drink. In this "**duet**" (Hartmann, 2016, p. 7), the server invited Daniel to co-create content by voicing what was being tasted. When the conversational dance unfolds like this, the frame altering practice of **Try(ing) Before You Buy** takes on a maieutic role, bringing a "person's latent ideas into clear consciousness" (OED, 2017c). Of course, lactose is, in part, what makes milk taste creamy—milk stout contains lactose—so it just might be that it is the creaminess from the lactose sugar in Orinoco that Daniel tastes and enjoys. . . . Balancing the science of taste, commerce and the art of craft beer serving in this manner, there might be an argument then, that, to Try Before You Buy serves to "enroll consumers into a field." (Kjeldgaard et al., 2017, p. 64), "ultimately affecting institutionionalized taste structures" (p. 61) where taste, craft and diversity is valued.

Viewed from within the production-consumption debate, the server cannot be a producer in as much as s/he does not produce beer in terms of an outcome achievement. A practice-theoretical perspective, however, draws attention away from the individuals (i.e. producer/ consumer) and looks at productive and consumptive **moments** as **practice performances**.

Through use of *things* carrying affective capacities with agentic properties, such as pipes/lines, nozzles, pump handles/clips, glasses, froth and the bar, by producing beer from the tap and offering their own interpretation on taste profiles, servers are productive of taste sensations in minds of consumers. Performing multiple practices—greeting, discussing options/flavors/taste, taking an order, receiving payment and dispensing beer—server "practices create value" (Hartmann, 2016, p. 7), producing consumptive and productive moments. "The term 'moment' refers on the one hand to a temporal dimension (moment as an episode) but also to the performative qualities of consumption and production by giving momentum to practice performance" (Hartmann, 2016, p. 9). Consumption and production are guided by the practices in which they take place—they are subject to "directions by **practice templates** that organize the activities within them" (pp. 9–10). As a practice template, which logic is used to alter organizing principles of bar work when 'Try Before You Buy' is encouraged? Like with guitarists "all looking for the perfect sound" (Hartmann, 2016, p. 14), in their quest for flavor, beer enthusiasts are all looking for the perfect pint (i.e. taste). How do beer servers navigate the 'good quality beer' cause and serving landscape?

Since BrewDog has been preparing its staff to engage in the craft conversation since 2013 by now requiring all staff to become Cicerone-certified beer servers, it could be argued that they are trying to establish a competitive advantage by instilling superior serving performances within practice moments to informally alter the logic of competition. As an "active market shaper", is BrewDog "reorienting the market institution" of serving a pint "for alternative valorizations" (adapted from Kjeldgaard et al., 2017, p. 52)? Could it be that taste, the logic of the taster and conversation are being used to alter organizing principles of bar work, producing social connection, emotional value and sharing of skill, knowledge, judgment and passion?

Linking Craft, Professions and Professional Identity

The development of the Cicerone organization and the associated set of qualifications, which certify bar staff as certified beer server (level 1), Cicerone (level 2), advanced Cicerone (level 3) and master Cicerone (level 4) constitutes the professionalization of an occupation. In this section, we reflect on the reasons why a profession is emerging around the activity of beer serving, before focusing on how professionalization impacts on workers, drawing on theory and examples from beer serving.

Why Professionalize?

Professionalization is a notoriously difficult, resource intensive and prolonged type of institutional entrepreneurship (Lounsbury, 2007). So, why do organizations embark upon it?Larson and Larson (1979, p. xvii) argues that the pursuit of material resources such as money and power are at the heart of professional project, stating, "Professionalization is thus an attempt to translate one order of scarce resources—special knowledge and skills—into another—social and economic rewards". While part of the explanation for the growth in professional projects lies in the pursuit of symbolic resources such as power (Larson & Larson, 1979), this doesn't entirely explain the reasons why brewing companies such as BrewDog support professionalization projects such as the Cicerone qualification.

Macdonald (1995) argues that the goal of professionalization is, in part, to achieve social mobility for individuals, but is also about obtaining market control for the professionalizing firm. Professions espouse autonomous expertise and a service ideal, and the pursuit of a set of service standards that align with producers' craft principles is also a plausible rationale for BrewDog's support of Cicerones. As the interface between producer and consumer, the bar server has an important role to play in enabling the prosumption activities which drive value in the industry.

The Cicerone qualification allows BrewDog's servers to join their cause for "craft beer conscientiousness" (BrewDog, 2013). In their own words, BrewDog "are passionate about doing everything we can to learn as much about craft beer as is humanly possible in order to spread the message far and wide", and sponsoring servers to undertake certification is seen as a way to promote this cause (BrewDog, 2013). Aside from craft beer evangelism, higher levels of product knowledge and better service standards among servers further distinguishes craft pubs' product and service offerings from those of wider pubs and restaurants, allowing them to attract customers and charge higher prices.

As *The Cask Report* 2017/18 states in relation to the "premiumisation" of cask ale: "The opportunity to raise profit from cask has never been greater" (Cask-Marque, 2017, p. 2). This is partly because cask ale drinkers spend more than other beer consumers (30% on average), drive the buying choices of their group, and because cask sales have remained steady or grown, at a time when many pubs are closing due to falling revenues (Cask-Marque, 2017). However, the growing margins in cask ale are not only driven by product improvements; they rely upon the licensees and bar servers who "create the proposition to the consumer" allowing the "craft ale offer" to distinguish true craft pubs from their rivals (2017, p. 7) and, as the report argues, training and professionalization of servers is key to establishing and delivering this distinguished service offering. It highlights a number of ways to convert consumers to the product during the service encounter, all of which rely upon the server having extensive knowledge of the beer, to engage in storytelling about the product, and many of which mirror the efforts of Italian producers to 'upsell' Grappa (Delmestri & Greenwood, 2016) by using "stylish glassware" and "tasting notes" to improve the perceived status of the product (Cask-Marque, 2017, p. 15).

Effects of Professionalization on the Worker (Bar Server)

While a profession may be established to ring-fence knowledge and promote a service ideal, and in so doing, to enable increases in the cost of products, many of the effects flow to the workers who are professionalized. Being considered to be a professional may confer certain resources onto an individual, such as autonomy and power. Professional certifications, such as the Cicerone qualification, and professional symbols (Macdonald, 1995), such as the Cicerone badge, act as markers of knowledge and status. Together, this knowledge, these qualifications and symbols constitute what Bourdieu (1984) calls cultural and symbolic capital. The notion of capital is helpful in this sense, because it illustrates how the symbolic and cultural value of a professional qualification can act as a form of currency in the job market. Indeed, this is what the Cicerone Certification Program alludes to when it states,

> Those who pursue a career in beer learn from many different sources and soon accumulate knowledge that sets them apart from those on the "customer" side of the bar. But without certification, it is hard to tell what people really know simply by looking at a resume or business card. . . . Certified Cicerones enjoy enhanced respect and prestige that can help improve their business success and career prospects.
>
> (Cicerone, 2017)

Indeed, a CBS at BrewDog mirrored this view, telling us that she would recruit someone with the qualification over a similarly experienced and knowledgeable applicant because "it shows a level of commitment and passion". This is a qualification which requires a great amount of "hours . . . effort . . . time . . . work" in order to achieve, making it a big investment for a server and symbol of valued attributes in recruitment decisions. Indeed, for Brie Shelley (2016), being a certified Cicerone was the minimum qualification required to land her a job as a manager at the American-based startup, Better Beer Society (an education-based beer business).

The benefits of a profession flow to the worker through not just the knowledge and prestige attained via the professional qualification process, but also through the development of a professional identity. In general, identities act on the individual by fixing their position in society, by establishing relationships between the individual and others. Ibarra (1999) famously outlined how individuals develop a self-concept from a universe of possible professional identities by examining the actions of role models, and experimenting with provisional selves. As such, professional identity is developed through socialization, career transition, and through life and work experiences which shape self-understanding (Ibarra, 1999). Seidel (2010), also focusing on a 'craft' profession (journalism), identifies three phases of the evolution of professional identity evidenced by the representations as a literary apprentice, as an entrepreneur, and as a knowledge worker. It is possible that as the beer serving profession increases in scope and legitimacy, the identities of Cicerones will also evidence such evolutionary characteristics.

A professional identity confers a sense of respectability on an individual (Macdonald, 1995), particularly through association with sets of symbols and places that act as a marker of distinction. As such, developing a professional identity also helps service workers to grapple with the negative aspects of their job and to cultivate a positive occupational image. As Eve outlined in the opening vignette to this chapter, bar work is often stigmatized, and, as she later elaborates, "for a long-time beer has not been taken seriously and now, with qualifications; that is changing". Stigma is defined by Erving Goffman (1986 [1963]) as any attribute of a person that is seen to be diverse from what is expected of their social identity, something *out of the ordinary* and less desirable for it. He reminds us, however, that stigma isn't an ontological property of a person's attributes, but rather a property of the relationships between that attribute and others. To use Goffman's example, a middle class person may perceive no stigma to result from visiting a library, yet a professional criminal will avoid being seen doing the same as the relationship between this act and their larger identity is likely to result in stigma. Thompson and Harred (2010) clarify the normative implications of visiting a Topless Bar and include bartending as one of the occupations vulnerable to stigmatization. They also note that occupants of such roles may use techniques of neutralization (Sykes and Matza, 1957) to point out that no harm is being done and that it is the clients who visit these locations or the owners of the premises who are in most moral jeopardy from their presence in these dubious premises or their responsibility for the behaviors exhibited there.

Despite the importance of stigma within sociology, little has been written on its relationship with professional identity. Slay and Smith (2011) show that constructing a professional self-concept alongside a stigmatized cultural identity requires *redefinition* of the profession, of the stigma and of the self. Their focus is on stigmatized cultural identities, rather than stigmatized occupational identities, but, for beer servers, a professional identity can act as a resource with which to buffer or repel occupational stigma. Being the holder of a Cicerone qualification may shield a beer server from social perceptions that their work is 'dirty' (Hughes, 1962) or low skilled. There are many gradations of "dirty work" (Ashforth & Kreiner, 2010) and bar work, while attracting some perceived stigma in the eyes of its participants as in the quote with which this chapter started does not seem to be at the really dirty end of this particular stick; but an imputation that qualification such as that offered by Cicerone can do something to mitigate. Nonetheless, the access offered by bar work to areas of fringe morality, semi-criminal opportunity and boundary-crossing transgression is always available, and is fluid in practice so this is an area of interest for further study (Minichiello, Scott & Callander, 2013).

Closing Comments and Future Research

The changes in beer serving are emblematic of a number of wider trends in the working world. They relate to the growth of craftwork, which has more broadly been enabled by technological platforms. The resurgence of craft products, craft mentality and, therefore, craftwork has been enabled by the existence of platforms (e.g. www.Notonthehighstreet. com and Pinterest) that allow producers to transcend the traditional geographic boundaries placed on craftwork through expanding their market. This chapter illustrates how this craft resurgence reshapes the demands on service workers (particularly beer servers). Craft servers need to be knowledgeable, even enthusiastic, about the product in order to deliver their service appropriately. In this context, bar work is not merely seen as crowd control and serving standardized lager, but increasingly invokes craft elements derived from the nature of production.

As we see in the case of beer, this resurgence of craft also leads to a convergence of producer and consumer, with further implications for the service worker. Such workers are called upon to not just excel in the act of service, but to cultivate a broad range of knowledge regarding the product and the means by which it is produced. This knowledge can then be used to bring the consumer closer to the production process, a consumer who is often a product enthusiast themselves. The producer-prosumer-consumer convergence is of course not unique to the beer industry; our insights may also apply in other areas of economic activity, for example, furniture retail (e.g. IKEA), fast-food restaurants and 3-D printers (Ritzer, 2014).

Alongside the increasing demands placed on beer servers we identify the emergence of a nascent profession of beer serving as represented by the Cicerone and Beer Education Alliance certification programs. The development of professional standards in beer serving are not singular and not value free, as with any other professional project, they are generated to benefit the interests of occupational elites. In the case of craft beer, professional standards offer standardized staff training and a bonus veneer of legitimacy to large scale (and fast growing) employers, such as Brew-Dog. For the servers, acquiring a certification confers a professional status which may act as a buffer between positive occupational self-concept and persistent perceptions of beer serving as 'dirty' or undesirable work. Furthermore, in certain organizations such certification may function as a symbol of commitment (to the beer, the industry, the employer), transforming the position of server from a dead-end position, to being the first rung of a well-paid service career ladder.

Professionalization of service work is more widespread than the beer industry, but it is not universal. We see a growing dichotomy between high end, professionalized service work and low value, low paid service work (across the occupational spectrum). In beer, for example, the servers in some areas of the industry have not and are unlikely to experience professionalization of their work, like waiters and waitresses in other organizations driven by a low-cost strategy they are paid minimum wage and often lose tips to balance tills. As such, the craft-prosumption-professionalization nexus that characterizes craft beer in the UK provides an interesting, but not universal, analysis into emerging trends within the service industries. Returning to where we started with Eve and to open up future research possibilities, in our ongoing research with servers, we are currently examining what 'work' Cicerone and BEA is doing in the world from the perspective of servers themselves by asking, what can a Cicerone qualification do? Do craft beer servers consider serving as a craft? And what are the implications or consequences, if any, of their thinking for the future of their profession?

References

Abarabove (2017). The Bar Career. Available from www.abarabove.com/the-craft-bartender-career-guide/ [Accessed 30.11.2017].

Andrews, D., & Turner, S. (2012). Is the pub still the hub? *International Journal of Contemporary Hospitality and Management, 24*(4), 1–11.

Argent, N. (2017). Heading down to the local? Australian rural development and the evolving spatiality of the craft beer sector. *Journal of Rural Studies.* Published online ahead of print Feb 2017, https://doi.org/10.1016/j.jrurstud.2017.01.016.

Ashforth, B. E., & Kreiner, C.E. (2010). Dirty work and dirtier work. *Management and Organization Review, 10*(1), 81–108.

Austin-Clarke, P (2017). Raise a glass of (craft) beer to new-style bars. *Telegraph and Argus.* Available from www.thetelegraphandargus.co.uk/features/15688576.PERRY_AUSTIN_CLARKE__Raise_a_glass_of__craft__beer_to_new_style_bars/ [Accessed 30.11.2017].

Avery, Z. (2011). The taste of beer. *Brewery History, 139,* 25–31. Available from www.breweryhistory.com/journal/archive/139/Avery.pdf [Accessed 30.11.2017].

Beercast (2017). The year Scottish brewing changed forever. Available from http://thebeercast.com/2017/01/2016-year-scottish-brewing-changed-forever. html [Accessed 30.11.2017].

Bourdieu, P. (1984). *Distinction: A Social Critique of Taste*. Trans. R. Nice. Cambridge: Harvard University Press.

BrewDog (2013). Brewdog and certified cicerone. Available from www.brewdog. com/lowdown/blog/brewdog-and-certified-cicerone [Accessed 05.12.2017]

Brookfield, S. D. (2015). *The Skilful Teacher*. London: John Wiley & Sons.

Cabras, I., & Bamforth, C. (2016). From reviving tradition to fostering innovation and changing marketing, *Business History*, 58(5), 625–646.

Cabras, I., & Higgins, D. M. (2016). Beer, brewing, and business history. *Business History*, 58(5), 609–624.

Campbell, C. (2005). The craft consumer. *Journal of Consumer Culture*, 5(1), 23–42.

Carlile, P. R., Nicolini, D., Langley, A., & Tsoukas, H. (Eds.) (2013). *How Matter Matters*. Oxford: Open University Pres.

Cask-Marque (2017). *The Cask Report 2017*. Available from http://cask-marque.co.uk/cask-matters/wp-content/uploads/sites/4/2017/09/Cask-Report-2017-18-final-version-1.pdf [Accessed 20.06.2018].

Chapman, N. G. (2015). *Craft Beer in the US*. Virginia Polytechnic Institute and State University, PhD Dissertation.

Chaucer, W. (1382). *The Parlement of Foules*. Oxford: Bodleian Library.

Cicerone (2017). Levels of certification. Available from www.cicerone.org/us-en/cicerone-certification-levels [Accessed 20.06.2018].

Clemons, E. K.; Gao, G. G., & Hitt, L. M. (2006). When online reviews meet hyperdifferentiation: A study of the craft beer industry. *Journal of Management Information Systems*, 23(2), 149–171.

Dale, K. (2007). *The Spaces of Organisation and the Organisation of Space*. New York: Palgrave Macmillan.

Delmestri, G., & Greenwood, R. (2016). How Cinderella became a queen. *Administrative Science Quarterly*, 61(4), 507–550.

Di Mario, A. (2013). *Indie Capitalism and Craft Beer Drinkers in Vermont*. PhD dissertation at University of Vermont.

Fehribach, D. (2017). *Crafting Craft Beer Brands*. PhD Dissertation at University of Central Florida.

Figueiredo, M. A. (2015). The Role of Aestheticized Markets in Contemporary Formations of Social Class and Gender, PhD Dissertation at University of Arizona Press.

Gibson, C. (2016). Material inheritances. *Economic Geography*, 92(1), 61–86.

Gioia, M., & Chaves, R. J. (2016). *A Sociocultural Approach to Craft Beer Production and Consumption*. VIII Encontro Nacional de Estudos.

Goffman, E. (1986 [1963]). *Stigma*. New York: Simon & Schuster.

Greer, B. (2014). *Craftivism: The Art of Craft and Activism*. Canada, BC: Arsenal Pulp Press.

Guardian (2016a). Number of pubs in UK falls to lowest level for a decade. Available from www.theguardian.com/lifeandstyle/2016/feb/04/uk-pubs-lowest-number-for-decade-2015-camra-beer-tax-campaign [Accessed 30.11.2017].

Guardian (2016b). Supermarket beer sales overtake pubs for first time. Available from www.theguardian.com/business/2016/sep/26/supermarket-beer-sales-overtook-pub-sales-first-time-last-year [Accessed 30.11.2017].

Guardian (2017). How the beery vision of brewing a small fortune can fall flat. Available from www.theguardian.com/business/2017/apr/15/how-the-beery-vision-of-brewing-a-small-fortune-can-fall-flat [Accessed 30.11.2017].

Hackley, C. (2007). Auto-ethnographic consumer research and creative non-fiction. *Qualitative Market Research: An International Journal*, 10(1), 98–108.

Hartmann, B. J. (2016). Peeking behind the mask of the prosumer. *Marketing Theory*, 16(1), 3–20.

Hartshorn, T. (2014). Manufacturing community. *The Journal for Undergraduate Ethnography*, 6(1), 47–62.

Hatch, M. J., & Schultz, M. (2017). Toward a theory of using history authentically. *Administrative Science Quarterly*, 62(4), 657–697.

Hede, A. M., & Watne, T. (2013). Leveraging the human side of the brand using a sense of place. *Journal of Marketing Management*, 29(1–2), 207–224.

HomebrewTalk (2008). East Kent Golding or Cascade for my Dunkel. Available from www.homebrewtalk.com/forum/threads/east-kent-golding-or-cascade-for-my-dunkel.63318/ [Accessed 30.11.2017].

Hou, Y. (2015). *An Ethnography of Taste*. Master's Theses. Available from https://aquila.usm.edu/cgi/viewcontent.cgi?article=1149&context=masters_theses [Accessed 30.11.2017].

Hughes, E. C. (1962). Good people and dirty work. *Social Problems*, 10(1): 3–11.

Ibarra, H. (1999). Provisional selves: Experimenting with image and identity in professional adaptation. *Administrative Science Quarterly*, 44(4), 764–791.

Innis and Gunn (2017). Dundee Brew School. Available from www.innisandgunn.com/bars/dundee/brew-school [Accessed 20.06.2018].

Jenkins, H. (1992). *Textual Poachers: Television Fans and Participatory Culture*. London: Routledge, Chapman and Hall.

Kjeldgaard, D., Askegaard, S., Rasmussen, J.Ø., & Østergaard, P. (2017). Consumers' collective action in market system dynamics: A case of beer. *Marketing Theory*, 17(1), 51–70.

Larson, M. S., & Larson, M. S. (1979). *The Rise of Professionalism* (Vol. 233). California: University of California Press.

Levy, S. J. (2015). Olio and intègraphy as method and the consumption of death. *Consumption Markets & Culture*, 18(2), 133–154.

Lewis, C. (2001). The future of British brewing. *Strategic Change*, 10(3), 151–161.

Lok, J.; Creed, W. E. D.; DeJordy, R., & Voronov, M. (2017). Living Institutions: Bringing Emotions into Organizational Institutionalism, in R. Greenwood, C. Oliver, T. Lawrence & R. Meyer (Eds.), *The SAGE Handbook of Organizational Institutionalism* (2nd ed.) (pp. 591–617), CA: Sage.

London, J. R. (2014). New Portlandia: Rock n' roll, authenticity and the politics of place in Portland, Oregon. PhD Dissertation at City University of New York.

Lounsbury, M. (2007). A tale of two cities: Competing logics and practice variation in the professionalizing of mutual funds. *Academy of Management Journal*, 50(2), 289–307.

Macdonald, K.M. (1995). *The Sociology of the Professions*. London: Sage.

Macnaught, A (2014). Cask vs Keg. *Cask-Marque*. Available from http://caskmarque.co.uk/beer-drinkers/cask-vs-keg/ [Accessed 20.06.2018].

Minichiello, V.; Scott, J., & Callander, D. (2013). New pleasures and old dangers: Reinventing male sex work. *The Journal of Sex Research*, 50(3–4), 263–275.

Murray, A., & Kline, C. (2015). Rural tourism and the craft beer experience. *Journal of Sustainable Tourism*, 23(8–9), 1198–1216.

Ocejo, R. E. (2010). What'll it be? Cocktail bartenders and the redefinition of service in the creative economy. *City, Culture and Society*, 1(4), 179–184.

Ocejo, R. E. (2017). *Masters of Craft*. New Jersey: Princeton University Press.

Ogilvie, S. (2007). Whatever is, is right? Economic institutions in pre-industrial Europe. *The Economic History Review*, 60(4), 649–684.

Orlikowski, W. J. (2007). Sociomaterial practices. *Organization Studies*, 28(9), 1435–1448.

Oxford English Dictionary (2017a). "craft". Available from https://en.oxford dictionaries.com/definition/craft [Accessed 30.11.2017].

Oxford English Dictionary (2017b). "craft beer". Available from https://en.oxford dictionaries.com/definition/craft_beer [Accessed 30.11.2017].

Oxford English Dictionary (2017c). "maieutic". Available from https://en.oxford dictionaries.com/definition/maieutic [Accessed 30.11.2017].

Peterson, R. A., & Anand, N. (2004). The production of culture perspective. *Annual Review of Sociology*, 30(1): 311–334.

Pirsig, R. (1999). *Zen and the Art of Motorcycle Maintenance*. New York: Random House.

Press, M, Bruce, F, Chow, R., & White, H. (2011). Rip+Mix. In *The Endless End*. Paper Presented at the 9th International European Academy of Design Conference, Porto, Portugal. May 4–7, 2011.

Prichep, D. (2013). *Wine Has Sommeliers. Now, Beer Has Cicerones*. Available from www.npr.org/sections/thesalt/2013/08/24/214582851/wine-has-somme liers-now-beer-has-cicerones [Accessed 20.06.2018].

Regan, G. (2004). *The Joy of Mixology*. New York: Random House.

Reynolds, A.S. (2010). *Experiencing Inebriation in Place*. Masters Dissertation at Virginia Polytechnic Institute and State University.

Ritzer, G. (2014). Prosumption: Evolution, revolution, or eternal return of the same? *Journal of Consumer Culture*, 14(1), 3–24.

Scotland, a Land for Food & Drink (2017a). *Scottish Food & Drink Industry Unveils New Vision*. Available from www.foodanddrink.scot/news/article-info/7436/scot tish-food-and-drink-industry-unveils-new-vision-to-double-size-of-industry-to-%C2%A330-billion-by-2030.aspx [Accessed 20.06.2018].

Scotland, a Land for Food & Drink (2017b). *Ambition 2030: A Growth Strategy for Farming, Fishing, Food and Drink*. Available from www. scotlandfoodanddrink.org/media/78130/strategy-brochure-smaller-size. pdf?Action=download [Accessed 20.06.2018].

Scotland Food & Drink (2013). *Insights & Analysis of the UK Retail Premium Bottled Ale Market*. Available from www.scotlandfoodanddrink.org/media/66118/sfdinsights_crafting-success.pdf [Accessed 20.06.2018].

Scottish Enterprise (2017). *Funding Boost for Scotland's Craft Brewing Industry*. Available from www.scottish-enterprise-mediacentre.com/news/funding-boost-for-scotlands-craft-brewing-industry [Accessed 20.06.2018].

Seidel, C. K. (2010). *Representations of Journalistic Professionalism*. PhD Dissertation: Case Western Reserve University.

Shanks, M. and McGuire, R. H. (1996). The craft of archaeology. *American Antiquity*, 61(1), 75–88.

Sheahan, T. (2018). Cicerone celebrates 10 years. *Brewers Journal*, Available from www.brewersjournal.ca/2018/01/03/%E2%80%A8cicerone-celebrates-10-years/ [Accessed 20.06.2018].

Shelley, B (2016). *How to Become a Certified Beer Geek*. Available from www.bevs pot.com/2016/02/02/how-to-become-a-certified-beer-geek/ [Accessed 05.12.2017]

Slay, H. S., & Smith, D. A. (2011). Professional identity construction. *Human Relations*, 64(1), 85–107.

Sykes, G., & Matza, D. (1957). Techniques of neutralization: A theory of delinquency. *American Sociological Review*, 22, 664–670.

Tap Taverns (2017). *FT/PT Bar Staff Required for New Independent Craft Beer Bar*. Richmond Upon Thames. Available from www.gumtree.com/jobs/job/1390345944/ft-pt-bar-staff-required-for-new-independent-craft-beer-bar richmond-upon-thames/ [Accessed 30.11.2017].

Thompson, W. E., & Harred, J. L. (2010). Topless dancers: Managing stigma in a deviant occupation. *Deviant Behavior*, 13(3), 291–311, DOI: 10.1080/01639625.1992.9967914

Thurnell-Read, T. (2014). Craft, tangibility and affect at work in the microbrewery. *Emotion, Space and Society*, 13, 46–54.

Tremmel, R. (1993). Zen and the art of reflective practice in teacher education. *Harvard Educational Review*, 63(4), 434–459.

Van Marrewijk, A.H. (2009). Corporate headquarters as physical embodiments of organisational change. *Journal of Organizational Change Management*, 22(3), 290–306.

Watt, J., & Dickie, M. (2017). *Defining Craft Beer*, Available from www.brew dog.com/lowdown/blog/defining-craft-beer [Accessed 30.11.2017].

Weir, D.T.H. (2008a). Liminality, sacred space and the diwan. In S. Brie, J. Daggers & D. Torevell (Eds.), *Sacred Space* (pp. 39–54), UK: Cambridge Scholars.

Weir, D.T.H. (2008b). Cultural theory and the Diwan. *The European Journal of Social Science Research*, 21(3), 253–265.

Weir, D.T.H. (2010). Space as context and content. In A. van Marrewijk & D. Yanow (Eds.), *Organizational Spaces: Rematerializing the Workaday World* (pp. 115–136), Cheltenham: Edward Elgar Publishing.

Wickens, M. (2010). Brandhouse and beer branding. *Brewery History*, 136, 64–69.

8 Wake Up and Smell the Coffee

Job Quality in Australia's Café Industry

Angela Knox

Introduction

As deftly noted by Lloyd and Payne (2016, p. i), "Across the developed world, most of us who work now earn our living in the service sector. However, the issue of what kind of service economy is sustainable and desirable, both in economic and social terms, is rarely debated". This debate is even more significant as poor quality, 'bad jobs' in hospitality, retail and care, for example, continue to expand. What is needed is more 'good jobs', particularly in the service sector. While significant growth in the service sector is creating new ways of working, the question of the quality of these jobs and whether or not such jobs have positive implications for workers is of fundamental importance. Policy makers across the advanced economies now agree on the importance of job quality, and there are demands to create 'good jobs', improve 'bad jobs' or simply encourage decent work (Findlay et al., 2017).

This chapter examines the café sector in Australia as an example of a burgeoning field of service work encompassing new ways of working. The café sector has experienced rapid growth in many developed countries, generating new and significant employment opportunities (Lloyd & Payne, 2016). Illustratively, the European branded café market (23 countries) encompassed 15,626 outlets in October 2014 and experienced a growth rate of around 4.9 per cent per annum (Allegra, 2014). In the UK, the dominant café chains—Costa Coffee, Starbucks and Caffe Nero—employ around 15,000 workers and Greggs, Subway and Pret a Manger employ an additional 35,000 employees (Lloyd & Payne, 2016). While the UK represents the most developed market, estimated at 5,664 outlets, growth across Europe has occurred in 14 out of 23 countries (Allegra, 2014). Across Europe, the expansion of the café sector is the result of specialty coffee and café culture becoming embedded into consumers' daily lifestyle (Allegra, 2014).

Similarly, Australia's café sector reflects significant and ongoing expansion (Kellner et al. 2016; Knox & Warhurst, 2018). Indeed, employment in cafés, restaurants and takeaway food is projected to grow by more than any other Australian sector and most of this growth will be in cafés (DEEWR, 2013). According to recent data, cafés and restaurants represent the third-largest sector of employment in Australia. Of those employed in Australia in 2016, 2.4 per cent (253,385) worked in cafés and restaurants compared to 1.8 per cent (178,462) in 2011 (ABS, 2017). Jobs in cafés are currently projected to grow more than occupations in any other Australian industry (DEEWR, 2013). Employment increased from 19,900 to 31,200 among café attendants and from 65,400 to 93,700 among baristas (combined with bar attendants/bartenders) over 2005–2015 (Australian Government, 2015). This expansion is linked to the growth of disposable incomes and longer working hours in Australia along with an 'entrenched coffee culture' driven by 'the nation's love of quality coffee' (Lin, 2013, p. 5–6).

Yet, the characteristics associated with the jobs available remains unknown. As such, we have virtually no understanding of new ways of working emerging within Australia's bourgeoning café sector or the implications of such work. This chapter examines work in Australian cafés, by analysing the front-of-house jobs of café attendant and barista. In doing so, it explores new ways of working within this emerging and rapidly expanding sector and whether café work is contributing to the proliferation of 'bad jobs' or creating 'good jobs', and how this might impact workers.

Job Quality and the Hospitality Industry

As a newly expanding and significant field of work, Australia's café sector provides an ideal context for exploring the potential emergence of new ways of working within the service industry. Using job quality as an analytical lens, this section examines the nature of work within the broader hospitality industry before considering preliminary evidence related to the café sector. This literature provides a useful backdrop for identifying and examining the nature of work within Australian cafés.

Broadly, job quality refers to the work and employment characteristics of a job, including work organization, skill development and training opportunities and pay and benefits (Knox & Wright, forthcoming). Extrapolating on these broad notions, researchers tend to confer high quality jobs, or so-called good jobs, as those offering financial and employment security while allowing workers to develop and utilize their skills with a degree of autonomy and control and to progress their careers (Findlay et al., 2013). In contrast, low quality jobs, or so-called bad jobs, are thought to offer little or no financial or employment security while restricting workers ability to develop and utilize skills, and providing workers with limited autonomy and control or opportunities to progress their careers. Not all jobs are the same, so extending research to consider the quality of jobs, particularly those that reflect new ways of working, is important because it affects attitudes, behaviour and outcomes at the individual, organizational and national level (Knox et al., 2015).

It is increasingly clear that job quality affects individual's job satisfaction and commitment as well as physical and mental health and well-being (Findlay et al., 2017). The individual outcomes of job quality also affect organizational performance along with social and national economic outcomes (Siebern-Thomas, 2005). Evidence of this nature illustrates the specific benefits that can be reaped from efforts to improve job quality. Studies highlight, for example, that job satisfaction is negatively correlated with absenteeism (Clegg, 1983) and turnover (Freeman, 1978). Thus, enhancing employee job satisfaction, through the development of better-quality jobs, can reduce the organizational costs associated with absenteeism and turnover substantially. Moreover, job quality and job satisfaction have been linked to labour productivity (Siebern-Thomas, 2005) such that improving job quality and job satisfaction will typically yield higher rates of labour productivity.

Within the hospitality industry, the quality of jobs is overwhelmingly thought to be 'bad'. Initial research focused on front-of-house jobs, in which employees interact directly with customers (Fine, 1996) overwhelmingly revealed 'bad jobs'. In hotels, these jobs have typically been associated with low pay and low skills combined with poor training and career opportunities (e.g. Bernhardt, Dresser & Hatton 2003; Lucas, 2004). Moreover, working conditions involve unsociable and often unpredictable working hours and increasing work intensification, driven by a cost minimization business strategy—even for upmarket 4–5 star hotels (Timo & Davidson, 2005). Subsequently, for workers in the industry, the outcome is a 'poor' employment experience (Lucas, 2004). Similarly, negative characterizations of jobs in the fast food sector led Etzioni (1986) to coin the term 'McJobs', characterized by routinization, low skills, low wages and poor career prospects (Etzioni, 1986; Leidner, 1993; Ritzer, 1993). Specifically, research examining the fast food sector highlights the dominance of young workers engaged to perform repetitive, boring and tedious jobs offering little in terms of wages or skill acquisition (Leidner, 1993; Lindsay & McQuaid, 2004; Ritzer, 1993). Additionally, research has highlighted the exploitation, deskilling and burnout associated with such jobs leading workers to become frustrated and fatigued (Leidner, 1993).

More recent research has examined back-of-house jobs, including room attendants and chefs, with the findings also revealing 'bad jobs'. Research examining hotel room attendants' jobs indicates that they are the least skilled and lowest paid in the hotel industry in Europe, the US (Vanselow et al., 2010) and Australia (Knox, 2010). These jobs offer minimal rates of pay, usually at the wage floor; at times, this pay may even be beneath national minimum wage rates. The work is routine, heavy and repetitive, requiring little formal training or qualifications, with training typically occurring on the job (Vanselow et al., 2010). Further training opportunities (such as customer service skills) can be constrained because of work pressures (McPhail & Fisher 2008) and progression opportunities are limited. In addition, increasing competitive pressures have led employers to intensify the work of housekeepers, requiring them to work harder and faster to complete their allocated duties (Vanselow et al., 2010; Oxenbridge & Moensted, 2011). Not surprisingly, housekeeping jobs are archetypal 'bad jobs' according to Bernhardt et al. (2003). Similarly, Fine's (1996) research portrayed back-of-house kitchen jobs as entailing low wages, long and unsociable working hours, intense pressure, low autonomy and subsequent dissatisfaction. More recently, Bernhardt et al.'s (2008) research examining both front- and back-of-house jobs in US restaurants reported high levels of worker exploitation marked by low (and illegal) wages, long working hours, poor training and high injury rates. Such findings echo those of Jayaraman's (2013) research in US restaurants, depicting poor working conditions and negative employment outcomes, including discriminatory labour practices, excessive working hours, exploitation and low/stolen wages. Such findings also resonate with those from the UK (Lane, 2014).

While far less research has been conducted within the expanding café sector, existing patchy findings suggest that café jobs in the UK are associated with young and poorly qualified workers who receive low pay and create high turnover (People 1st, 2009). At the same time, the British Hospitality Association (BHA) and the sector skills council, People 1st, are endeavouring to challenge the 'dead end' café job stereotype, asserting,

> We want to see the industry held out as a great vehicle for social mobility . . . it is a huge engine for recruiting people with few or no qualifications and giving the chance to progress.
>
> (BHA, 2010, p. 16)

This goal remains unfulfilled, at least within the UK café sector (Lloyd & Payne, 2012). Based on case studies within the UK, Lloyd and Payne (2012) reported limited higher-level positions, long working hours and low rewards, factors that led most workers to express disinterest in progression or to feel that they were unlikely to succeed. Even among managerial jobs, Lloyd and Payne (2014) highlighted poor quality jobs, noting low pay, routinization and limited autonomy and discretion. Preliminary research in Australia examining the use of international student labour in cafés, restaurant and take away food outlets similarly suggested that their work is characterized by poor wages and working conditions, extensive avoidance of minimum labour standards, insecure employment and high turnover (Campbell, Boese & Tham, 2015).

More recent research examining café workers in the UK, Norway and France indicates that while some variation exists in terms of job quality, "the job of café worker is essentially a low-skilled [and low paid] position", which is frequently routinized and controlled (Lloyd & Payne, 2016, p. 182). In the UK, job quality is said to be poor, reflecting low-skill forms of work organization, standardization and low pay. Among French café workers, job quality is said to be somewhere between café workers in the UK and Norway as a result of France's higher national minimum wage and working time regulations. In Norway, café workers possess a broader job role and more discretion and autonomy than their counterparts, however, the authors affirm that they remain low skilled and low paid, overall. Furthermore, Lloyd and Payne (2016, p. 183) argue, "There seems little potential to raise the technical knowledge and skill requirements or the interaction with customers in these jobs to levels that might equate to intermediate skilled employment". Lloyd and Payne (2016) conclude that national institutions and regulations are critical in terms of 'blocking off' the 'low road' and improving pay and working time provisions. Moreover, they argue that the development of such responses may be facilitated by pressure from trade unions and other social groups. The presence of unions at company or workplace level created a union effect that improved pay and conditions across all three countries (Lloyd & Payne, 2016). Further progress might be achieved via union pressure for stronger employment regulation at the national level and improved approaches to union organizing in hard-to-reach sectors.

In contrast, evidence from the US suggests that the 'third wave' of coffee production is leading to the emergence of 'coffee connoisseurship' (Bookman, 2013). The so-called third wave is a movement that emphasizes the production of higher quality coffee, including the use of higher quality beans, single-origin coffee and higher quality roasting and extraction techniques; it is marked by the introduction of specialty coffees that are presented to customers "like fine wines, with an emphasis on origins as a distinguishing factor in discriminating coffee quality and taste" (Roseberry, 1996) (Bookman, 2013, p. 61). Perhaps most significantly, this phenomenon has been associated with the expansion of so-called coffee intelligentsia, who reject standard 'low road' strategies in favour of 'high road' approaches that improve work processes and outcomes, including skills, wages and benefits (Weissman, 2008, p. xvi). While such reports signal that changes may be occurring within the café sector, our understanding of the extent and nature of any such changes remains limited.

In Australia, the characteristics and related quality of jobs performed within cafés have been the subject of very little research. This oversight is particularly concerning given the expanding significance of the café sector in terms of employment growth. In line with the significance of this industry and its expansion, the federal government has highlighted the need to increase supply of skills in order to address demand and enhance productivity and quality in the industry (DEEWR, 2013). Despite such calls, the café industry, and more importantly, café jobs remain poorly understood, leaving policy developers at a cross-road. This chapter seeks to improve understanding by analysing the nature of jobs in Australian cafés. In doing so, the chapter examines the cost-based and quality-based café segments and characterizes front-of-house café jobs in relation to three areas: work organization, skills and training and pay and benefits. The findings provide important data reflecting new ways of working by illustrating the characteristics and relatedly the quality of jobs in Australia's rapidly expanding café sector. Such data are essential to enhancing our understanding of new ways of working as they emerge in the café sector, and the hospitality industry more generally, and informing policy development aimed towards improving job quality and its implications for workers.

Methods and Data

For the purposes of this study, a café was defined as an establishment selling coffee and other non-alcoholic drinks and limited food offerings, such as sandwiches and cakes, with a seated area for consumption (Lloyd & Payne, 2012). Subsequently, a case study approach was deployed, allowing these concepts to be explored in-depth and in context (Yin, 2003). Sites were purposively selected on the basis of product market strategy, focusing on 'standard cafés' that were cost-focused and 'specialty cafés' that were quality-focused, thereby encompassing the major market segments (Lloyd, Warhurst & Dutton 2013). In total, eight sites participated—four standard cafés and four specialty cafés and a range of ownership structures were included. Sites were defined as independent if they were a single site/café, group if they included between two and three sites and chain if they included more than three sites (Ivanov, 2014). Workforce size ranged from 6 to 15 employees. All of the sites were located within a five kilometre radius of the business centre of one Australian city.

Within each site the jobs performed by café attendants and baristas were examined, thereby encompassing the non-managerial frontline work that is performed in cafés. Café attendants sell and serve food/beverages for consumption on premises in cafés, whilst baristas prepare and serve espresso coffee and other hot beverages (ABS, 2014).

To envelop a range of perspectives, interviews were conducted with the manager, café attendants and baristas in each site, with a total of four to six interviews per site. Additional interviews were conducted with key informants in the wider café industry, including wholesale coffee managers, roasters and trainers. In total, 52 interviews were conducted. Interviews were semi-structured, enabling questioning in line with the research aims whilst also allowing interviewees to discuss additional issues. This approach enables the interviewer to elicit interviewee viewpoints more effectively than a standardized interview or questionnaire (Flick 1998). Interview schedules ranged over the key themes related to job quality: work organization, skills and training and pay and benefits (e.g. Bernhardt et al., 2003; Knox et al., 2015; Lloyd & Payne, 2012; Lloyd et al., 2013). The data were content analysed by the researcher to identify common trends and relationships within and between key concepts (Yin, 2003) using an iterative thematic process (Corbin & Strauss, 2008).

Findings

The key aspects of the jobs performed by café attendants and baristas across café segments are explored sequentially.

Work Organization

In broad terms, café attendants and baristas performed similar tasks across the café segments, and they universally indicated that their work was physically demanding, as they were on their feet for long periods of time and carrying heavy items, including stacks of plates and bags of coffee beans. The work tasks performed by café attendants included taking orders, preparing and serving food/beverages, cleaning and preparing tables for use, clearing away used dishes/cutlery, washing dishes and cleaning equipment. For baristas, work tasks focused on preparing, serving and selling a variety of coffee beverages (short black, long black, café latte, cappuccino, macchiato, ristretto) and other hot drinks (tea, hot chocolate, chai), promoting products, collecting payments and operating cash registers, setting up espresso machines/grinders and cleaning/maintaining coffee machines, grinders and coffee-making areas.

Despite these broad similarities, differences existed in terms of the standards followed and levels of monitoring, discretion and work intensity. Within standard cafés, attendants and baristas followed relatively standard procedures that involved basic tasks. In standard sites, food and beverage menus tended to be simple and café attendants followed routine procedures. Attendants tasks were relatively basic and routine, and fragmentation existed as a result of a strong reliance on food supplied premade by external wholesalers, including muffins, biscuits and pies, for example. Other food items, such as sandwiches and salads, were simple to prepare. Similarly, baristas tasks were basic as espresso machines were largely automated in standard cafés, particularly in chain sites, allowing baristas to press a button rather than manually operating the machine in order to extract coffee. Alternate coffee extraction techniques (such as filtering, cold drip and siphon) were not offered by any of the standard cafés and generally only one blend of coffee was available. Thus, baristas in standard cafés possessed minimal expertise across a narrow range of equipment and coffee blends. Both standardization and routinization were especially common in the chain café.

In specialty cafés, attendants' tasks were comparable with those of their standard counterparts but attentiveness and attention to detail was more strongly emphasized:

> My staff must greet every customer as soon as they walk through the door . . . every dish taken out has to look the same, the plates can't have any spills on them and as soon as they finish the plates must be cleared away.
>
> (Manager, specialty independent café)

In this respect, the work performed by attendants in specialty cafés was more intensive than that of their standard counterparts, yet the tasks could not be said to require qualitatively different or higher-level skills. By comparison, specialty baristas performed some qualitatively different tasks as they were required to operate and calibrate espresso machines manually. Manual operation demanded technical skills as well as extensive tacit knowledge gained through experience:

> It's not like pressing a button and it comes out magically, you've actually got to do a tamp [grind, measure and pack the coffee], . . . watch the way that coffee comes out . . . and . . . look at . . . whether or not you've dosed it properly. You've also got to heat the milk properly. . . —you could overheat it and it could split. You could under heat it, you could give it too much air and it will just be really bubbly. . . —but in practice [you can learn and develop these skills] if you do it every single day for eight hours.
>
> (Manager, specialty group café)

Another barista noted the knowledge and problem-solving skills involved in ensuring high quality coffee, explaining,

> For example, if the shot [of coffee] started pouring a little bit too fast you would know that the weather has changed so I need to fix that problem by changing the grind and making it courser and increase the dose [of ground coffee] to compensate for the humidity, there are situations like that.
>
> (Manager, specialty group café)

Moreover, in several of the specialty cafés baristas used additional preparation techniques requiring different equipment and procedures, such as cold drip, chemex and siphon; these different extraction techniques also required understanding different coffee blends and flavour profiles.

Relatedly, specialty café baristas were required to possess an extensive knowledge of coffee cultivation, roasting, blending and grinding as such factors affected the flavour of the coffee and how it should be extracted to optimize quality. Illustratively, baristas and managers made comments to the following effect: "It's a bit like wine—it's all about where it's grown, who's making the wine, what vineyard it's from . . . understanding coffee a lot more than just being in a café" (Barista, specialty group café).

Relatedly, baristas noted the importance of developing their palates in order to improve their coffee-making expertise:

> If you don't have a naturally strong palate, then you have to develop one by tasting lots of coffees and going to cupping sessions [sampling coffee at roasting warehouses], and that's how you become more refined and better able to detect different flavors, how they reflect different terroir [the specificity of place of cultivation, including the soil in a region, the climate, the weather, and the aspect of where the coffee has been cultivated], like with wine vineyards and wine tasting. . . [and] once you have that sort of palate you can bring out the best in the coffee [by adjusting the way that you grind it, extract it and serve it so as to minimize any bitterness and highlight sweetness or caramelization, for example].

Subsequently, specialty baristas were required to perform a wider range of tasks involving additional technical skills and experience along with a scientific understanding of coffee cultivation, roasting and extraction, as well as high-level sensory skills.

In addition to these differences, levels of worker discretion, intensity and monitoring varied across the café segments. Workers in standard cafés possessed relatively low levels of discretion, particularly those working in chain sites where policy and procedure was standardized, and technology was automated. Work intensity was moderate as working time schedules were closely aligned with patterns of customer demand and automation eased the intensity of work. Monitoring ranged from moderate in independent sites to high in chain sites. Work was monitored most intensively in the chain sites as it was aided by sophisticated technology, including work flow monitors, surveillance cameras and real-time sales data.

In specialty cafés, staff possessed greater discretion than their counterparts in standard cafés. Specialty workers were allowed some freedom to experiment in aid of improving quality standards. For example, both attendants and baristas in specialty cafés were encouraged to innovate in order to produce new food and coffee options for customers. Such discretion was thought by managers and their staff to be an integral aspect of the cafés ability to position itself at the high end of the industry. Relatedly, specialty café workers tended to experience more intensive work demands, at least among the sites examined, associated with the absence of automation, strong and very particular customer demand as well as the higher level of detail and precision demanded of specialty café workers. During peak periods of customer demand, the intensity of work was high. Monitoring was moderate among the specialty cafés and work flow monitors and surveillance cameras were not deployed but management maintained a 'close eye' on operations.

Skills and Training

In line with the differences in work tasks and organization, differences in skills and training were also apparent. In standard cafés, initial on-the-job training was conducted by the manager/supervisor or an experienced worker, outlining work tasks and procedures. This initial training varied from one day to two weeks. Most commonly around two days were required for attendants and approximately one week for baristas. Overall, training was relatively basic as tasks were routine and the technology/equipment was simple to operate. Following initial training, new staff worked alongside a more experienced worker until they reached proficiency. In the chain café, training tended to be highly standardized and structured, based on formalized training policies and procedures, and online learning modules were available; training in independents was more ad hoc and informal with few written elements and no online options. Additional ongoing training was relatively limited, associated with the introduction of any new technology/equipment, such as point of sale hardware and/or software upgrades, or the introduction of new menu items.

In specialty cafés, initial on-the-job training was similarly focused on work tasks and organization. Training was conducted by the manager/supervisor, and it varied in duration from two days to two weeks, typically requiring around three days for both attendants and baristas. Baristas initial training was compressed as only experienced baristas were hired by specialty cafés, but baristas then received ongoing training, as explained next. Average duration of initial training was slightly longer for café attendants in specialty cafés than standard cafés because attention to detail was emphasized:

> Food needs to be prepared just right and it has to be consistently of high standards or customers will go somewhere else. . . [and attention must be paid to other details, including] making sure that the saucer is wiped clean of any spills, that the spoon is polished [and oriented correctly] and there is a napkin placed squarely on the saucer under the cup.
>
> (Manager, specialty independent café)

Several managers noted the importance of ensuring that small details were attended to, including the use of chilled glasses to serve cold drinks and warm cups/glasses to serve hot drinks, for example. In this sense, specialty attendants performed work that was more detailed, but the skills required were not qualitatively different to those evident among attendants in standard cafés. Beyond initial training, further training occurred on an ongoing basis though frequency and content varied as outlined next.

For attendants, ongoing training related to seasonal variations in menus and/or new equipment. As such, the skills developed did not tend to be qualitatively different or higher level than those already possessed. In contrast, baristas received more regular ongoing training, which related to further developing their skills:

> A barista . . . is becoming more like a sommelier. You need . . . to be able to talk about coffee, you need especially be able to talk about filter coffee and the way filter coffee highlights different nuances of origin the way a sommelier would be able to talk about the differences between a . . . burgundy to a Marlborough Sauvignon Blanc to Loire Valley.
>
> (Barista, specialty café)

Relatedly, baristas received training regarding different coffee blends and the selection and grinding of different coffees to satisfy customer preferences. One specialty manager explained,

> We have blends and single origins, so they get to work like all the different coffees . . . from different regions. . . —you can have different extractions from that . . . totally different flavour profiles. . . . So they get to experience different varieties and different profiles.

Ongoing training also involved additional techniques/equipment used to heat and texture milk and to calibrate and operate espresso machines and grinders more precisely in order to enhance coffee quality. Developing baristas sensory skills was also important as optimizing quality of coffee extraction involved monitoring and controlling the colour, viscosity, smell and taste of coffee: "You have to taste it throughout the day and watch the color of the shot and its viscosity and constantly adjust your grind and tamp to get consistent shots" (barista, specialty independent). In several cases, baristas spent time at coffee roasting sites to develop their knowledge of roasting and to enhance their sensory skills, especially to refine their palates. Moreover, most of the specialty baristas participated in cupping sessions (tasting freshly roasted coffee blends) and competitive 'smackdowns' (informal competitions and training) on a regular basis to further enhance their sensory and technical skills. Associated with this ongoing training/education, the most skilled specialty baristas were referred to as 'coffee geeks'. 'Coffee geeks' were constantly seeking

Table 8.1 Key Characteristics of Standard and Specialty Cafés

Key Characteristics	Standard Cafés	Specialty Cafés
Work Organization		
Tasks	Attention to procedure, greater automation in chains, basic skills	Strong attention to detail, more specialized/ upgraded skills among baristas
Discretion	Low	Moderate to high
Intensity	Moderate	Moderate to high
Monitoring	High in chains Moderate in independents	Moderate
Skills & Training		
Initial training	One day–two weeks	Two days–two weeks
Time needed to become competent	Two weeks for café attendants One month for baristas	Two weeks for café attendants At least two years for baristas
Training process	Formal, structured in chains, informal, ad hoc in independents	Informal, ad hoc in independents, more structured in group cafés
Pay and Benefits		
Pay per hour (ordinary time)	$17.23 junior rate applicable to workers aged 18–19 years $20.27 adult rate applicable to workers over 19 years of age	$17.23–$20.27 café attendant $20.27–$32 baristas
Benefits	Discounted food/drinks	Free drinks/meal during shifts

to enhance their coffee knowledge—from the horticulture involved in coffee cultivation to cutting-edge technology/techniques used in processing, roasting, grinding and extraction, and they earned something of an elevated status, akin to the 'celebrity chef' (Fine, 2009).

The time taken to become competent, which often included periods of prior experience, varied marginally for attendants and markedly for baristas across the market segments (see Table 8.1). Among café attendants in standard and specialty sites, reaching full competence took around two weeks, whilst it required one month and at least two years, respectively, for baristas.

Pay and Benefits

Overall, the pay and benefits offered to workers varied between the café segments. Within the standard cafés, pay rates were based on the industry award[1] and pay varied in line with the age of workers. In the cafés examined, most juniors were aged 18–19 years, and they received $17.23

per hour. Adult workers, aged over 19 years, were paid the adult award rate of $20.27 per hour. Café attendants and baristas of equivalent ages were paid the same award rates, and 'above award' payments were not reported at any of the standard sites. As such, minimum wage rates were the norm in the standard cafés examined.

Among the specialty sites, some junior café attendants existed but adult workers dominated and pay rates varied in line with the job performed. While the award rates received by café attendants were consistent with the award-based rates provided in the standard cafés, 'above award' payments were commonplace for baristas in specialty cafés. Baristas earned higher (above award) rates of pay than café attendants as baristas were said to be more highly skilled and experienced. Attendants earned the minimum award rates stipulated on the basis of their age—$17.23 to $20.27 per hour, while baristas earned a minimum of $20.27 per hour, but more typically they earned $25 to $32 per hour, with rates increasing in line with levels of skill/experience. Individual agreements existed in some specialty cafés. In such cases, the annual salaries of baristas ($70 000 to $85 000 per annum) often exceeded the average salary for all industries in Australia (around $75 600 per annum) (ABS, 2014).

Additional benefits were provided by all of the cafés, with workers receiving discounted or free food and drinks during their working time. Tips and gratuities were received occasionally, but they were small and after pooling and division employees tended to receive between $5 and $20 each per week.

Discussion

In seeking to analyse the nature of work in the bourgeoning café sector, the findings highlight both old and new ways of working within the services industry. Typically, the old, or traditional, ways of working persisted in standard cafés, whereas distinctive new patterns of working were emerging within the specialty cafés, particularly among specialty baristas. These new ways of working signal encouraging new developments and opportunities for workers, including reduced automation, enhanced worker discretion and autonomy, increased skills and higher wages. Importantly, market segment (standard or specialty) appeared to be a more important factor in shaping the development of new ways of working than ownership structure (chain, group or independent). Few differences existed between chain, group and independent cafés, other than the level of standardization in the chain site. The lack of further differences is likely to be associated with the Australian café industry being overwhelming dominated by independent owners (Lin, 2013), as reflected in the sample. Café chains have a small presence (less than 15 per cent of market share) in Australia. Starbucks was a massive failure, for example, and Café Nero, Costa Coffee and Peet's have no presence in Australia.

Within the standard (cost-based) segment, traditional ways of working persisted. Work organization was relatively standardized and tasks were basic, involving routine procedures that revealed fragmentation and deskilling. Work performed in standard cafés was associated with low levels of discretion, moderate levels of work intensity and moderate to high levels of monitoring; work was monitored most intensively in the chain site where technology was deployed to monitor employees and sales. Standard cafés tended to provide basic initial training, which was more standardized and formalized in the chain site, and relatively limited ongoing training. Typically, skill demands were low involving simple technical skills. Within this segment, minimum rates of pay were provided, and employees received discounted/free food and drinks and minimal tips/gratuities.

Within the specialty (quality-based) segment, some aspects of work organization/tasks were consistent with those in standard cafés but others, including levels of attentiveness and attention to detail, were higher. In addition, specialty baristas were required to operate espresso machines manually while also demonstrating a greater knowledge of other coffee extraction equipment/techniques and a more extensive understanding of coffee cultivation, roasting, blending and grinding. Reduced automation represents a novel departure from the threat of increased automation facing many other workers. This significant departure led to positive work developments emerging in specialty cafés, involving moderate to high levels of discretion and autonomy, increased training and skill development and higher wages among specialty baristas. Typically, attendants required simple technical skills, whereas baristas jobs involved advanced technical skills, a scientific understanding of coffee cultivation, roasting and extraction along with superior sensory skills, akin to those of sommeliers. Within this segment, minimum rates of pay were provided to attendants, while baristas received substantially higher rates of pay, exceeding the award rates significantly. All workers received discounted/free food and drinks and minimal tips/gratuities.

These findings reveal that for some workers, particularly those working in standard cafés, certain aspects of their jobs could be termed 'bad', including low/minimum wages, low skills, limited training, standardization, fragmentation and routinization. Although such findings are broadly consistent with the majority of evidence regarding job quality in the hospitality industry, the café jobs examined did not exhibit the sorts of characteristics associated with the worst examples of 'bad jobs' evident in the hospitality industry, including wage theft, excessive working hours, unsafe work practices, injuries and burnout (Bernhardt et al., 2008; Campbell et al., 2015; Fine, 1996; Jayaraman, 2013; Leidner, 1993). It must be noted, however, that any employers engaging in exploitative practices would have been inclined to avoid participating in this research. Further research is therefore necessary in order to more fully examine the extent of 'bad jobs' within the café industry.

In contrast, other café jobs, especially those of baristas in specialty cafés, entailed 'good' characteristics, including superior wages, higher-level skills and training, self-regulated work and enhanced discretion. The improved job quality among these workers signals a new direction in terms of hospitality work and a significant departure from the 'bad jobs' previously documented in cafés (Lloyd & Payne, 2012, 2014, 2016) and the wider industry (Bernhardt et al., 2003; Dutton et al., 2008; Fine, 1996; Lucas, 2004). Compared to findings from the UK, France and Norway (Lloyd & Payne, 2016), the quality of jobs among Australia's café sector, particularly for specialty baristas, suggests that 'better jobs', perhaps even 'good jobs', can be created within the hospitality industry. The development of 'better jobs' is significant as it reveals new and expanding job opportunities within a sector previously associated with poor employment experiences (Knox 2010; Lucas, 2004) and 'dead-end' prospects (Bernhardt et al., 2003; Dutton et al., 2008). Such findings are important as they illustrate the potential of hospitality jobs to be improved if employers are willing to pursue different, quality-based ('high road') approaches as asserted by Weissman (2008) and Bookman (2013).

In addition, specialty baristas' job quality was maximized through improved skills utilization, ensuring their abilities were harnessed, deployed and developed to heighten organizational performance (UKCES, 2010). Compared to other workers, specialty baristas were more effectively supported by their employers, in terms of developing and deploying the skills needed to do their job. Indeed, specialty baristas exhibited greater "depth and quality of informal learning . . . inside the workplace and the opportunities . . . to develop and utilize their skills at work" (Payne, 2012, p. 421), reflecting improved skills utilization (Grant, Maxwell & Ogden, 2014; Payne, 2012). Notably, improved skills utilization coincided with higher levels of pay.

In the UK, evidence suggests that levering higher skill and pay in low-skilled service work is unlikely to occur based on product market repositioning alone (Lloyd et al., 2013). While there is growing recognition that supply-side interventions targeting employee qualifications are not the solution either (Lloyd et al., 2013), some have suggested that demand-side interventions, including approaches that emphasize skills utilization, may be more effective (e.g. Grant et al., 2014; Payne, 2012). This research lends support to the potential value of such interventions. Indeed, voluntary employer-driven approaches directed towards skills utilization may be a useful way forward.

In sum, the 'bad jobs' said to exist in fast food and other hospitality sectors typically reflect a dominance of 'low road' approaches (e.g.

Bernhardt et al., 2008); however, employers can and do deviate from typical 'low road' approaches and invest in their workforces, creating new and better-quality job opportunities and outcomes. In cafés, these approaches were associated with the 'third wave' of coffee production (Weissman, 2008), a phenomenon that, while still relatively new, is producing significant and beneficial changes within the industry. These changes offer substantially better job opportunities and outcomes. Such opportunities/outcomes benefit employees and prior research suggests that they also improve recruitment and retention, thereby benefitting employers by way of reduced turnover costs along with enhanced labour/ skill retention and productivity (Siebern-Thomas, 2005). Overall, these findings suggest that policy development should be directed towards the expansion of 'high road' approaches (facilitated by pressure from trade unions) along with improved skills utilization in order to grow 'better', and even 'good jobs', within the café industry and beyond.

Note

1. The award system enshrines legally binding minimum wages and conditions at the industry level, though it does not prohibit employers from paying discretionary over-award payments to their employees. Most hospitality employers do not pay over-award amounts (RCA, 2009).

References

ABS. (2014). Average Weekly Earnings, Australia, Cat. No. 6302.0.

ABS. (2017). *2016 Census Quick Stats*. Available from www.censusdata.abs.gov. au/census_services/getproduct/census/2016/quickstat/036

Allegra. (2014). *Allegra Project Café: UK Retail Coffee Shop Market: Strategic Analysis, December 2014*. London: Allegra.

Australian Government. (2015). *Job Outlook*. Available from http://joboutlook. gov.au/ [Accessed 30.03.2017].

Bernhardt, A., Boushey, H., Dresser, L., & Tilly, C. (Eds.) (2008). *The Gloves-off Economy: Workplace Standards at the Bottom of the Labour Market*. Champaign: University of Illinois.

Bernhardt, A., Dresser, L., & Hatton, E. (2003). The coffee pot wars: Unions and firm restructuring in the hotel industry. In E. Appelbaum, A. Bernhardt & R. Murnane (Eds.), *Low Wage America* (pp. 33–76). New York: Russell Sage Foundation.

British Hospitality Association (BHA). (2010). *Creating Jobs in Britain: A Hospitality Economy Proposition*. London: BHA.

Bookman, S. (2013). Branded cosmopolitanisms: "Global" coffee brands and the co-creation of "Cosmopolitan Cool", *Cultural Sociology*, 7(1), 56–72.

Campbell, I., Boese, M., & Tham, J. (2015). Welcome to Melbourne: International Students and Precarious Work in Cafes, Restaurants and Takeaway Food Services, *Proceedings of the 29th AIRAANZ Conference*, February 3–5.

Clegg, C. (1983). Psychology of employee lateness, absence and turnover: A methodological critique and an empirical study, *Journal of Applied Psychology*, 68, 88–101.

Corbin, J., & Strauss, A. (2008). *Basics of Qualitative Research: Techniques and Procedures for Developing Grounded Theory*. London: Sage.

Department of Education, Employment and Workplace Relations (DEEWR). (2013). *Employment Outlook to 2017*. DEEWR, Canberra.

Dutton, E., Warhurst, C., Lloyd, C., James, S., Commander, J., & Nickson, D. (2008). Just like the elves in Harry Potter: Room attendants in UK hotels. In C. Lloyd, G. Mason, & K. Mayhew (Eds.), *Low wage work in the UK* (pp. 96–130). New York, NY: Russell Sage Foundation.

Etzioni, A. (1986). McJobs are Bad for Kids, *The Washington Post*, August 24, B170.

Findlay, P., Kalleberg, A., & Warhurst, C. (2013). The challenge of job quality. *Human Relations*, 66(4), 441–451.

Findlay, P., Warhurst, C., & Keep, E. (2017). Opportunity knocks? The possibilities and levers for improving job quality. *Work and Occupations*, 44(1), 3–22.

Fine, G. (1996). *Kitchens*. California: University of California Press.

Fine, G. (2009) (2nd Ed.). *Kitchens: The Culture of Restaurant Work*. California: University of California Press.

Flick, U. (1998). *An Introduction to Qualitative Research*. London: Sage.

Freeman, R. (1978). Job satisfaction as an economic variable. *American Economic Review*, 68, 135–141.

Grant, K., Maxwell, G., & Ogden, S. (2014). Skills utilisation in Scotland: Exploring the views of managers and employees. *Employee Relations*, 36(5), 458–479.

Ivanov, A. (2014). *IBISWorld Industry Report OD5489: Chain Restaurants in Australia*. Australia: IBISWorld.

Jayaraman, S. (2013). *Behind the Kitchen Door*. Cornell University Press, USA.

Kellner, A., Peetz, D., Townsend, K., & Wilkinson, A. (2016). "We are very focused on the muffins": Regulation of and compliance with industrial relations in franchises. *Journal of Industrial Relations*, 58(1), 25–45.

Knox, A. (2010). "Lost in translation": An analysis of temporary work agency employment in hotels. *Work, Employment and Society*, 24(3), 449–467.

Knox, A., & Warhurst, C. (2018). Occupations, the missing link? A new theoretical and methodological approach to product markets, skill and pay. *Work, Employment and Society*, 32(1), 150–168.

Knox, A, Warhurst, C., Nickson, D., & Dutton, E. (2015). More than a feeling: Using hotel room attendants to improve understanding of job quality. *International Journal of Human Resource Management*, 26(12), 1547–1567.

Knox, A., & Wright, S. (forthcoming). Understanding and conceptualizing job quality based on qualitative research. In *Oxford Handbook of Job Quality*, in press.

Lane, C. (2014). *The Cultivation of Taste: Chefs and the Organisation of Fine Dining*. Oxford: Oxford University Press.

Leidner, R. (1993). *Fast Food, Fast Talk: Service Work and the Routinization of Everyday Work*. California: University of California Press.

Lin, R. (2013). *IBISWorld Industry Report H4511b: Cafes and Coffee Shops in Australia*. Australia: IBISWorld.

Lindsay, C., & McQuaid, R. (2004). Avoiding the "McJobs": Unemployed job seekers and attitudes to service work. *Work, Employment and Society*, 18(2), 297–319.

Lloyd, C., & Payne, J. (2012). Flat whites: Who gets progression in the UK café sector? *Industrial Relations Journal*, 43(1), 38–52.

Lloyd, C., & Payne, J. (2014). It's all hands on, even for management: Managerial work in the UK café sector. *Human Relations*, 67(4), 465–488.

Lloyd, C., & Payne, J. (2016). *Skills in the Age of Over-Qualification*. Oxford: Oxford University Press.

Lloyd, C., Warhurst, C., & Dutton, E. (2013). The weakest link? Product market strategies, skill and pay in the hotel industry. *Work, Employment and Society*, 27(2), 254–271.

Lucas, R. (2004). *Employment Relations in the Hospitality and Tourism Industries*. London: Routledge.

McPhail, R., & Fisher, R. (2008). It's more than wages: Analysis of the impact of internal labour markets on the quality of jobs. *International Journal of Human Resource Management*, 19(2), 461–472.

Oxenbridge, S., & Moensted, M. (2011). The relationship between payment systems, work intensification and health and safety outcomes: A study of hotel room attendants. *Policy and Practice in Health and Safety*, 9(2), 7–26.

Payne, J. (2012). Fronting up to skills utilisation: What can we learn from Scotland's skills utilization projects? *Policy Studies*, 33(5), 419–438.

People 1st. (2009). *Skills Priorities for the Hospitality, Leisure, Travel and Tourism Sector. People* (1st ed.). UK: Uxbridge.

RCA (Restaurant and Catering Australia) (2009). *Submission to the Australian Fair Pay Commission Minimum Wage Review 2009*. Available from www.fair pay.gov.au/NR/rdonlyres/ . . . /0/RandCA_ submission_2009.pdf.

Ritzer, G. (1993). *The McDonaldization of Society*. California: Sage.

Roseberry, W. (1996). The rise of yuppie coffees and the reimagination of class in the United States. *American Anthropologist*, 98(4), 762–775.

Siebern-Thomas, F. (2005). Job quality in European labour markets. In S. Brazen, C. Lucifora, & W. Salverda (Eds.), *Job Quality and Employer Behaviour*. New York: Palgrave Macmillan.

Timo, N., & Davidson, M. (2005). A survey of employee relations practices and demographics of MNC chain and domestic luxury hotels in Australia, *Employee Relations*, 27(2), 175–192.

United Kingdom Commission for Employment and Skills (UKCES) (2010). *High Performance Working: A Policy Review*, Evidence Report 18, UKCES, London.

Vanselow, A., Warhurst, C., Bernhardt, A., & Dresser, L. (2010). Working at the wage floor: Hotel room attendants and labor market institutions in Europe and the United States. In J. Gautie' & J. Schmitt (Eds.), *Low wage work in a wealthy world* (pp. 269–318). New York, NY: Russell Sage Foundation.

Weissman M (2008). *God in a Cup*. Boston: Houghton Mifflin Harcourt.

Yin, R. (2003). *Case Study Research: Design and Methods*. 3rd ed. California: Sage.

Part IV

Harnessing Technological and Digital Information

The Need for Workforce Agility

9 Digital Workplace Design

Transforming for High Performance

Nick van der Meulen, Kristine Dery and Ina M. Sebastian

MIT Sloan Center for Information Systems Research (US)

Introduction

Advances in digital technologies and global competitive pressures have caused a rising tide of uncertainty, ambiguity, and complexity for organizations.[1] To survive and succeed in such environments, organizations need to 1) restructure their internal operations to make it easier for employees to get things done in the organization and 2) create an information-driven, test-and-learn environment that enables experimentation and enhanced data gathering (Bennett & Lemoine, 2014; Mocker, Weill & Woerner, 2014). We learned that in response to these two requirements, organizations are fundamentally redesigning how their employees work by changing various physical, cultural, and digital arrangements—and doing so in a tightly coupled fashion. We refer to the outcomes of these initiatives as "digital workplaces."

The discourse on digital workplace design is difficult to grasp for management practitioners and academics alike (Köffer, 2015). For managers, the large variety of its possible constituent practices makes it difficult to distinguish which design parameters matter most. After all, in practitioner outlets they are encouraged (often by parties with a vested interest) to invest in everything from the latest technological solutions (e.g. Miller & Cain, 2016), to redesigning the physical work environment (e.g. Entis, 2016), and/or transforming into a self-managed organization (Bernstein et al., 2016). For academics, this problem of scope is exacerbated by the large number of disciplines (e.g. computer science, management, psychology), theories, and levels of analysis that these interrelated components of a digital workplace touch upon. In the field of Information Systems alone there are already four major categories of digital workplace-related research streams (Köffer, 2015): 1) collaboration (e.g., computer supported cooperative work, media synchronicity, social networks), 2) compliance (e.g., IT consumerization, information security), 3) mobility (e.g., empowerment, management control, telework), and 4) stress and overload (e.g., cognitive load, technostress, work-life balance). A recent systematic literature review by Lee (2016) has shown that even when limited to the organizational level of analysis, from an academic viewpoint, there are 194 different variables that relate to the digital workplace. Since these disjointed research streams and components of the digital workplace have been investigated in isolation, there is no framework for doing so in unison. As such, we do not know how the components of the digital workplace compare in terms of impact and how they might combine to collectively affect organizational performance. In this chapter, we therefore focus on the following two research questions:

1. How are organizations designing digital workplaces to cope with uncertain, ambiguous, and complex environments?
2. How do the digital workplace design choices of organizations collectively contribute to organizational performance?

Answering these questions requires insight into management practice, which is why we have conducted two separate, yet complementary, empirical studies. In the next section, we will first elaborate on the methodological details of this mixed methods research design. After doing so, we draw on our qualitative results to develop a framework that unpacks the digital workplace into a series of design and management levers. This framework is subsequently applied to our quantitative results section, where we explore how these levers combine and relate to organizational performance. We illustrate our findings with examples from organizations that consider the digital workplace an integral part of their organizational strategy and discuss the relationship of these findings with prior literature. In conclusion, we provide a set of recommendations to management practitioners as well as several possible avenues for further research.

Research Method

The datasets used in this chapter originate from two separate studies conducted independently at two universities. The quantitative data was collected between 2011 and 2014, when the first author worked at Erasmus University Rotterdam, whereas the second and third author collected the qualitative data at the MIT Center for Information Systems Research (MIT CISR) in 2015. While these studies were designed independently, they shared the similar objective of figuring out how organizations were going about designing and implementing digital workplaces for high performance. To leverage the mixed-method benefit of combining the two studies, the authors collaborated closely during the analysis of the datasets and were co-located for several months to enhance the critical perspective that has resulted in this chapter. More specifically, we used a 'concurrent triangulation mixed methods' research design (Cresswell, 2014) in which we draw on the unique methods employed by both studies to confirm and cross-validate our qualitative and quantitative research findings. These methodologies are discussed in detail in the following subsections.

Qualitative Research Study

Our qualitative data was collected via exploratory semi-structured expert interviews, which invited participants to openly share their experiences regarding the digital workplace. In particular, we aimed to understand 1) how organizations defined the digital workplace, 2) what activities or areas of work were given new consideration, 3) why organizations considered it important to focus on the digital workplace to build new capabilities, and 4) how they were going about designing and implementing digital workplaces. Note that we were interested more in what they were doing and why they were doing it, rather than the change management practices that surrounded the transition to the digital workplace. Organizations self-selected into the study based on their response to a 'request for participation' email that was distributed to a broad industry cross-section of large organizations (consisting of at least 500 employees) in the United States of America, Europe, and Australia. Participating interviewees were executives identified as responsible for digital workplace initiatives in their organizations. Each interview was between 30 and 45 minutes long, and in some organizations, multiple people with responsibilities across IT, HR, Facilities, and Digital were interviewed. This led to a total of 63 interviews in 27 organizations. Most interviews were recorded and transcribed, although, occasionally, it was only possible to gather written notes due to confidentiality restrictions. Interview transcripts were utilized for within-case and cross-case analysis. During the analysis phase, the interview data was coded based on emerging categories that were debated and agreed on by the second and third author. Additional feedback was acquired from the broader MIT CISR research team as the work was presented frequently throughout the data collection and analysis period.

Quantitative Research Study

Our quantitative data was collected by means of an online survey, which was developed in collaboration with a team of ten subject matter experts from three Dutch research institutes and subsequently pretested with the help of six corporate partners. The goal of the research instrument was to explore the prevalence of digital workplace practices as well as their effects on organizational performance. Invitations to participate in the survey were sent to senior managers and corporate policymakers (i.e., informed respondents) throughout the data collection period by the first author's research team and

Table 9.1 Quantitative Sample Characteristics

		Absolute	Relative
Usable Responses		113	100%
Organizational size	1–50 employees	33	29
	51–100 employees	13	12
	101–500 employees	22	19
	>500 employees	45	40
Years in operation	0–5 years	19	17
	6–25 years	40	35
	26–100 years	37	33
	>100 years	17	15
Industry	Banking and Insurance	15	13
	Business Services	24	21
	Construction	1	1
	Consultancy	15	13
	Government	15	13
	Healthcare	1	1
	ICT and Media	14	12
	Industry	1	1
	Logistics	2	2
	Research and Education	7	6
	Utilities	3	3
	Undisclosed	15	13

affiliated research partners. In an attempt to improve their participation rate and the truthfulness of their responses, participants were informed in the introduction of the survey that their data was collected completely anonymously. This meant that even though the data collection process spanned several years, the research setup had to be cross-sectional.

In total, 318 participants completely filled out the survey for their organizations. Among these, there were 113 organizations that had experience with the digital workplace; other organizations indicated that they were either still learning about or preparing themselves for the digital workplace. Considering our focus on digital workplace design, we examined the 113 organizations in our dataset that had made conscious choices to design a digital workplace. Table 9.1 summarizes the characteristics of this sample, which represents a wide range of industries, organizational sizes, and years in operation.

The 6S Digital Workplace Framework

Our qualitative investigation shows that the digital workplace is about a fundamentally different way of working, in which organizations shifted from models with a focus on command and control toward a focus on connect and collaborate. Doing so required a holistic approach that revolves around the employee, as isolated efforts by facilities, human resources, or IT departments were considered insufficient for effecting meaningful change in the way work was conducted. As one senior executive lamented,

> *If you just imagine the microcosm of an individual workplace in our company, then every part of it is owned by a different part of the company. The screen, laptop and video camera belong to IT, the phone to communications, the desk and chair to facilities, and the person sitting at it is governed by HR. Without all of these parts moving together we are in danger of simply playing an old game with new rules. This is not workplace transformation.*
> (Facilities manager at a global insurance organization)

This description, which depicts a common concern among workplace management in our research sample, supports the viewpoint of an organization as an ecosystem where physical, cultural, and digital elements either mutually reinforce one another, or place individual constraints on organizational performance. All elements needed to be aligned and changed in dynamic harmony to create a competitive advantage.

We established that organizations typically transform their workplace using three design levers: 1) physical and virtual space, 2) systems that support getting work done, and 3) enterprise social media. In addition, we identified that successful organizations guide digital workplace transformation with three additional management levers: 1) symbols (branding) that communicate the strategic significance of the digital workplace design, 2) leadership with a sustained focus on supporting the digital workplace design, and 3) systemic learning processes that ensure continuous improvements in the way work is conducted. Without these management levers, organizations' efforts to transform the workplace tended to stagnate in pilot projects and suboptimal designs. Figure 9.1 provides a graphical overview of the entire framework with its three design and management levers; we will discuss each of these and illustrate them with typical practices derived from our interviews.

Design Levers

Space

The physical work environment is the traditional embodiment of the workplace, and therefore also remained an important cornerstone of the digital workplace. Whether physical or virtual, space refers to those elements that provide choice in the work environment and allow for

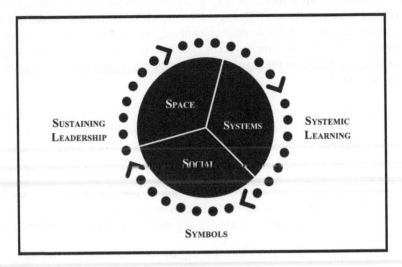

Figure 9.1 Six Design Levers for the Digital Workplace

collaborative behaviors. That is why in nearly all organizations we studied, decisions regarding the work environment were taken with interaction in mind. The ways in which these goals were to be achieved, however, differed. For instance, some organizations deliberately designed (specific parts of) the work environment in such a way that it maximized collaboration and the number of 'collisionable hours':[2]

> We consider the decision to have a central open staircase a major cause for our success. People meet there by chance and if we wouldn't have these open stairs, they would need to go through several doors to reach another floor. In our view that would lead to a separation of people; obstructing the cooperation and communication that we aimed for.
>
> (Digital workplace steering committee member at a European research and advisory organization)

Employee mobility within offices was further enabled by the use of open work environments with flexible seating. Interviewees indicated that these make employees more visible and approachable and also across hierarchies. Yet while removing office walls altogether may increase interaction, there is a risk of doing so at the cost of privacy and focus. Several organizations therefore envisioned their work environment around personas, each with its own specific requirements and experiences. These personas extended to requirements for remote working (at home, at co-working spaces, or on the go), resulting in an integrated perspective on workplace experiences where employees can choose environments in which they can perform optimally. In the physical office, different work requirements by individuals and teams typically led to more nuanced work environments, providing a variety of work settings for specific activities or job functions:

> *We're really looking at a distributed work model now, where we'll have hoteling, we'll have client space, we'll have focus space, we'll have community areas, and we'll have touchdown points where teams can touch down and sit near each other but not have an assigned desk.*
>
> (CIO at a large North American management and consulting services organization)

Systems

Digital workplace systems comprise the technologies that support new ways of working. These technologies differ from those that are directly associated with specific work processes and tasks, such as customer relationship management systems, or research analysis software. Organizations that successfully leveraged the systems lever addressed three elements (mobility, unified communications and collaboration (UCC), and personalized support) in a coherent approach that focused on simplifying the way work is conducted:

> *A digital enterprise [. . .] demands a company whose business rules and policies are completely digital, where people's jobs are represented in a digital fashion and, most importantly, a technology ecosystem that makes the company's information both secure and, for those with the right access, easy to find and share. It's a philosophy of how work is going to get done.*
>
> (CIO at a large North American financial services organization)

Most organizations have enhanced employees' mobility by virtualizing their workflow: all required work-related information is digitized and made available at any time and any place through external access to corporate systems. Whereas some organizations use dedicated devices to achieve this, others rely on virtualization tools in combination with a 'Bring Your Own Device' (BYOD) policy. These policies are typically supported by cloud-based solutions and UCC systems, especially in large, distributed organizations. Organizations in our research sample sought to facilitate collaboration by providing searchable knowledge bases to connect with others, and by making it easy for employees to work together both physically and virtually.

We also learned that organizations are increasingly focused on 1) providing the right technologies to get work done (faster) and 2) removing potential barriers to employee performance. Organizations commonly found it difficult to alleviate complexity of workplace systems (such as difficulties with technologies in virtual meeting rooms, log-in issues, printer connectivity, complex travel systems, etc.). Providing technological support quickly whenever and wherever it is needed, as well as by constantly servicing technologies to pre-empt problems were crucial elements to personalized support. Additionally, organizations were experimenting with ways to augment office space through location and presence indicator systems, which help employees to find available spaces to work quickly and create awareness of where and when colleagues are available to collaborate (e.g. Randall, 2015). Several organizations have started to extend personalization even further: a large financial services organization for instance enabled employees to choose from personalized technology toolkits based on their work needs:

> We created a user needs map, which basically said, what are we trying to do from an employee technology perspective? It's to communicate, to get people to collaborate, to improve knowledge management, to facilitate them to get things done on a day-to-day basis. And if that's the goal, then how do you [. . .] measure it and see progress? How would an employee see a difference? That was an equally important thing.
> (CIO at a large North American financial services organization)

Social

In many of the organizations in our study, social media played a role in simplifying working life and facilitating access to corporate conversations at different levels. Enterprise social media (ESM), such as Yammer, Chatter, or Jive have the potential not only to build communities to share ideas but also for discussions to be transparent in ways they have never had been before. Organizational listening via ESM provided opportunities to understand more about customers, identify new ideas and new talent within the organization, find the speed bumps to effective work practices, and to change conversations through interactions across silos and hierarchies. Just as the amplification of the customer voice constitutes one of the fundamental pillars of successful digital business models, the employee voice seems to underpin the digital workplace:

> We had to find ways of shining the spotlight into dark corners of our organization to find those people who had much to say, but [who] found it hard to be heard [. . .] in a traditional hierarchical structure.
> (Partner digital transformation at an Australian professional services organization)

While some organizations found social media useful to build the corporate conversation and enable broader and more diverse participation, others found that take-up was patchy. Active networks where employees share and build ideas create value for organizations. In many cases, creating such active networks was challenging, and smaller communities did not always progress to larger communities:

> *[The employees in innovation departments] need the social network tools, and they're very engaged with the technology, and that's a much easier call, but getting it to process oriented work is much more difficult.*
>
> (Senior architect manager at a large
> North American insurance organization)

IT leadership responsible for ESM often pursued a different and parallel approach for ESM on the team/group level with the purpose of simplifying work flows and collaboration within groups. Some organizations let teams choose which social media platforms they wanted to use for sharing information. Yet other organizations changed how team used ESM through integration into frequently used systems. One executive responsible for ESM in a large North American software organization, for example, indicated that the most successful implementations occurred when social capabilities were placed in virtual environments where people were already working.

Management Levers

Sustaining Leadership

The sustaining leadership lever proved critical to support, project, and promote the strategic role of the digital workplace in the organization. In organizations with successful digital workplace initiatives, a broad management mind shift that cascaded throughout management layers reinforced the new ways of working that the design levers enabled. For instance, managers had to provide employees with autonomy to benefit from teleworking arrangements; they had to trust that employees would use BYOD arrangements responsibly; and they had to stimulate transparency in work practices in line with open work environments and digitized work flows:

> *In a world that speeds up it is inevitable that decisions are made lower in the organization. It means that you have to give employees access to required information [. . .] and also that managers let go of certain responsibilities [. . .] which means trusting employees.*
>
> (Regional director at a global information
> services and technology organization)

Collaboration of digital workplace leadership with management at different levels is needed to ensure alignment of the capabilities of digital workplace design and the day-to-day management of employees. Equally important—and likely critical for this broad management mind shift to occur—is that we found that organizations with a successful digital workplace establish a dedicated digital workplace leadership team with its own accountabilities, goals, and access to ensure strategic relevance and allocation of sufficient resources. These leadership teams were increasingly cross-functional for the benefit of collective expertise and governance, and were typically headed by a member of the C-suite (such as the chief information officer or the chief people officer). While it was this leadership team's responsibility to design the digital workplace, we saw that successful leadership did not usually organize this design process in a top-down or directive manner, but rather in an organic, facilitative fashion in conjunction with the rest of the organization.

Systemic Learning

The systemic learning lever refers to the process by which the digital workplace leadership team continuously adapts the design of the digital workplace through real-time experimentation and feedback. Organizations following such an approach recognized that not every element of the design could be an immediate success, and therefore 'failed forward' by continuously fine-tuning or replacing individual elements rather than maintaining suboptimal designs or lingering complexity. In order to learn what works, these organizations openly and continuously gathered input throughout their ranks by such means as employee surveys, ESM discussions with digital workplace champions, or even Internet of Things sensors.

Organizations in transitional phases sought to accelerate learning in several ways. In one particular case, a monthly trophy was awarded to the employee who did the best job in implementing digital workplace principles. We also found that training and coaching were considered essential for the realization of new behavioral norms, as well as for creating employee buy-in and legitimacy through storytelling and shared experiences:

> We spent a lot of time training and talking to managers, to groups, and to all employees. Because we considered the changes as major. It is a completely different way of working where everyone has his own challenges, his worries, his way of accepting it. We had several ways and moments to share information and listen to each other's input.
>
> (Digital workplace steering committee member at a
> European research and advisory organization)

Ultimately, as organizations learned how to measure the digital work-place effectively, systems also began to take a greater role in systemic learning, as data on the use of workplace capabilities and associated out-comes were openly provided to employees with complete transparency in real time. One organization created a dashboard, at which employees could see their individual performance indicators, as well as their use of laptops, printing, and communications platforms, and benchmark all results with best practices in the organization:

> *That's the place where employees can get information about how they're using the tools that they have at their fingertips [. . .] We're going to propose a challenge to see how many employees use it, and we'll gather metrics to show how effective they are in using the tech-nology and translate that to savings for the company.*
> (VP of communications at a large North American financial services organization)

Symbols

The third important lever for guiding transitions is management com-munication through meaningful as well as powerful symbols and actions. Lasting change required that senior and middle management 'live' and communicate the importance of the digital workplace strategy to employ-ees and provide them with a clear vision.

Senior management actions provide high symbolic value for reinforc-ing the workplace strategy to employees. Many organizations found it essential that senior management exemplified new ways of working—for example, by initiating discussions about innovative ideas with employees on ESM, or by sharing open office space with employees and engaging in more frequent, ad hoc, informal meetings:

> *The main purpose [. . .] is to spur collaboration, that you get peo-ple to meet that otherwise wouldn't have. We converted all manager offices into collaboration space, and everybody just sits at a table. So I think that's the other, the cultural message we want to send, that this is a flat organization. We no longer have a hierarchy. Everyone has the ability to collaborate with each other without perceived silos, you know, boundaries that people had.*
> (CIO at a large North American financial services organization)

Organizations that conducted major workplace changes with strategic, well thought-out initiatives typically utilized symbols to reinforce com-munication of how they were transforming to be competitive in the digital economy, and how they expected employees to change with them through the adoption of new behavioral norms (such as being more collaborative, creative, or innovative). Brands or graphic symbols that identify digital workplace initiatives (and the digital workplace team as an entity in the organization) are much more than communication campaigns. Their goal was to initiate changes in the way people in the organization define their working lives:

> *You want to be in a situation where you are able to challenge things that have never been challenged before, whether business ideas or processes. Too often we see things being done because that's how they've always been done.*
>
> (Director of strategy at an Australian professional services organization)

Quantitative Results

With the 6S digital workplace framework in place, we proceeded to analyze our quantitative data regarding how digital workplace design affects organizational performance. To this end, we mapped a total of 23 statements representing the six digital workplace levers on our framework. Respondents answered each statement on a five-point Likert scale ranging from 1 = 'completely disagree' to 5 = 'completely agree.' In addition, we measured organizational performance relative to direct competitors on five dimensions: revenue growth, profit growth, growth in market share, ability to attract new customers, and employee satisfaction. For this measure, we used a five-point Likert scale ranging from 1 = 'far worse' to 5 = 'far better.' Scores on the five dimensions were averaged to create an overall organizational performance score. Table 9.2 shows the survey items mapped to the six digital workplace design levers, the means and standard deviations of all measures, as well as their correlations with organizational performance.

By examining the correlation coefficients, we can deduce that workplace design elements for five of the levers (all except Social) are significantly related to organizational performance. However, not all design elements (items) are equally important. More specifically, we find the most and highest correlations for elements of the three management levers, such as stimulating transparency ($r = 0.37$, $p < 0.01$), finding a balance between trust and control ($r = 0.37$, $p < 0.01$), and enabling autonomous work ($r = 0.35$, $p < 0.01$). With regards to the Space design lever, we see that popular office designs focused on flexible open work environments ($r = 0.10$, $p = 0.33$), specific activities ($r = 0.12$, $p = 0.22$), or the reduction of floor space ($r = 0.08$, $p = 0.42$) do not significantly relate to performance. Instead, organizations seem to derive more value from environments specifically designed to enable and support collaboration ($r = 0.33$, $p < 0.01$) as well as from active telework arrangements (r = 0.30, p < 0.01). The use of co-working spaces was very uncommon within our sample and proved non-significant (r = 0.08, p = 0.43). In terms of the Systems and Social levers, we see that technologies that support autonomous and remote work—i.e. any time/any place (r = 0.27, p < 0.01) as well as digitized work and information flow technologies (r = 0.20, p = 0.04)—relate to performance, but BYOD policies (r = −0.08, p = 0.41) and the use of enterprise social media (r = 0.14, p = 0.15) do not. Finally, we found that providing direction to the digital workplace by means of a clear mission and/or vision is also an important element to take into account, as this Symbols lever is also significantly related to performance (r = 0.24, p = 0.01).

Yet while such correlations provide useful insights, they fail to shed any light on the ecosystem as a whole or on whether elements from the various levers work in dynamic harmony or constraint. We, therefore, conducted an additional K-means clustering analysis to determine groups with differing digital workplace strategies. Differences between these groups were subsequently examined using one-way analysis of variance, as reported in Table 9.3. Consistent with our qualitative findings, we find that those organizations that act on all three design levers as well as the three management levers tend to outperform their competitors the most (as shown in cluster 4: 'Hybrid' with an average performance score of 3.84)—especially compared to those organizations that primarily focus on opening up space (cluster 1, scoring 3.02). There are, however, two clusters with intermediate organizational performance. The first (cluster 2, scoring 3.43) focuses primarily on Space and Systemic Learning levers that derive value from co-location (i.e. activity-based working environments and an open knowledge sharing policy), yet severely limits autonomy and remote working practices and technologies. Whereas the other cluster (cluster 3, scoring 3.64) seems to take the exact opposite approach, here we see hardly any focus on traditional Space elements, but a lot of attention to remote working, autonomy, and employee voice (management being more open to employee initiatives). We shall elaborate further on these findings and their potential implications in the discussion section.

Discussion

Our qualitative results point out that organizations consider the digital workplace an important strategic asset for 1) simplifying ways of working, enabling employees to handle more complex work and 2) creating information-driven test-and-learn environments that cross traditional working silos and hierarchies to tackle uncertainty and ambiguity. We learned that this is not a finite transformation project, but rather a constant reevaluation of work and subsequent iterative change processes. Evidence-based decision making is critical in these environments to

Table 9.2 6S Statement Means, Standard Deviations, and Correlations With Organizational Performance (N = 113)

Statements	Mean	Std. Dev.	Correlation with Org. Performance
Organizational performance	3.46	0.77	–
Space			
1. Our work environment is based on flexible (open) workspaces	3.58	1.14	0.097
2. Employees consider our work environment to be inspiring	3.29	0.92	0.185
3. Our work environment enables and supports collaboration	3.57	0.90	0.329**
4. Our work environment follows 'activity-based working' principles	3.48	1.22	0.120
5. We found an optimal balance between required and available workspaces	3.07	0.96	0.079
6. We enable the use of co-working spaces	2.52	1.19	0.079
7. We actively support employees who telework	3.60	0.96	0.300**
Systems			
8. We provide our employees with the technological solutions they need to work (together) at any time and any place	3.68	0.98	0.273**
9. All the work-related information our employees need is made digitally available to them	3.68	1.00	0.203*
10. Our employees' (corporate) technology use is not limited to the solutions we provide to them	2.59	0.90	–0.081
Social			
11. We use enterprise social media to foster social cohesion/collaboration	3.05	1.16	0.142
Symbols			
12. Our organization has a clear mission/vision that provides direction (to the digital workplace)	3.71	0.81	0.239*
Sustaining Leadership			
13. Our employees are enabled to work autonomously	3.67	0.90	0.347**
14. Our employees can determine their own working hours/times	3.72	0.89	0.206*
15. We hold our employees accountable to pre-set goals or targets	3.54	0.86	0.111
16. We found a good balance between employee trust and control	3.39	0.89	0.366**

Statements	Mean	Std. Dev.	Correlation with Org. Performance
17. We follow an organic management approach without strictly defined job roles and tasks	2.96	0.98	0.139
18. We see management's role as facilitative rather than directive	3.24	0.91	0.265**
19. Our organization stimulates transparency in work activities	3.69	0.80	0.374**
Systemic Learning			
20. Our top management team is open to employees' initiatives	3.72	0.90	0.277**
21. It is our corporate policy to openly share knowledge and information	3.53	1.00	0.256**
22. Our employees openly share their mistakes and failures so that everyone may learn from them and find solutions	3.31	0.81	0.332**
23. We train our employees on aspects of the digital workplace	3.24	0.98	0.084

*Significance (two-tailed) at 5%, **Significance (two-tailed) at 1%

Table 9.3 6S Statement Means and ANOVAs for K-Means Clusters

Clusters	1 (n = 34)	2 (n = 14)	3 (n = 19)	4 (n = 38)	ANOVA
Measure	Open	Activity Based	Mobile	Hybrid	F
Organizational performance	3.02	3.43	3.64	3.84	10.08
Space					
1. Flexible open work environment	3.76	2.43	2.37	4.47	41.37
2. Inspiring work environment	3.21	2.86	2.68	3.82	9.91
3. Designed for collaboration	3.24	3.21	3.16	4.21	12.97
4. Activity-based work environment	3.44	3.71	1.89	4.16	24.12
5. Optimal use of space (reduce m²)	2.91	3.43	2.11	3.61	16.15
6. Enable use of co-working space	2.47	2.14	1.95	2.95	3.80
7. Enable + support telework	3.24	2.93	3.42	4.24	12.46

(*Continued*)

Table 9.3 (Continued)

Clusters	1 (n = 34)	2 (n = 14)	3 (n = 19)	4 (n = 38)	ANOVA
Measure	Open	Activity Based	Mobile	Hybrid	F
Systems					
8. Any time/any place technology	3.32	2.79	3.84	4.16	10.70
9. Digitized work/ information flow	3.29	3.07	3.37	4.42	15.06
10. BYOD policy	2.79	2.50	2.37	2.58	1.00
Social					
11. Use of (enterprise) social media	3.00	3.00	2.47	3.37	2.55
Symbols					
12. Providing a clear mission/vision	3.29	3.43	3.84	4.16	8.96
Sustaining Leadership					
13. Enable autonomous work	3.21	2.64	3.74	4.34	29.35
14. Allow flexible hours	3.35	2.57	3.68	4.47	36.87
15. Output-based management focus	3.18	3.57	3.47	3.89	5.20
16. Trust versus control balance	2.59	3.36	3.37	4.13	32.57
17. Organic management	2.68	2.86	2.89	3.26	2.40
18. Facilitative management	2.94	2.93	3.00	3.74	6.57
19. Stimulating transparency	2.79	3.57	3.16	3.71	32.26
Systemic Learning					
20. Management open to initiatives	3.09	3.56	3.95	4.29	16.47
21. Open knowledge sharing	2.94	3.93	3.63	4.29	16.62
22. Learning from failure (culture)	2.97	3.07	3.42	4.29	10.43
23. Digital workplace training	3.04	2.71	3.20	3.56	2.04

identify the speed bumps that make work difficult. Significant digitization is required to gather data, in combination with effective informal feedback channels.

The primary contribution of this chapter lies in the formulation of a framework that unpacks the components (levers) of digital workplace designs that can be used to examine organizational transformations in a more structured way. One of our expectations was that in order to derive a competitive advantage from the digital workplace, organizations would need a holistic approach in which all design levers from our 6S digital workplace framework are addressed in conjunction with its additional management levers. Our quantitative findings confirm this assertion, showing that such 'dynamic harmony' (as per Becker, 2007) indeed provides the highest average level of competitive advantage, leading to higher scores than the other clusters across the entire portfolio of practices. Yet, we also find support for idiosyncratic combinations of individual practices in other clusters, indicating that even partial digital workplace designs (or even pilots) can add some value above industry averages.

By examining the extent to which such individual elements relate to organizational performance, we provide a unique comparison between several organizational practices that are rarely investigated in conjunction. Of particular interest is the finding that practices with the strongest relationship to organizational performance belong to the sustaining leadership lever. This is in keeping with the resource-based view (RBV) of the firm (Barney, 1991), which argues that durable competitive advantage comes from the unique interactions between the characteristics of the firm, its management practices, and cultural norms. The RBV would suggest that the adoption of several universal 'plug and play' elements from our space or systems levers might be too easily imitated, thereby lacking the scarcity to be of true competitive value. This does not mean, however, that these elements are unimportant. Open, inspiring, or activity-based work environments and BYOD policies might not directly relate to organizational performance, but our study participants have indicated that these are most definitely pivotal in dealing with expectations from millennials that form today's top talent in the digital economy. The scores on several of these elements by the high performing cluster of organizations further indicate that such elements have become so-called table stakes.

The results of our studies enable a more nuanced understanding of the space lever. While previous academic research has found "no common elements of the physical environment (e.g. enclosures and barriers in work spaces, adjustable work arrangements, personalized work spaces, and ambient surrounding) that are consistently and exclusively associated with desired outcomes" (Elsbach & Pratt, 2007), we find that digital workplace designs focused on supporting collaboration as well as telework do seem to add competitive value on an organizational level. These findings are in line with prior research that pointed out the need for appropriate and adaptable workspaces that meet the dual needs of collaboration and concentration (Roper & Juneja, 2008), as well as previous studies on the organizational effects of telework (e.g. Bloom et al., 2015; Martínez-Sánchez et al., 2007). Our interviews have shown that supporting collaboration means more than opening up floor space, however: it requires thought about how employees will be able to interact easily and find each other in physical and virtual space—also with the help of various systems levers.

Enterprise social media may prove beneficial for supporting collaboration within the organization, as they provide networks that enable employees to share and participate in activities outside of their traditional work boundaries. Yet despite the rapid uptake of social media outside of the organization, social media platforms varied in their uptake and importance to the workplace design in the organizations we studied. Choudrie and Zamani (2016) found that several bottom-up and top-down pressures can result in user resistance and the creation of workarounds in relation to ESM. In our study, we found that large organizations see value in their global reach, ability to bridge hierarchies, and their use as a transparent form of communication. For some organizations, this purpose is akin to the metaphor of a 'leaky pipe' (Leonardi, Huysman & Steinfield, 2013), which means that organizations do not make full use of ESM capabilities in building communities (i.e. the 'echo chamber') and supporting interpersonal connections (i.e. the 'social lubricant'). For others, however, we saw a centrality of social media that was having a significant impact on collaborative practices. While our quantitative study did not indicate a correlation between social media adoption and performance, we had more positive perceptions reported in the interview data. Given the rapid growth of ESM over the last three years, the time difference between our qualitative and quantitative investigations may account for this difference. It could also be explained by the need for better communication systems that offer more than email. The high focus on collaboration as a desirable outcome of the digital workplace leads us to surmise that social media might start to significantly relate to organizational performance when organizations manage to make full use of the range of ESM capabilities.

Of further importance is that organizations in our study treated employee choice and segmentation as part of the digital workplace design rather than idiosyncratic deals on a per-employee basis (e.g. Rousseau, Ho & Greenberg, 2006). This presents a challenge, however, as organizations need to take a whole-systems perspective on work that accounts for individual requirements. In terms of technology, we thus find that those systems that enable autonomy and collaboration drive organizational performance, whereas BYOD policies do not. Our expectation is that the latter might be due to potentially limited technological support and/or limited integration of employees' own devices into organizational systems, which would only serve to make working life more complex. In that regard, we also learned that the organizations in our study typically define just a few (golden) rules to counter complexity. Instead, employees are given a lot of autonomy and trusted to use good judgment and common sense. This approach is in line with findings from previous studies that have found that managerial control must be transformed in more mobile, flexible work environments (Sewell & Taskin, 2015) and that work stress is reduced when employees feel supported and have control over the dimensions involved in the execution of their work (e.g. Besseyre des Horts, Dery & MacCormick, 2012). In some organizations, these approaches were combined with an output-only focus by management, although we have found no demonstrable relationship with organizational performance in those cases. We did find anecdotal evidence of particularly successful organizations in which employees were also involved in making (or adjusting) the rules. One such organization used a crowdsourcing platform to formulate its social media usage rules. This approach reduced the size of the document outlining the rules by over 80%, it created a wording in plain English that was readily understandable, and it placed control back in the employees' hands.

To ensure that the ambitions for the digital workplace are clearly understood and 'lived,' organizations use comprehensive communication strategies and symbols. Whether these are heavily branded campaigns, a regularly repeated set of mission statements, or other symbolic actions by management (such as a tolerance or encouragement of failure), these enacted statements of strategic intent play an important role in the digital workplace success of competitive organizations. This seems particularly evident in arenas where innovation is an important strategic driver and organizations are focused on workplace attributes that encourage sharing and contributing to new ideas.

Finally, we found correlations between systemic learning capabilities and facilitative, open leadership in higher performing organizations—supporting previous findings regarding this type of leadership in the digital workplace (van Heck et al., 2012). Leadership teams were dedicated to amplifying the effect of employee voice (including using digital channels) and had a management style that was more facilitative than directive. There was little quantitative evidence to suggest that the digital workplace leadership of the higher performing firms was more distributed. Instead, we found that successful digital workplace leadership could be top-down or bottom-up, provided there were clearly recognizable channels for employees to provide their input and voice their concerns. Feedback was thus being accessed in many ways, and a dedicated management function or team facilitated decisions on how such input was used for continued redesign of the workplace.

Conclusion

In this chapter, we have combined two consecutive studies to build an understanding of the digital workplace. We clarified what is meant by the digital workplace, developed a framework that can be used by academics as well as practitioners for design and research purposes, and offered insights into how successful organizations gain a competitive advantage with digital workplace design. Our study is likely to invite as many questions as it answers, yet we would like to provide several suggestions to management practitioners, as well as proposals for further academic research.

First and foremost, we encourage managers to develop a holistic digital workplace design, in which the three design elements are supported by related leadership and learning practices. In terms of top management support for the digital workplace, a combination of IT, human resources, facilities, and communications expertise is recommended. Efforts will come to nothing, however, without buy-in from middle management. We, therefore, also advise organizations to invest in middle management to generate their support and help them transition into a more supportive role.

Furthermore, we suggest that managers create solutions that support a wide variety of personas within the organization and offer choice in where, when, and how employees can work. Learning about the various needs within the organization requires engagement of employees as well as a (management) mindset in which it is common practice (also for employees) to experiment with new ways of working (and occasionally to fail). To this end, governance should move from risk minimization to opportunity maximization.

Finally, managers must recognize that a new approach to data is required for reducing uncertainty in the organization. It is therefore important to invest in digital capabilities that enable the organization to collect data easily as well as to analyze and present it in meaningful ways. Effectively gathering meaningful feedback, amplifying the voice of employees, and making evidence-based decisions about workplace design are critical steps to making it easier to get work done in complex environments.

Future Research

This chapter provides a fertile starting ground for future research on whether organizations are deriving value from the digital workplace. First, the 6S framework can be used to identify digital workplace elements that have not been quantitatively examined. After all, the digital workplace is ever evolving, with new developments such as proactive search, peer-to-peer level IT support, and virtual personal assistants just around the corner (Miller & Cain, 2016). We, therefore, invite researchers to replicate our findings across larger and wider samples and with additional elements.

Second, larger samples would enable additional tests on the subject of dynamic harmony and constraint. By testing for necessary and sufficient conditions of how design elements impact organizational performance, we could obtain a better understanding of the interaction between the various design and management levers.

Third, it is important to note that our study only draws on the perspectives of managers, which results in a limited view of the organization. We anticipate that more detailed studies that incorporate the perspective of employees will be able to bring more nuance to this work.

Last, we also encourage researchers to develop quantitative models that include causal chains with intermediary effects. A particularly fruitful effort would involve unpacking the relation between digital workplace elements, specific behavioral norms (such as collaboration, creativity, or proactivity) and organizational performance. Alternatively, researchers could investigate the various ways in which the digital workplace reduces off-task complexity.

Notes

1. Business complexity deals with the amount of variety as well as the number of connections or dependencies in an organization (Mocker et al., 2014), whereas uncertainty and ambiguity respectively refer to a lack of knowledge and a lack of clarity (difficulty in identifying or defining potential outcomes) in an organizational decision making process (Schrader, Riggs & Smith, 1993).
2. Collisionable hours refer to the frequency of chance encounters and unplanned interactions between employees due to deliberate design choices in the physical environment (Waber, Magnolfi & Lindsay, 2014).

References

Barney, J. (1991). Firm resources and sustained competitive advantage. *Journal of Management*, 17(1), 99–120.

Becker, F. (2007). Organizational ecology and knowledge networks. *California Management Review*, 49(2), 1–20.

Bennett, N., & Lemoine, G. J. (2014). What a difference a word makes: Understanding threats to performance in a VUCA world. *Business Horizons*, 57(3), 311–317. http://doi.org/10.1016/j.bushor.2014.01.001

Bernstein, E., Bunch, J., Canner, N., & Lee, M. (2016). Beyond the holacracy hype. *Harvard Business Review* (July–August), 38–49.

Besseyre des Horts, C.-H., Dery, K., & MacCormick, J. (2012). Paradoxical consequences of the use of Blackberrys: An application of the Job Demand-Control-Support Model. In C. Kelliher & J. Richardson (Eds.), *New Ways of Organizing Work: Developments, Perspectives, and Experiences* (pp. 16–29). New York & London: Routledge.

Bloom, N., Liang, J., Roberts, J., & Ying, Z. J. (2015). Does working from home work? Evidence from a Chinese experiment. *The Quarterly Journal of Economics*, 130(1), 165–218. http://doi.org/10.1093/qje/qju032

Choudrie, J., & Zamani, E. D. (2016). Understanding individual user resistance and workarounds of enterprise social networks: The case of Service Ltd. *Journal of Information Technology*, 31(2), 130–151. http://doi.org/10.1057/jit.2016.9

Creswell, J.W. (2014). *Research Design: Qualitative, Quantitative, and Mixed Methods Approaches* (pp. 1–273). London: Sage.

Elsbach, K. D., & Pratt, M. G. (2007). The physical environment in organizations. *The Academy of Management Annals, 1*(1), 181–224.

Entis, L. (2016). The open office concept is dead. Available from http://fortune.com/2016/05/12/the-open-office-concept-is-dead/ [Accessed 6.3.2017].

Köffer, S. (2015). Designing the digital workplace of the future: What scholars recommend to practitioners. In *Proceedings of the Thirty-Sixth International Conference on Information Systems* (pp. 1–21). Fort Worth, TX.

Lee, J. (2016). Drivers and consequences in transforming work practices. In J. Lee (Eds.), *The Impact of ICT on Work* (pp. 71–92). Singapore: Springer.

Leonardi, P., M., Huysman, M., & Steinfield, C. (2013). Enterprise social media: Definition, history, and prospects for the study of social technologies in organizations. *Journal of Computer-Mediated Communication, 19*(1), 1–19. http://doi.org/10.1111/jcc4.12029

Martínez-Sánchez, A., Pérez-Pérez, M., De-Luis-Carnicer, P., & Vela-Jiménez, M. J. (2007). Telework, human resource flexibility and firm performance. *New Technology, Work and Employment, 22*(3), 208–223. http://doi.org/10.1111/j.1468-005X.2007.00195.x

Miller, P., & Cain, M. W. (2016). Hype cycle for the digital workplace, 2016. Available from www.gartner.com/document/3366717

Mocker, M., Weill, P., & Woerner, S. L. (2014). Revisiting complexity in the digital age. *MIT Sloan Management Review, 55*(4), 73–81.

Randall, T. (2015). The smartest building in the world: Inside the connected future of architecture. Available from www.bloomberg.com/features/2015-the-edge-the-worlds-greenest-building/ [Accessed 8.5.2016].

Roper, K. O., & Juneja, P. (2008). Distractions in the workplace revisited. *Journal of Facilities Management, 6*(2), 91–109. http://doi.org/10.1108/14725960810872622

Rousseau, D. M., Ho, V. T., & Greenberg, J. (2006). I-Deals: Idiosyncratic terms in employment relationships. *Academy of Management Review, 31*(4), 977–994.

Schrader, S., Riggs, W. M., & Smith, R. P. (1993). Choice over uncertainty and ambiguity in technical problem solving. *Journal of Engineering and Technology Management, 10*(1–2), 73–99. http://doi.org/10.1016/0923-4748(93)90059-R

Sewell, G., & Taskin, L. (2015). Out of sight, out of mind in a new world of work? Autonomy, control, and spatiotemporal scaling in telework. *Organization Studies, 36*(11), 1507–1529. http://doi.org/10.1177/0170840615593587

van Heck, E., van Baalen, P., van der Meulen, N., & van Oosterhout, M. (2012). Achieving high performance in a mobile and green workplace: Lessons from Microsoft Netherlands. *MIS Quarterly Executive, 11*(4), 175–188.

Waber, B., Magnolfi, J., & Lindsay, G. (2014). Workspaces that move people. *Harvard Business Review* (October 2014), 69–77.

10 Agile Working

The Case of TechSci, a Global Technology Company

Deirdre Anderson and Clare Kelliher

Introduction

The evolution of working practices (such as remote working, flexitime, annualized hours) in recent decades has been enabled by advancements in information and communication technology and the development of the global marketplace, although the way in which such practices have developed is related to national context (Stavrou, Parry & Anderson, 2015). A further driver has been the changing profile of the workforce, including increased numbers of women in paid employment, migration of workers across national borders and people continuing to work till a greater age (Perry-Smith & Blum, 2000; Ashford, George & Blatt, 2007; Eurofound, 2016). Employers, keen to attract and retain these workers who may wish to interact with work in different ways, have responded by offering alternative working arrangements, often in the form of greater flexibility in relation to where and when work is done. These different forms of working arrangements have attracted attention from researchers and many studies have examined the implementation of flexible working arrangements and have explored the contribution of flexibility to the work-life integration of employees. Here, we seek to understand the concept of workforce agility, a more recent term preferred by some employers over flexibility, as they deem flexibility to have been narrowly defined, principally as a benefit for employees and seen as a cost to employers (Agile Future Forum, 2013). Workforce agility is a broader term which refers to a range of 'agile working practices', concerned with four key dimensions: who is employed, where they work, when they work, and the roles undertaken. A defining feature of agile working practices is that they are, in principle, designed to provide benefit for both the employee and the employer (Agile Future Forum, 2013).

This chapter draws on findings from a study which was designed to examine the perspectives of senior managers regarding both the challenges and benefits associated with the management of a set of evolving working practices, in an organization whose primary aim is to develop and connect global networks. We analyse the implementation of workforce agility within a global technology company (referred to in this chapter as TechSci), exploring the implementation of key initiatives which are part of their new ways of working. We begin with a brief review of the literature on changing working practices that seek to enhance different forms of workforce flexibility, considering the contrasting aims of the employer and the employee. This is followed by a section outlining the methods used for data collection and analysis in the study. We then present empirical evidence from interviews with 12 senior managers within TechSci, beginning with a section giving contextual background about the organization. Conceptualizations of workforce agility are detailed, followed by descriptions of three organizational initiatives which demonstrate the organization's particular understanding, interpretation and enactment of agility. Finally, we discuss the implications for practice and make suggestions for future research.

Background

We begin this section with an introduction to flexible working arrangements, which are usually deemed to include flexitime, homeworking, compressed working hours and job sharing (Stavrou, Parry & Anderson, 2015), and are principally designed to enable the achievement of a better work-life balance. The intention has been to facilitate employees attending to both work and personal responsibilities (Kelliher & Anderson, 2008; Beauregard & Henry, 2009). A key element in implementing flexible arrangements has been the choice offered to employees over where, when and how much to work (Hill et al., 2008). In contrast, flexible working arrangements, involving numerical flexibility (Institute of Manpower Studies, 1985) and temporal flexibility (Deery & Mahony, 1994), such as zero-hours contracts and shift work, are driven from the perspective of the employer, since they allow labour resources to be managed more efficiently, by matching working patterns to business activity (Coe, Johns & Ward, 2007; Desombre et al., 2006; Kalleberg, 2003).

Thus, flexible working policies have often been concerned with *either* the interests of the employer *or* the employee (Alis, Karsten & Leopold, 2006). Governments and policy bodies have sometimes pursued these different approaches in tandem. For example, in the UK labour market, flexibility has been encouraged as a means to make the economy attractive to foreign investment (Legge, 2007). At the same time, legislative support has been provided for the adoption of flexibility policies designed to assist employees balance work and non-work commitments (DfEE, 2001) initially for working parents and carers, and since June 2014 for all employees following a qualifying period of service. This was stimulated by the desire to support working parents, but also by the mounting case of business benefits to be gained from giving employees greater control over their working arrangements in the form of talent attraction and retention, enhanced job satisfaction and organizational commitment (Beauregard & Henry, 2009; CIPD 2010; De Menezes & Kelliher, 2011; Stavrou & Kilaniotis, 2010). Employers may also benefit from reduced accommodation costs (Anderson, Swan & Lewis, 2016) and the ability to extend operating hours when employees work at different times and in different locations. Organizations have therefore been increasingly expected to implement policies, which contribute towards both organizational competitiveness and employee work-life balance.

This 'dual agenda' has been the focus of a number of studies (e.g. Rapoport et al., 2002; Lewis, Rapoport & Gambles, 2003; Kim, Bailyn & Kolb, 2016), which have highlighted the mutually beneficial nature of many flexible working arrangements. However, work-life balance remains a contested term (Fleetwood, 2007; Ozbilgin et al., 2011; Bloom, 2015), and its operationalization linked to flexible working arrangements has associated ambiguities. Although flexible working arrangements introduced for different reasons may at one level appear to be similar (e.g. part-time working, working at non-standard times or from different locations), there have been few attempts, to date, to examine the potential of initiatives for matching the differing interests in flexibility between employers and employees. The term 'agile working' has been coined to describe practices, which attempt to do this. This new focus on 'workforce agility' has therefore added a further perspective to this debate by examining the ways in which agility initiatives which contribute to the achievement of business goals, and those providing value to employees, might be brought together. This study reveals deeper understanding of the complex and multi-faceted nature of workforce agility.

Method

A purposive sampling technique was used in order to gain in-depth understanding of workforce agility in the context of evolving working practices in this global technology company. Following discussion with the country CEO, 12 senior executives working in varying locations around the world, and from different functional backgrounds, were selected for interview. Semi-structured virtual interviews were conducted using WebEx over a period of three weeks. Interview questions were sent to participants a few days before the interview took place in order to allow them to familiarise themselves with the areas under investigation. The questions covered a range of topics, including their understanding of agility, organizational drivers for the changes to work practices, benefits and downsides of using agile working practices, and any unanticipated consequences. Permission was gained in each case for the interview to be audio recorded and they were subsequently transcribed verbatim. For the purposes of this study, a thematic approach to the analysis was undertaken, supported by the use of NVivo software.

Contextual Background

TechSci has over 70,000 employees based in nearly 100 countries and sells a broad range of technologies. According to the interviewees, the company places high value on the skills and expertise of its employees who are geographically widely distributed. Their market has shifted significantly over the last 20 years and changing demands from customers have driven them to develop new products and services. In order to remain competitive and responsive in an uncertain environment, workplace practices have evolved along all the four dimensions of workforce agility: source (who is employed), location (where they work), times (when they work) and role (what they do) (Agile Future Forum, 2013). As a technology company, agility in TechSci has a particular focus on the provision of technology which facilitates collaborative and secure working, thus enabling employees to connect and interact with colleagues and clients, whether they are at the workplace, at home or travelling (in airports, other transport hubs, hotels, etc). Agility was reported to be inherent in the organization's approach to work, integrating space and technology and moving people to the work as required.

In presenting the findings we discuss the interpretation of agility within TechSci and the subsequent benefits which were seen to emerge. We then report on the TechSci Office, which was the major initiative discussed by interviewees, illustrating TechSci's approach to integrated and consistent agility. The TechSci Office was described as the organization's model of the 'workplace of the future'. It was deployed globally and used integrated technology and change management practices to drive adoption of the newly designed work environments at company locations. Two further initiatives are then discussed which support and contribute to the effectiveness of the TechSci Office. The TechSci Way has involved extensive consultation with staff about the company's "inspirational culture" to ensure that employees have an open and agile environment to facilitate their working. TechSci Global Jobs provides an internal forum for advertising projects which require a fractional commitment from staff and can be undertaken as an "additional role". This allows the company to draw on employee skills from anywhere in the business across the world and allows individuals to gain experience beyond their local environment. In all of the interviews, respondents emphasized the importance of integration and coherence in striving for agility within and throughout the company.

Agility Within TechSci

Although there was no formal definition of agile working, responses from interviewees suggested that they shared a common perception of agile working and felt that it was an embedded way of working within TechSci with significant business benefits. The interviews revealed a strong focus on agility as a means of facilitating connections between people and in particular, the ability to bring clients and employees from across the organization together in physical and virtual meetings on an everyday basis. The provision and use of space were also mentioned by most interviewees in their understanding of agility, and several also explained that the increasing speed of delivery expected and the need for greater innovation were important drivers. A specific business benefit mentioned by one manager was related to the growth of business in new markets, which often occurred very quickly as a result of new acquisitions.

Because of the highly agile environment that we have, both from a productivity, a people perspective and technology perspective that we use in the workplace, we're very, very quick and able to acquire new companies and the incorporation of those companies into Tech-Sci's culture is very, very quick. As a consequence, we're able to redefine our position in the market as a result of that acquisition much, much, much quicker than most of our competitors.

Peter

Some interviewees also mentioned a technical meaning of agility in terms of agile software developed for project management, such as Lean or Scrum, but were quick to point out that their approach to agility went beyond such methodologies and was embedded within the culture of TechSci. As explained next, the company fosters creativity and innovation within the organization with associated benefits for both employees and their customers.

[Agility refers to] a set of values that we have in terms of how we approach the work and how we produce the end result. It's the ethos of trying something, doing it quickly, finding that it doesn't work in all cases and then refining it to something that does work. It's more about the attitude I guess, of "Let's play with this and find something that really works for us". It allows us to be authentic to our values and deliver good software.

Danny

The nature of TechSci's business requires involvement in the high-level design of technical solutions for clients. For TechSci's own working practices, as well as the delivery of products and services, high-quality connections are seen as essential between different locations to enable collaboration in teams even when they are physically dispersed. For example, Derek, talked about the importance of employees being able to bring their expertise to conversations with clients, no matter where they are based, describing such ability to be agile as a key competitive advantage. He went on to say,

Agility is one of the cornerstones of our success. The agile working environment has a very positive impact on the business because it allows us to adapt to client requirements but also people's own personal lives, and it also helps us in terms of retaining employees and providing a better quality of work, and a better working environment overall.

Derek

This quote illustrates the benefits to the company in terms of meeting objectives, but that it was also seen to play an important role for staff. The ability to work from anywhere, while having secure access to and sharing highly technical or confidential data, was seen as essential for employees. Knowledge-based workers often worked in virtual teams, in different time zones, necessitating working hours outside of what might be traditional business hours locally. In its broader understanding within TechSci, agility was perceived as an evolving process related to the provision and use of space, and making communication better or faster. Respondents in technical roles pointed out that there is an element of continuous delivery inherent in the solutions which were designed and used by TechSci's own staff, as well as meeting client specifications. Such continuous delivery occurred due to feedback on systems and processes being readily available and used for improvement and development on an ongoing basis. This highly mobile approach to working was reported to lead to reductions in travel time. Interviewees explained that increased use of technology to enable virtual attendance at meetings had been found to maintain high quality outcomes. In this way, TechSci was able to take full advantage of the skills of the staff without being limited by the physical geography of their location.

Respondents indicated that the company was able to meet client needs, while at the same time recognizing the importance of giving individual employees the autonomy to decide where the best location is for them to work. This was seen to work in part because staff were seen to be very self-motivated and because they were working in a highly technical environment and completing self-directed work. All of the interviewees referred at some stage to flexibility of the workforce generally, or in their own teams. When questioned further, they talked in more depth about the volume of work undertaken and the company's expectation that individuals were responsible for managing their own time. They were clear about their own autonomy and without exception they explained that it was a very positive feature for them, as well as an inherent part of the roles they undertook. In most cases, their roles involved frequent communication with colleagues in other time zones, and they talked about adjusting the times they worked accordingly. This might involve shifting their working hours if they had a lot of evening meetings, but also taking a couple of hours off in the middle of the day to go to the gym. For example, one individual reported that because of liaising with colleagues literally on the other side of the world, they worked from midnight to 10.00 am on three or four occasions each month. A few of the managers mentioned potential lack of downtime as a negative aspect of working globally. In particular, they referred to their managerial responsibility to younger employees to ensure that they did not overload themselves. Several also mentioned the need to respect other people's space and time when arranging meetings, and therefore the need to be conscious of "normal working hours". Most of the managers made a direct link between the benefits of workforce agility for the business, and the need to ensure employees could also achieve a satisfactory level of work-life integration. As Peter explained,

> *Broadly speaking, agility is about talent. If we don't make TechSci a great place to be, we won't attract the right talent, we won't retain the right talent. If we don't make TechSci a highly agile workforce that addresses the work life balance issue, then we're not going to attract and retain that talent. Quite frankly, if we don't do that then we're not going to be competitive because we need to do that in order to meet the challenges of that landscape that's changed and continues to change.*

> Peter

Although the main emphasis of creating workplace agility was the introduction of the TechSci Office around the world, one interviewee also talked about using virtual desk space in public innovation environments, such as science parks. Embedding high quality collaboration technology in such open offices enabled further flexibility of location for employees. A local science park with open access might be much nearer to home than the TechSci location, provide all the necessary facilities and reduce commuting time. This was described as a successful initiative in several European cities.

TechSci Office

The TechSci Office, or their model of the workplace of the future, is based on three elements: the use of physical space, the integration of technology and flexible work policies. Interviewees stressed the need for employee consultation throughout the process of designing the workplace and the need to engage in a process of change management. Many examples were given of moving to a new site, or the complete redesign of existing office space and the introduction of the TechSci Office. Ensuring that the newly designed offices reflected the TechSci culture was seen as a fundamental premise underpinning the concept of the TechSci Office. The in-house Office Innovation Group was responsible for working with local business unit partners, including IT and HR staff, to deliver a workplace that adheres to the values and ethos of TechSci.

Interviewees emphasized the need for working spaces designed for a changing workforce and evolving marketplace. A wide range of both open and closed spaces of different sizes, such as rooms which afford privacy, conference rooms, creativity and gaming areas were provided to facilitate effective working individually and collectively. Open collaborative areas were designed to have an informal, more 'residential' feel with couches and a coffee table and lamps rather than office lighting, all aiming to facilitate more comfortable and relaxed conversations, rather than sitting in a formal meeting room. It was recognized that open plan working spaces can fail, however (and indicated that they have failed in other organizations), if they are seen as a big landscape of work stations. The TechSci approach acknowledged varying needs as described earlier and aimed to provide for them.

Senior managers were united in their views that the company needed to capitalize on its own expertise and ensure that the latest technology was available in its own new offices, including digital signage, ideas walls, touch screen booking and maps of rooms when entering a workplace, colour and lighting options designed to ensure personal comfort, as well as high speed visual and audio connectivity. It was also interesting to note the acknowledgement of the demands of employees' personal lives and several of the interviewees commented that the company's flexible working policies were key in the retention of staff. Nevertheless, they indicated that the organization strived to create vibrant and energetic workplaces, which would be attractive to staff. A prime consideration when designing the changing workspaces was the need to maintain a sense of community among staff, trying to ensure that people can work together effectively and supportively.

> *So what I think the TechSci Office drives is that you have to be much more thoughtful in how you get people to want to come to an office. Whether you bring them in for an event, whether you bring them in for a certain way of working, you have to be deliberate about that; it doesn't happen in the way that it would if people are mandated to come in every day. I certainly see us having no inclination to bring everyone back into the office because of this idea of people feeling like they can be their whole self and that they're fulfilling all areas of their life. That's really important.*
>
> Ashley

Managers indicated that cultural priorities in different countries and regions were respected, and that these were incorporated into the design of each TechSci Office. This was achieved through extensive consultation with staff which began with sponsorship at a local level for the change management process which was to take place. The Office Innovation Group worked closely with local management, and consultation took place with staff at all levels to try and ensure that the needs of working groups were explored and understood. Agility and working practices were not necessarily seen to be the same around the globe, not least because local leaders might choose to implement things in subtly different ways. One interviewee illustrated the focus on cultural differences when he spoke about the introduction of the TechSci Office in a country in Asia Pacific,

> *The project managers [in the Office Innovation Group] are the experts and they discuss ideas with regional IT managers and explore the accepted ways of working, getting input into specific ideas. You know, they might say, "I'm about to roll out a new telepresence unit or this other service over there. Is it going to work? So is there a culture of doing face-to-face video? Is that something which everyone would accept? If you're rolling out a social collaboration tool do you think people would engage openly in writing what their thoughts are, or would they be very constrained in making comments"?*
>
> Martin

Similarly, the design considered demographics, such as the age of the workforce. For instance, it was observed that an office with a large graduate intake may wish for a more informal working environment. Similarly, in some countries, it may be difficult for people to work from home due to lack of space or poor connectivity. In such circumstances, employees have little choice but to work in the office, so full occupancy has to be catered for.

The first stage of a new TechSci Office involved gaining current data about the use of facilities through monitoring occupancy of existing workspaces and then using this data to plan the design.

> *We've all got our TechSci badges that gets us into any building and logs entry in and out of any building, so we know exactly where everyone is if they're on TechSci premises. So the work place resources team have a lot of analytics on exactly how people are working, how often they come into an office, how often they don't come into an office, so it's down to individuals. So we've got great data that we can leverage to decide on exactly what the swing space should be, how many virtual desks can be accommodated.*
>
> Chris

Design decisions were made by local teams to ensure the best use of resources to support and enhance existing work practices, although it was reported that inevitably some adjustment was required to a different working environment. One example given referred to a lease for a large building taken on immediately prior to the global financial crisis, which was only utilised to 60%–70% of its capacity. The anticipated growth had not happened, so when the lease came up for renewal, they exited and moved into a smaller space, involving a redesign from the ground up, with all the very latest technology and design principles and enabling full occupancy.

> *We work very closely with the businesses to define what attributes of their space are required to implement the agile work environment or the agile process, and that can be anything from furniture types, to areas where they can collectively join and collaborate and stand, to idea walls or white walls that they can work with, to digital signage, etc., as well as the introduction of our technology throughout.*
>
> Michael

There was a strong emphasis on being able to bring people together virtually from across the organization, allowing face-to-face meetings with people locally, but bringing in colleagues from elsewhere in the organization, potentially in a different time zone from the host office, or working from home or when travelling. This agile approach then enabled adaptation to client requirements, as well as to people's own personal lives. Interviewees observed a link to staff retention and high-quality work output. However, Derek (and others) pointed out that there can be a negative pushback from clients who may expect a more physical presence of experts.

> *The only downside is that sometimes some customers are taken aback initially saying, "Well you are going to do this, we would like to see people sitting here at the table." What we say is, "Well that's fine but actually that's not the most efficient way of doing things," and, once they see how we do it, they actually embrace it.*
>
> Derek

As well as the design of the physical space and required technology, it was also seen as necessary to decide on size of the new facilities which involved working out the optimum capacity. For instance, a building may have only 20% or 25% of the people there for most of the time (the "show-up rate") and yet more than 80% may attend a weekly meeting for two hours. The challenge is obvious, finding a compromise which is acceptable to the employees and cost-effective for the organization. Participants emphasized that a critical feature of the success of a project was the engagement of the local teams in decisions about size and capacity so that they felt that the design represented who they were and how they worked. One manager referred to a particular example where there was a lack of engagement during the project in this location, which led to significant resistance from one section of the workforce, resulting in the need to bring together representatives for the various groups and work to redefine protocols and expected behaviours post-occupancy.

It's not a great example of implementation of the TechSci Office, but it is a good example that shows if you don't engage and have them be a part of the process, and feel like this is our space, feel a sense of ownership, I have these concerns, or I have these needs or requirements, if they don't feel that they are being heard through the process then once you put them into that space the space doesn't feel comfortable to them, they are not sure how to behave in the space.

Alex

This demonstrated the need for extensive consultation mentioned by most of the interviewees.

TechSci Way

The organizational culture of TechSci was reported to embrace a multi-faceted approach to agility, and it was seen as part of the ethos of the company. The change management processes used for the introduction of the TechSci Office around the world required extensive consultation throughout all levels of the company. Consultation was seen to play an important part in the development and understanding of the company culture, by exploring employees' perceptions and ideas about the way they wanted the organization to be. The TechSci Way was reported as recognizing and celebrating that the success of the company rested on the skills and expertise of its staff. Similar to the implementation of the TechSci Office, consultation was seen as a key feature of the development of the TechSci Way, exploring the views and ideas of employees.

We went out and we asked people, many people, many employees, what does TechSci look like on a good day? We didn't just ask them to tell us; we asked them to sing it; we asked them to draw it; we asked them to do all these different creative ways of sharing with us what it was like, and people gave us differing amounts of information, but the key message was that on the best day TechSci has amazing technology, brilliant people and an environment where you can make a difference.

Ashley

In this consultation process, employees shared experiences and ideas about *"making a difference"* and creating impact through corporate social responsibility initiatives, or driving the local agenda in the business, for instance. The TechSci Way was designed to celebrate and drive success through a clear commitment about what TechSci expects of its employees, and what they can expect from the organization.

> *[The TechSci Way] talks about the fact that we want it to be flexible; we want people to be able to be flexible in the way they do work, but we also want to make sure that people are productive. Imagine if you become too flexible in a working environment, and you start to lose your culture because people are not in offices anymore; you've always got to have a trade-off of the things that are going to make a good productive working relationship. The TechSci Way is really advocating for balance in how we do things.*
>
> Ashley

Innovation throughout the organization was reported to underpin this approach, which aimed to benefit staff through embedded agile working practices, including sophisticated technology which facilitated remote working and participation in virtual teams. Respondents emphasized the importance of human connection and interaction, which was achieved in ways other than physical proximity, while at the same time recognizing the challenges this may bring.

> *I think the one difficulty would be that many managers are not local to their teams. So their teams are virtual teams, so they might have people dotted all round Europe, and they might be based in Barcelona, and they might be managing people across five countries. Well, the ability to bring that team together and really create that team culture can be quite problematic. We spend a lot of time in the soft-skills training looking at how teams develop. How can you bond a team remotely when you don't have that physical contact on a regular basis? So I would call that one out because I think, as human beings, we interact better when we're physically connected, when we're physically in the same location. So doing that remotely for a long period of time is a challenge.*
>
> Chris

Agile working practices were seen to facilitate autonomy so that people could manage their own time, attending to the demands from their home life while fulfilling their work responsibilities. Some interviewees reflected that this independence can add to the challenge of creating collaborative working and a sense of community. A commitment within the TechSci Way was to deliver new workspaces to employees through the introduction of the TechSci Office around the world. The aim was to support the introduction of the physical workplace while working with local employees to create an environment that reflected how they wanted to work, while still maintaining the branded look and feel of a TechSci office. An important element was the encouragement and support for staff in attending the workplace so that they could develop relationships and facilitate effective working including creativity.

One perhaps surprising outcome of the introduction of the TechSci Way was the decision to remove the annual performance appraisal process and rating of staff. The feedback and views from the consultative process indicated that the appraisal process had not achieved its aims and in keeping with the commitment to agility throughout the organization and the ways of working, the decision was taken to remove it. Instead, employees and managers exchanged information on a weekly basis using a specific software tool designed for internal use. This involved employees answering a number of questions about their experiences that week, including whether they felt they had added value, whether they played to their strengths and what their priorities were for the next week.

Every manager is expected to read their check-in emails from their team. There's a question to address about what an individual needs from their manager this week. People will tell me they might want a call, or they might want, say, "Help me progress with the requisition" or "Help me think about this project", so I know immediately what they need. For me, it's been absolutely ground-breaking. I've never done anything that's so real time before and I think that that is . . . (pause) . . . when you think about engagement surveys and things like that that you run as a company, you might do that every 12 months so you're getting a pulse once a year. We've moved away from all of that and it's so much more immediate.

Ashley

Managers were, therefore, able to grasp quickly the nature of their team's experiences, whether successes or challenges, business critical or steady state. As Sam explains next, this process was supported by conversations with individuals and teams:

It results in very informal conversations between you and your manager but very regular. Those are just you as an individual building you up in terms of your strengths rather than a discussion about you've not done this, and you've not done that conversation. Those kinds of conversations are almost controlled by the team. The team themselves know what they want to do and they themselves pull each other up or say we don't want that sort of thing in our team's kind of conversations. It has really changed our ability to move quicker significantly.

Sam

Global Job Market

The third key initiative which was explained by interviewees was the Global Job Market and in particular the "extra roles" which staff were able to take on. As discussed earlier, there were many teams with members based in different locations, so employees tended to develop wide reaching networks throughout the company. Recognizing the value of the expertise of staff and being able to identify and access it whatever their location was seen as essential within TechSci. Participants talked about "capability search" when explaining that they may not have identified who they needed for a particular project, but knew the skills that were required. Being able to find the right person to contribute and deliver particular objectives was seen as key to growing the business and working more efficiently—the Global Job Market represented a forum for that search and identification process to occur. Posts were advertised with details of the nature of the task and the experiences and skills needed. Interestingly, these posts were often extra roles which might require, for example, 25% of someone's time for a 12-month period to work on a particular assignment.

> *So we have a project at the moment running globally and we've posted that there, we go all round the world and we let people put their hat in the ring for that opportunity. We tell them that we're going to need them for, I don't know, that opportunity; we say maybe for a year but on the basis of say 25% of your job, so can you come and do it for that period of time. Then people apply, and we look at their qualifications, as in what experience they've got of that topic; do they have support from their manager to take some time out to come and work on something? Is that practical? Then we make a decision on who is the best fit and then we give them that assignment. Then that assignment becomes an add-on to their day job.*
>
> Ashley

Numerous benefits were reported, for both individuals and the organization, particularly because geographical location was not important when applying for assignments. People came together in virtual teams across the world using either video or meeting technology. This increased the marketplace for talent because it focused on specific experiences and could be quite prescriptive about what was needed because of the virtual nature of the team. Delivery on the project was seen as more efficient and the project manager was able to draw on a more diverse skill set. If the time required was substantial, (in some cases, it was 50%+), then a negotiation took place between the individual, the home manager and the project manager. Without exception, the interviewees were very enthusiastic about this initiative, and when asked about the potential conflict of interest, they pointed out that everything was done in the interests of trying to drive the company's goals and delivering to clients whether internal or external. From an individual perspective, the Global Job Market was seen as a tremendous opportunity for personal development, not just in terms of skills, but also in extending understanding of the work of the organization and in developing new relationships and widening one's personal network.

Discussion

In this chapter, we have explored the implementation of agile working at TechSci. We have examined how agile working was conceptualized in this global technology company and looked in some detail at the implementation of three initiatives—TechSci Office, TechSci Way and the Global Job Market. TechSci Office represented the integration of physical space, technology and flexible working. This initiative was designed to allow the organization to achieve greater efficiency and to be more responsive to client needs. At the same time, the TechSci Office enabled employees to have some flexibility over where and when they worked, allowing for local differences in different parts of the organization. The initiative was seen as an important factor in their ability to attract and retain high calibre staff in different country contexts. The TechSci Way was underpinned by a strong commitment to consultation with staff, including in delivery of the changes required for the TechSci Office. It also was designed to foster innovation and to give staff greater control over their working arrangements. These two initiatives appear to present an appropriate environment for the needs of the employer and the employee for flexibility to be reconciled. The Global Job Market provided opportunities for managers of projects to source input from across the organization and also for employees to have access to different opportunities, allowing them to gain a broader portfolio of experience by taking on involvement in other projects as an additional role.

The use of agile working at TechSci yielded a number of benefits found in other studies of the use of flexible working. For example, talent attraction and retention were seen as a major driver for offering autonomy over work arrangements to employees (Beauregard & Henry, 2009; CIPD, 2010; De Menezes & Kelliher, 2011). Likewise, albeit with a number of considerations taken into account, the company was able to tailor their space to usage more closely (Anderson et al., 2016). This would suggest that the dual agenda was being realized (Rapoport et al., 2002). However, we argue that the evidence presented here suggests more than mutual benefit from the use of agile working, but that there was some evidence of mutual flexibility being achieved. In other words, these practices both allowed the employer to operate on a model where they could use labour in flexible ways (e.g. through the use of technology to connect expert staff to clients, or to source part-time, limited duration commitments to projects through the Global Job Market) and the employee to exercise some degree of control over their working arrangements to facilitate a better work-life balance. However, it is noteworthy that work intensification was seen as a potential consequence of allowing greater autonomy (Kelliher & Anderson, 2010) and in line with the so-called autonomy paradox (Mazmanian, Orlikowski & Yates, 2013).

This suggests that, at least for large organizations, there is the potential to match the needs for flexibility which they require, with employees' needs for flexibility. As such other organizations may also be able to gain the benefits of mutual flexibility. In this case technology featured as a significant enabler, but cultural factors also appeared to be important, together with a commitment to consult with employees and support work-life balance. Other employers may need to consider their own context in order to ascertain how this can be best achieved. It does, however, need to be acknowledged that this study was small in size, drawing on 12 interviews with managers in 1 organization. It may be that the employees who were agile workers may have experienced the implementation in different ways that were not reported by our managerial respondents.

References

Agile Future Forum (2013). *Understanding the Economic Benefits of Workforce Agility*. London: Agile Future Forum.

Alis, D., Karsten, L., & Leopold, J. (2006). From Gods to Goddesses: Horai management as an approach to coordinating working hours. *Time & Society*, 15(1), 81–104.

Anderson, D., Swan, J., & Lewis, S. (2016). Towards a triple agenda beyond recession and austerity: Innovations in policy and practices. In S. Lewis, D. Anderson, C. Lyonette, N. Payne & S. Wood (Eds.), *Work-life Balance in Times of Recession, Austerity and Beyond* (pp. 180–190). London: Routledge.

Ashford, S. J., George, E., & Blatt, R. (2007). 2 old assumptions, new work: The opportunities and challenges of research on nonstandard employment. *The Academy of Management Annals*, 1(1), 65–117.

Beauregard, T.A., & Henry, L.C. (2009). Making the link between work-life balance practices and organizational performance. *Human Resource Management Review*, 19(1), 9–22.

Bloom, P. (2015). Work as the contemporary limit of life: Capitalism, the death drive, and the lethal fantasy of "work–life balance". *Organization*, 23(4), 588–606.

Chartered Institute of Personnel and Development (CIPD) (2010). *Flexible Working: Working for Families, Working for Business*. London: CIPD.

Coe, N.M., Johns, J.L., & Ward, K. (2007). Mapping the Globalisation of the Temporary Staffing Industry. *Professional Geographer*, 59(4), 503–520.

Deery, S.J., & Mahony, A. (1994). Temporal flexibility: Management strategies and employee preferences in the retail industry. *Journal of Industrial Relations*, 36(3), 332–352.

De Menezes, L.M., & Kelliher, C. (2011). Flexible working and performance: A systematic review of the evidence for a business case. *International Journal of Management Reviews, 13*(4), 452–474.

Desombre, T., Kelliher, C., Macfarlane, F., & Ozbilgin, M. (2006). Re-Organizing work roles in health care: Evidence from the implementation of functional flexibility. *British Journal of Management, 17*(2), 139–151.

Department for Education and Employment (DfEE) (2001). *Work Life Balance 2000: Results from the Baseline Study.* London: DfEE.

Eurofound (2016). *Working Time Developments in the 21st Century: Work Duration and its Regulation in the EU.* Luxembourg: Publications Office of the European Union.

Fleetwood, S. (2007). Why work—life balance now? *The International Journal of Human Resource Management, 18*(3), 387–400.

Hill, E.J., Grzywacz, J.G., Allen, S., Blanchard, V.L., Matz-Costa, C., Shulkin, S., & Pitt-Catsouphes, M. (2008). Defining and conceptualizing workplace flexibility. *Community, Work and Family, 11*(2), 149–163.

Institute of Manpower Studies. (1985). *Flexibility, Uncertainty and Manpower Management, IMS Report No. 89.* Brighton: Atkinson, J.

Kalleberg, A.L. (2003). Flexible firms and labor market segmentation: Effects of workplace restructuring on jobs and workers. *Work and Occupations, 30*(2), 154–175.

Kelliher, C., & Anderson, D. (2008). For better or for worse? An analysis of how flexible working practices influence employees' perceptions of job quality. *The International Journal of Human Resource Management, 19*(3), 419–431.

Kelliher, C., & Anderson, D. (2010). Doing more with less? Flexible working practices and the intensification of work. *Human Relations, 63*(1), 83–106.

Kim, H., Bailyn, L., & Kolb, D.M. (2016). Revisiting the dual agenda: Why companies miss the point if they retract flexible work arrangements during bad times. In S. Lewis, D. Anderson, C. Lyonette, N. Payne & S. Wood (Eds.), *Work-life Balance in Times of Recession, Austerity and Beyond* (pp. 165–179). London: Routledge.

Legge, K. (2007). Putting the missing H into HRM: The case of the flexible organisation. In S. Bolton & M. Houlihan (Eds.), *Searching for the Human in Human Resource Management.* Basingstoke: Palgrave Macmillan.

Lewis, S., Rapoport, R., & Gambles, R. (2003). Reflections on the integration of paid work and the rest of life. *Journal of Managerial Psychology, 18*(8), 824–841.

Özbilgin, M.F., Beauregard, T.A., Tatli, A., & Bell, M.P. (2011). Work—life, diversity and intersectionality: A critical review and research agenda. *International Journal of Management Reviews, 13*(2), 177–198.

Perry-Smith, J.E., & Blum, T.C. (2000). Work-family human resource bundles and perceived organizational performance. *Academy of Management Journal, 43*(6), 1107–1117.

Mazmanian, M., Orlikowski, W. J., & Yates, J. (2013). The autonomy paradox: The implications of mobile email devices for knowledge professionals. *Organization Science, 24*(5), 1337–1357.

Rapoport, R., Bailyn, L., Fletcher, J.K., & Pruitt, B. (2002). *Beyond Work-family Balance. Advancing Gender Equity and Workplace Performance.* New York, NY: Wiley.

Stavrou, E., & Kilaniotis, C. (2010). Flexible work and turnover: An empirical investigation across cultures. *British Journal of Management, 21*(2), 541–554.
Stavrou, E.T., Parry, E., & Anderson, D. (2015). Nonstandard work arrangements and configurations of firm and societal systems. *The International Journal of Human Resource Management, 26*(19), 2412–2433.

Conclusion

11 Observations and Conclusions on Work, Working and Work Relationships in a Changing World

Clare Kelliher and Julia Richardson

This final chapter aims to draw together the material presented in the book and pull out emerging overarching themes from the respective studies about the changing world of work. It will take stock of the issues raised in each of the chapters and consider these in the broader context of the drivers of change raised in the introductory chapter, namely, developments in technology, greater global integration, increased competitive pressures and societal and demographic changes. These wider developments have, in turn, led to changes in the nature of work and work relationships including the use of technologies and innovations to allow work to be done in different ways; changes to the structure of employment, increasing concern for work-life balance and autonomy, the refinement of product and service offerings and changes to the nature of professional work.

The nine empirical chapters in this book each considered different aspects of work, working and work relationships, and how they have evolved in contemporary labour markets. They have dealt with different types of changes, driven by different contextual influences. In the first part of the book, 'Work Opportunities and Experiences in the New Economy: A Double-Edged Sword?' three chapters examined the various dimensions of current work opportunities and experiences. In Chapter 2, 'The Fur-Lined Rut': Telework and Career Ambition', Beauregard, Canonico and Basile explored how the ability to work on a flexible basis (in this case telework) is highly valued by employees, to the extent that they eschew opportunities for career advancement which they believe would threaten their working arrangement. This adds to the continuing debate about the extent to which flexible work arrangements have a negative impact on career advancement, work opportunities and earnings (Cohen & Single, 2001; Weeden, 2005; Leslie et al., 2012) and whether employers interpret employee requests for flexible working arrangements as a sign of lower levels of organizational commitment (Lero, Richardson & Korabik, 2008).

In Chapter 3 'Performing the "Ideal Professional": Insights From Workers' Accounts of Emotional Labour in Contemporary Workplaces',

Linehan and O'Brien examined the challenges of meeting the expectations of being an 'ideal professional' in the field of HRM. The central focus in that chapter was on emotional labour and revealed an expectation of specific prescribed and proscribed displays of emotion. The findings presented show that although there have been ongoing calls for leaders and professionals to be more authentic, embedding their 'true selves' in their work performance (e.g. Avolio & Gardner, 2005; Steffens et al., 2016; Weiss et al., 2018), which is in contrast to the concomitant expectations for emotions to be managed. This is in line with Bolton and Houlihan's (2007) observation that while there are calls for 'thicker' relationships between HR professionals and other organizational members, expectations about how the nature of those relationships are demonstrated is heavily prescribed.

In the final chapter in this part, Chapter 4, 'Working as an Independent Professional: Career Choice or the Only Option?', McKeown focused on self-employment, examining the relationship between the worker and the organization they carry out work for and the reasons why people enter self-employment. The chapter distinguished between the drivers of entrepreneurial pull and unemployment push as motivations, highlighting some of the challenging dimensions of working as an independent professional. These findings add to the growing criticisms of conceptions of the 'boundaryless career' (Inkson et al., 2012), as being overly optimistic and underestimating the difficulties of pursuing a career that evolves across, rather than within, organizational boundaries. A key contention is that although those who contract independent workers may well benefit from their independence, they might, paradoxically, gain further benefit by supporting those workers in order to recruit their services in the future. This view, however, is in contrast to contemporary recommendations about the need for individuals to take charge of their career management and moves more towards encouraging collaboration between the employer and the employee irrespective of the duration of relationship. Taken together, the chapters in this part demonstrated the composite and dynamic nature of contemporary work opportunities and experiences. Although, there may be much to be gained from the new economy, there are also potential drawbacks.

In the second part of the book 'Making the Most of Flexible Work Practices: The Need for Spatial Job Crafting and Boundary Management', two chapters examined flexible working through the lens of time and spatial flexibility. In Chapter 5, 'Reflecting on and Proactively Making Use of Flexible Working Practices Makes All the Difference: The Role of Spatial Job Crafting, Wessels and Schippers examined spatial flexibility and extended the notion of job crafting to spatial aspects of work. They demonstrated that spatial job crafting can foster work engagement and innovation and argued the need for employees to be proactive in its use. In Chapter 6, ' "Bounded Flexibility": The Influence of Time-Spatial

Flexibility and Boundary-Management Strategies on Women's Work-Home Interaction', Peters and Van der Heijden examined the extent to which women's opportunities for time-spatial flexibility impacts on their work-home balance. They also investigated the extent to which the relationship between the two are moderated by their enacted work-home and home-work segmentation strategies. They argued that time-spatial flexibility can be seen as a job resource since it can result in less time and strain-based, work-home interference and more positive work-home interference. A central message in this part is the need for employees to be proactive in crafting their work arrangements and experiences according to their own personal and professional needs. Yet, it also acknowledges that in order to benefit fully from flexible work arrangements then employees also need to appreciate both their own requirements and those of their employer.

The third part of the book 'Professionalization in the Service Industry: Cicerones and Baristas' examined the trend towards professionalization in some service industries, led by changes to the nature of the service provided. The implications of this trend for individual workers' experiences are examined, particularly with respect to job autonomy and increased skill requirements. Both chapters, Chapter 7 'Craft Beer, Cicerones and Changing Identities in Beer Serving' by Clarke, Weir and Patrick, and Chapter 8 'Wake Up and Smell the Coffee: Job Quality in Australia's Café Industry' by Knox presented an alternative to Ritzer's (2009) classic thesis on the increasing 'McDonaldization' of social processes and products. Knox's explored the bifurcation of outlets in the Australian café industry—first the standard, cost-based cafés where traits of Ritzer's thesis were reflected with a high level of standardization and deskilled, routine work and second, speciality cafés with non-standardized, individualized service placing greater skill requirement on servers. Clarke, Weir and Patrick demonstrated a similar finding with their exposition of the development of the Cicerone beer server, whom they equated with wine sommeliers.

Both chapters make a contribution to our understanding of how the nature of work has changed and how changes in product offerings can have implications for the level of skill required in a job. In both these instances what might have been deemed relatively low-skilled jobs have become more specialist, requiring more sophisticated skills and in the case of craft beer bar servers, the opportunity to acquire a qualification linked to their profession. In doing so they challenged assumptions about the increasing ubiquity of standardization and commodification of service sector work, demonstrating that in some cases, changes to the product offerings require increased skill and are likely to be characterized by greater employee discretion.

The final part of the book 'Harnessing Technological and Digital Innovation: The Need for Workforce Agility' examines the implementation of new ways of working and in particular insights into the opportunities offered by agile working in two case studies. These case studies demonstrated the complexity of integration and the challenges that organizations may encounter. Chapter 9 'Digital Workplace Design: Transforming for High Performance' by van der Meulen, Dery and Sebastian, and Chapter 10 'Agile Working: The Case of TechSci, a Global Technology Company' by Anderson and Kelliher examined the implementation of workforce agility. An important issue in these discussions is the extent to which the implementation of flexible and agile working practices can satisfy the interests of both the employer or the employee and going beyond the 'dual agenda' (Bailyn, 2006) to achieve mutual flexibility.

Emerging Themes

Having presented an overview of each of the chapter's findings, we turn now to explore the overarching themes and connections which have emerged between the chapters.

The Increasing Ubiquity of Technology

Technology is a theme which runs through several of the chapters, echoing more general interest in the impact of technological innovation on the future of work, work relationships and the consequent experiences and opportunities for employees (e.g. Howcroft & Taylor, 2014; Levy, 2015; Moore & Hayes, 2017; PriceWaterhouseCoopers, 2018). Most obviously, Chapters 9 and 10 look at how technology has been used to facilitate different ways of working and of organizing. These chapters align with other recent work suggesting an increasing trend among employers to use technology to detach work from place (Felstead & Henseke, 2017). Both chapters noted that technology has often been implemented in an isolated sense, but if it is to be used to change the operation and geographical organization of how work is done, it is important that technological innovation is integrated with changes in the use of physical space and the way in which people are managed. This conveys an underlying message that whereas work might be physically detached from the workplace, the relational nature of work should be maintained by supporting appropriate relational connectivity between the respective worker and the organization. It calls for technology to be integrated into a holistic workplace design with buy-in from, and catering to, the needs of stakeholders including different levels of management, as well as employees and their representatives. This implies engagement with and understanding of the diversity of stakeholder needs with respect to how technology might be utilized.

Chapters 2, 5 and 6 are also strongly underpinned by the use of technology in the workplace. The issues examined in these chapters emanate from developments in technology and how the relationship between employees' work and non-work lives is experienced. The people studied in Chapter 2 traded career advancement for the ability to work remotely and those in Chapters 5 and 6 made choices about where and when to work, but were only able to do so because of technological mechanisms. The use of technology in this regard enables employees working remotely to access information resources in the same way as their office-based counterparts, allowing them to fulfil their work obligations from another location. The facilitation of connectivity with co-workers thus enables coordination, collaboration and knowledge transfer, despite physical separation.

Yet, it should be acknowledged that other studies (Golden, 2007) have found that non-teleworking colleagues may experience a sense of injustice for having to 'pick up' the work of their teleworking counterparts, perceiving themselves to have a heavier workload. Matos (2013) observes that organizations such as Yahoo, Hewlett-Packard and IBM, which previously encouraged the use of flexible work practices, have reduced opportunities for remote working, reportedly due to the potential implications for collaboration and knowledge transfer. It is possible these organizations were looking for a degree of connectivity between employees/clients/customers that current technology does not allow. It is also notable that the ubiquity of technology may result in too much connectivity, resulting in negative spillover between work and life as reported by the women workers in Chapter 6. This finding adds weight to calls for space and connectivity to be understood as 'processes' to be managed (Beyes & Steyaert, 2011), and in particular for the space and connectivity between home and work domains to be managed. It also reflects the findings of other studies where employees perform space and the connectivity between work and home domains in fluid and dynamic ways—including when work spills over into the non-work domain (Richardson & McKenna, 2013). These findings demonstrate the paradox of technology facilitating flexible working practices and thus benefitting the employee, but at the same time potentially having negative implications for the relationship between the work and non-work domains.

The Challenge of Achieving a Satisfactory Work-Life Balance

Chapters 5 and 6 examine the interface between work and life and related concern about access to work-life balance in the contemporary context, an area of increasing interest to organizations, individuals and public policy makers. This reflects growing awareness of the positive impact of achieving satisfactory work-life balance for both individual well-being and performance (Kalliath & Brown, 2008). Furthermore, although much of the extant literature has focused on caring responsibilities and how they might be managed to achieve satisfactory work-life balance, it must be acknowledged that those who do not have caring responsibilities may also wish to balance work with other activities in their lives, such as religious and cultural commitments, sports and leisure, education, etc. Those with caring responsibilities may also have commitments and interests beyond caring (Kelliher, Richardson & Bioiarentseva, 2018). Thus, changes in work, working arrangements and relationships need to engage with the implications for the work-life balance of a wider range employees non-work activities.

In addition, there has been considerable exploration of technology and the role it plays in the work-life interface (Folotcad & Henseke, 2017; Halford, 2005; Towers et al., 2006; Wheatley, 2017); and specifically the paradoxical nature of its role. On the one hand, technology has been widely recognized as a facilitator of flexible working by providing the means for work to be done from almost any location where an Internet connection is available. This can lead to a more satisfactory relationship between work and life by allowing employees to reduce or avoid commuting time through to 'digital nomads' who may engage in work at the same time as travelling and who may work outside of normal working hours. In large centres of population, the need to avoid long commutes has been found to be a primary motivator to engage in flexible working practices (Richardson & McKenna, 2013). However, there has also been findings that working in a technologically enabled way can contribute to work intensification (Kelliher & Anderson, 2010), and in recent years, there has been a growing literature on the consequences of being 'always on' and expectations about employees being available for work contact outside their designated working hours via smartphones and tablets (Besseyre Des Horts, 2012; Felstead & Henseke, 2017). A key concern is that employees working from home may be unable to 'switch off' and thus suffer from increased levels of stress and potentially eventually burnout.

Refinement of Service Offerings and Skills in Service Work

The development of more refined service offerings in some sectors and the implications of this for what work involves is the subject of Chapters 7 and 8. In both cases a more sophisticated offering (craft beer and coffee) is accompanied by more personalized and informed service giving rise to the reformulation of some service jobs in these sectors. In each situation, staff working in these jobs are expected to acquire detailed product knowledge and knowledge about the ingredients and production processes, and to share that knowledge with and offer advice to customers. Thus, the jobs of these coffee and beer servers have become more skilled, acquiring a 'professional' job title, and in the case of those serving craft beer, the potential for a qualification as well. The point here is not that technology has overtaken this work, but that in some sub-sectors there is a movement towards 'de-automation' and work developments regarding increased complexity and autonomy. This part of the book speaks directly to debates about the putative *re/upskilling* of work, versus the putative *deskilling* of work, stemming from Braverman's (1998) early thesis as well as Ritzer's (2009) conception of the increasing 'McDonaldization' of social processes and products. In particular, we observe how there are instances of both deskilling and upskilling taking place within the same sector. This presents a different image to that of Carey's (2007) examination of changes in how social work is done in the context of agency care management, which reports the increasing 'proletarianization' of social work, predicting that it is likely to become further deskilled and marginalized. It may be instructive, therefore, to explore the extent to which this kind of bifurcation has occurred in other service industries with implications for the nature of work.

De-coupling of Workers From Organizations

The de-coupling of workers from the organizations they carry out work for has been observed in a number of ways in several of the chapters in this book. First, physical de-coupling, with employees working away from the workplace in the form of telework, but also co-operation on projects of people working in different parts of the world in global organizations and operating as virtual teams. Second, one chapter has examined a de-coupling of employer-employee relationships as a result of an increasing number of individuals engaging in self-employment. In this instance, professional workers are de-coupled from the organizations that make use of their services, often moving from employment to a series of short-term work contracts. This 'de-coupling' of workers from organizations is also witnessed elsewhere in the form of looser employment relationships, such as the use of zero-hours or temporary contracts. Finally, we see de-coupling in relation to personal or emotional involvement in the work undertaken with the emotions displayed being more prescribed and proscribed for professional workers. The chapter which examines HR professionals shows how they engage in emotional labour, managing their emotions to remain seemingly rational and detached, and where emotion is displayed, it is constrained and managed.

The de-coupling of the individual from the organization in the form of self-employment has been a recent feature in many economies (*The Economist*, 2018; International Labour Organization, 2017). In some instances, it has been promoted by governments as a route to foster economic growth and for employees it may provide an opportunity for more freedom and autonomy over working experiences, and provide opportunities and work-life balance (Deloitte Insights, 2018). There is also a link between growing self-employment and technology, most clearly illustrated by the development of the gig economy, where workers are connected with those requiring their services through platforms, such as Uber, UBerEats, AirTasker, etc., or Deliveroo. In the UK, for example, Lepanjuuri, Wishart, and Cornick (2018) have reported that 4.4% of adults have engaged in some form of work in the gig economy in the previous year. Even while this form of work provides earning opportunities to a range of populations (The Taylor Review, 2017), it has also been the target of criticism with charges that it may augment precariousness and fragmentation (Rubery, Keizer & Grimshaw 2016). Gig workers may be doubly de-coupled from the employer, in the sense that they work on a contract for the job basis but also, may be physically de-coupled in that they have no direct physical interaction either with the organization they do work for, or with their co-workers or sometimes with customers. Yet, some scholars have pointed to the possibility of 'freelancer unionism', where such disparate workers might unite in gig workers communities for the purposes of mutual support (Wood, Lehdonvirta & Graham, 2018).

Reasons for entering self-employment have been found to vary from those who do so because they want to go it alone, to those who do so for lifestyle reasons, through to those who become self-employed due to the lack of employment opportunities available to them. At the same time in some countries there has been a growing trend towards what has been termed 'bogus self-employment' (Keizer, 2013), whereby employers change the nature of the work relationship making former employees as independent contractors (*The Economist*, 2017). Furthermore, the extent of de-coupling may vary and particularly where those who are self-employed may have an ongoing relationship with a single organization as in the case of 'sessional academics'. Williams and Beovich (2017) have reported how universities employ teaching-focused sessional academics on short-term contracts, considering them to be self-employed. However, in reality, these teaching staff may be working for a particular university on this basis for many years. Therefore, the extent to which they are truly de-coupled from the respective organization is debatable, because they differ from the full-time employee only in the sense that they do not receive contractual employment related entitlements, such as medical and pension benefits.

Future Research

The findings about changes to the nature and organization of work and work relationships detailed in this book paint a striking picture of how the experience of workers have evolved in the early years of the 21st century. What emerges is a complex picture made up of different, although sometimes interconnected, types of change, driven by a range of factors. In many ways, the factors driving changes identified have remained consistent; however, what has changed is how they have impacted on work, working and work relationships and, in some cases, the pace of the change.

It is noteworthy, however, how little is known about how these changes impact workers and what might be some of the broader societal implications. Given that significant changes have taken place in a relatively short time, there is a clear need for researchers to monitor these developments on an ongoing basis and to further understanding of their implications for work and work relationships. It is interesting to note that whilst many of the driving factors for these changes have been present for some time (e.g. developments in technology, increased competitive pressures), the way in which they have influenced work and work relationships has altered over time. For example, whereas developments in technology may have digitized work and allowed for work to be done in almost any place and at any time, developments in artificial intelligence are likely to become increasingly important in the future, in terms of replacing jobs, creating new jobs and also in assisting humans with work. These will be important developments to monitor, as will the experiences of remote working and virtual teams as they become more pervasive in organizations. It will be important to assess the longer-term implications of people working in this way, such as the costs to meaningful communication, collaboration and knowledge sharing, alongside the benefits of higher-level job satisfaction and organizational commitment for employees, and savings on the cost of workplace accommodation for employers. Understanding the relationship between work and technology more fully will assist governments, policy makers, employers, employees and their representatives to negotiate a pathway which allows maximization of benefits to all stakeholders. How technology enables the relationship between home and work also merits further exploration, not least to addresses the lack of empirical studies on the extent to which technology may generate home-work conflict. Whereas it may be used to connect to work when at home, or to home when, for example, travelling for work, this means it also enables employees to connect to home during work hours.

Changes to the nature of work relations also deserve attention by future researchers. The increase in self-employment, whether via the use of digital platforms or otherwise, changes the structure of the labour market. It is important to understand the implications of these changes, since if fewer individuals are employed, then what is typically offered as part of an employment package (e.g. holiday and sick pay, training, etc.) cannot be assumed, and the legal protections given to employees no longer applies. This raises challenges for how economies operate and are regulated and may require rethinking of government policy and legislation in relation to work, and may imply a role for collective organization of these workers, or a role for non-governmental organizations.

The provision of services plays an important role in many economies and increased competitive pressures are likely to mean that organizations will continue to look for ways to differentiate service products, in line with changing consumer preferences. In particular, the search for authenticity and customization is in contrast to a move to standardization to enable low-cost delivery. Such changes have implications for the nature and organization of work and influence the degree to which the human element can be replaced by automation. It is important for researchers to monitor these developments and to further understanding on how they influence what work involves, how it is done and the implications for those who perform it.

Whereas much of the extant career theory has tended to focus on professional career actors, with a relative paucity of research on careers in the service industries, these chapters indicate that given these changes, careers in the service industries merit further investigation. In particular, it would seem appropriate to investigate the extent to which changes in the nature of the service offerings impact on the career trajectory of the respective worker. A central key theme in this regard is that further work is required on the relationship between product offerings and respective career trajectories. For example, how do changes in the nature of the product or service impact on the individual's career opportunities and experiences? Research might also consider the extent to which professionalization in some service industries may shield the employee from social perceptions that they are engaged in 'dirty work' (Ashforth, Kreiner & Fugate, 2010)

Conclusion

The studies of changes to work, working and work relationships depicted in the chapters of this book represent only a segment of the type of changes taking place in workplaces across the globe in recent times. However, they provide rich insights into the experiences of workers whose work has changed, who have different working arrangements and whose relationships with the organizations they do work for have moved away from the model of full-time, permanent employment.

References

Ashforth, B.E., Kreiner, G.E., & Fugate, M. (2000). All in a day's work: Boundaries and micro role transition. *Academy of Management Review*, 25(3), 472–491.

Avolio, B.J., & Gardner, W.L. (2005). Authentic leadership development: Getting to the root of positive forms of leadership. *The Leadership Quarterly*, 16(3), 315–338.

Bailyn, L. (2006). *Breaking the Mold: Redesigning Work for Productive and Satisfying Lives* (2nd ed.). Ithaca: ILR Press.

Besseyre Des Horts, C., Dery, C., & MacCormmick, J. (2012). Paradoxical consequences of the use of Blackberrys: An application of the job demand-control-support model. In C. Kelliher & J. Richardson (Eds.), *New Ways of Organizing Work: Developments, Perspectives and Experiences* (pp. 16–29). New York: Routledge.

Beyes, T., & Steyaert, C. (2011). The ontological politics of artistic interventions: Implications for performing action research. *Action Research, 9*(1), 100–115

Bolton, S., & Houlihan, M. (2007). Beginning the search for the H. In S. Bolton & M. Houlihan (Eds.), *Searching for the Human in Human Resource Management: Theory, Practice and Workplace Contexts.* London: Palgrave Macmillan.

Braverman, H. (1998). *Labor and Monopoly Capital: The Degradation of Work in the Twentieth Century.* New York: Monthly Review Press.

Carey, M. (2007). White-collar proletariat? Braverman, the deskilling/upskilling of social work and the paradoxical life of the agency care manager. *Journal of Social Work, 7*(1), 93–114.

Cohen, J.R., & Single, L.E. (2001). An examination of the perceived impact of flexible work arrangements on professional opportunities in public accounting. *Journal of Business Ethics, 32*(4), 317–328.

Deloitte Insights (2018). *The rise of the social enterprise.* 2018 Deoitte Global Human Capital Trends, Deloitte Development LLC.

Felstead, A., & Genseke, G. (2017). Assessing the growth of remote working and its consequences for effort, well-being and work-life balance. *New Technology and Employment, 32*(3), 195–212.

Golden, T. (2007). Co-workers who telework and the impact on those in the office: Understanding the implications of virtual work for co-worker satisfaction and turnover intentions. *Human Relations, 60,* 1641–1667.

Halford, S. (2005). Hybrid space: Re-spacialisations of work, organisation and management. *New Technology, Work and Employment, 20,* 19–33.

Howcroft, D., & Taylor, P. (2014). Plus ca change, plus la meme chose?—Researching and theorising the "new" new technologies. *New Technology, Work and Employment, 29*(1), 1–8.

International Labour Organization (ILO) (2017). *World Employment Social Outlook 2017 Trends.*

Inkson, K., Gunz, H., Ganesh, S., & Roper, J. (2012). Boundaryless careers: Bringing back boundaries. *Organization Studies, 33*(3), 323–340.

Kalliath, T. J., & Brough, P. (2008). Work-life balance: A review of the naming of the construct. *Journal of Management and Organization, 14*(3), 323–327.

Keizer, A. (2013). Unions and their representation of contingent workers: A comparative analysis of Japan, the Netherlands and the UK. *10th European ILERA Conference,* 20–22 June, Amsterdam, The Netherlands.

Kelliher, C., & Anderson, D. (2010). Doing more with less? Flexible working practices and the intensification of work. *Human Relations, 63*(1), 83–106.

Kelliher, C., Richardson, J., & Bioiarentseva, L. (2018). Work life balance in the 21st Century: What work, what life, what balance?, *Human Resource Management Journal,* forthcoming.

Lepanjuuri, K., Wishart, R., & Cornick, P. (2018). *The Characteristics of Those in the Gig Economy: Final Report.* London: BEIS.

Lero, D., Richardson, J., & Korabik, K. (2008). *Cost-Benefit Analysis of Work-Life Balance Practices.* Canadian Association of Labour Administrators, Canada.

Leslie, L.C.M., Manchester, C.F., Park, T.Y., & Ahn Mehng, S.I. (2012). Flexible work practices: A source of career premiums or penalties? *Academy of Management Journal, 55*(6), 1407–1428.

Levy, K. (2015). The contexts of control: Information, power and truck driving work. *The Information Society, 31*(2), 160–174.

Matos, K. (2013). HP & Yahoo's telecommuting breakup: It's not you, it's me!. *Huffington Post Business*, 23 October.

Moore, S., & Hayes, L.J.B. (2017). Taking worker productivity to a new level? Electronic monitoring in homecare—The (re)production of unpaid labour. *New Technology, Work and Employment, 32*(2), 101–114.

Price Waterhouse Coopers (2018). *Workforce of the Future: The Competing Forces Shaping 2030.*

Richardson, J., & McKenna, S. (2013). Reordering spatial and social relations: A case study of professional and managerial flexworkers. *British Journal of Management, 25*(4), 724–736.

Ritzer, G. (2009). *The McDonaldization of Society*. Los Angeles: Pine Forge Press.

Rubery, J., Keizer, A., & Grimshaw, D. (2016). Flexibility bites back: The multiple and hidden costs of flexible employment practices. *Human Resource Management Journal, 26*(3), 235–251.

Steffens, N.K., Mols, F., Haslam, S.A., & Okimoto, T.G. (2016). True to what we stand for: Championing collective interests as a path to authentic leadership. *The Leadership Quarterly, 27*(5), 726–744.

Taylor, M., Marsh, G., Nicol, D., & Broadbent, P. (2017). *Good Work: The Taylor Review of Modern Working Practices*. UK: UK Government.

The Economist (2017). Self employed or employee? Britain wrestles with the gig economy. *The Economist*. Available from https://www.economist.com/britain/2017/07/13/self-employed-or-employee-britain-wrestles-with-the-gig-economy

The Economist (2018). GrAIt Expectations. *The Economist*. Special Report AI in Business, March 31, 2018, March 31–April 6 (Print Edition)

Towers, I., Duxbury, L., Higgins, C., & Thomas, J. (2006). Time thieves and space invaders: Technology, work and the organization. *Journal of Organizational Change, 19*, 503–618.

Weeden, K.A. (2005). Is there a flexiglass ceiling? Flexible work arrangements and wages in the United States. *Social Science Research, 34*(2), 454–482.

Weiss, M., Razinskas, S., Backmann, J., & Hoegl, M. (2018). Authentic leadership and leaders' mental well-being: An experience sampling study. *The Leadership Quarterly, 29*(2), 309–321.

Wheatley, D. (2017). Employee satisfaction and use of flexible working arrangements. *Work, Employment and Society, 31*(4), 567–585.

Williams, B., & Beovich, B. (2017). Experiences of sessional educators within an Australian undergraduate paramedic program. *Journal of University Teaching Learning & Practice, 14*(1). Available from https://ro.uow.edu.au/jutlp/vol14/iss1/13

Wood, A.J., Lehdonvirta, V., & Graham, M. (2018). Workers of the Internet unit? Online freelancer organisation among remote gig economy workers in six Asian and African countries. *New Technology, Work and Employment, 33*(2), 95–112.

Contributor Biographies

Deirdre Anderson is Head of Department: People and Organizations in Lincoln International Business School and a Director of the Eleanor Glanville Centre, an interdisciplinary center for inclusion, diversity and equality at the University of Lincoln. Her research interests include flexibility and work-life integration, inclusion and diversity, gendered careers and work and family (especially in different cultures). Deirdre frequently presents her research at academic and practitioner conferences within the UK and internationally, and publishes in journals of recognized international excellence. She has recently edited a book *Work-Life Balance in Times of Recession, Austerity and Beyond*. Prior to academia, Deirdre spent over 20 years working within organizations and then as an independent business psychology consultant and trainer in the private sector.

Kelly A. Basile is an Assistant Professor at the School of Business and Management at Emmanuel College in Boston, Massachussetts. She holds a PhD in Organizational Behavior from the London School of Economics and Political Science. Her research interests include work-life boundary management, technology, culture and diversity in organizations. In addition to her academic experience, Dr. Basile worked in commercial research and consulting for over a decade. She also holds a Master's in Business Administration from Babson College and a Master's in Social Work from Boston University and is a Fellow of the Higher Education Academy.

T. Alexandra Beauregard is a Reader in Organizational Psychology at Birkbeck, University of London. She holds a PhD from the London School of Economics and Political Science. Her research interests are centered on the work-life interface, flexible working arrangements and diversity in the workplace, with a particular focus on gender equality and gender identity. She has published widely on these topics in academic journals and in practitioner outlets, as well as authoring chapters in a number of edited scholarly books and teaching-oriented texts.

Esther Canonico is a Fellow in the London School of Economics Department of Management. She holds a PhD in Organizational Behavior from LSE and an MBA from London Business School. Her research interests include diversity in the workplace and flexible working practices. In addition to her research expertise, Esther has a deep understanding of organizational practices based on her extensive experience in senior management for over a decade. She is a Fellow of the Higher Education Academy and a member of several international organizations, such as the Gender and Diversity in Organizations Division of the Academy of Management and the Work and Family Researchers Network.

Daniel Clarke researches and teaches management, marketing and qualitative inquiry at the University of Dundee School of Business, Scotland, where he is the Program Director of Bachelor of Science (Hons) Business Management. Daniel's scholarship operates in the intersection of organizational space and place, and his work has been published in *Management Learning, Qualitative Inquiry and Forum: Qualitative Social Research*. His academic interests are to do with bringing the use of imaginative-creative, visual and experimental practices of pedagogy and research in to management learning. He is currently researching the range of 'origin cues' in brand origin architecture within the marketing of craft beer.

Kristine Dery is a Research Scientist at the MIT Sloan School's Center for Information Systems Research (CISR), where she explores how companies design work and working environments to enable companies to engage employees to excel in the world of digital. Her projects explore the Digital Workplace, Employee Experience, Managing Talent for Digital and Agile at Scale.

Clare Kelliher is Professor of Work and Organization at Cranfield School of Management, United Kingdom. She has a long-standing interest in flexible working and has published widely on this topic. She co-chairs the International Labour and Employment Relations Association Study Group on flexible work practices. With Dr Richardson, she has convened several conference streams and symposia, and they edited *New Ways of Organizing Work: Developments, Perspectives and Experiences*, published by Routledge in 2012. Professor Kelliher is a member of the Editorial Board of Human Resource Management Journal and has served as an elected member of the editorial board for Work, Employment and Society.

Angela Knox is an Associate Professor of Work and Organizational Studies at the University of Sydney Business School. Her research focuses on job quality, insecure and precarious work and employment regulation. She has co-edited a book and published in *Gender, Work* *and Organisation*, the *Human Resource Management Journal*, the *International Journal of Human Resource Management* and *Work, Employment and Society*.

Carol Linehan is a Senior Lecturer in the School of Applied Psychology, University College Cork, and a Chartered Work and Organizational Psychologist (C.Psychol. P.S.I.). Her main teaching and research interests are in the domain of work psychology. She has particular interest in emotion labor in organizations, and the impact of contemporary work practices on employees' identities and experiences of work. Recent work has appeared in the *International Journal of Human Resource Management, Culture and Organization*, the *British Journal of Management* and the *Journal of Management Studies*.

Tui McKeown is an Associate Professor in the Department of Management within the Monash Business School at Monash University, Australia. Her research focuses on an active examination of the changing world of self-employment in general, and on independent contracting in particular. She has coined the terms 'independent professional' (IPro) and 'nano business', as a key philosophy informing this research is the desire to explore, debate and share ideas that develop a broader understanding of what constitutes work in the twenty-first century.

Elaine O'Brien is an Oganizational Psychologist (C.Psychol, BPS) and Lecturer in Management at University College Cork where she teaches Human Resource Management and Organizational Behaviour. She has considerable industrial experience in both public- and private-sector organizations, working as a Human Resources Manager and Human Resources Consultant. Her current research interests lie in the area of Emotion Labour, Work/professional Identities, Employee Resilience and Employee Engagement. Elaine's work is published in leading journals including *Journal of Management Studies, Journal of Business Ethics* and *International Journal of Human Resource Management*.

Holly Patrick is Lecturer in Human Resource Management at Edinburgh Napier University, where she teaches leadership, contemporary human relations and leads an overseas Bachelor of Arts (Hons) program for practicing managers. She has conducted research in the Creative Industries in the UK and Australia, into leadership and in the craft beer segment in the UK. Her work has been published in scholarly journals in the UK and Australia. When not researching or teaching, Holly enjoys spending time on the family farm with her husband and their high-spirited gang of sheep, chickens, goats and dogs.

Pascale Peters holds a position as Associate Professor at Radboud University Nijmegen [Institute for Management Research (IMR/GAINS)] and is Full Professor Strategic Human Resource Management at Nyenrode

Business Universiteit in the Netherlands. She is a member of the editorial board of *Community, Work and Family* journal. She publishes and supervises PhD-students, master's- and bachelor's students on topics such as the (gendered) labourmarket participation, work-life balance, boundary management, sustainable HRM (employability, workability and vitality) and the contemporary and sustainable organization of work, in particular, home-based telework, New Ways to Work, and working carer support.

Julia Richardson is Professor of Human Resources Management and Deputy Head of the School of Management, Curtin University, Perth Australia. Her research interests center on 'the future of work', career sustainability, flexible work practices and life balance in international careers. A member of the New Zealand Business Performance Panel and former Chair of the Career Division of the Academy of Management, Julia also sits on several editorial boards. She has enjoyed a global career in the public and private sectors in UK, New Zealand, Japan, Singapore, Canada and Australia, and has won multiple awards for her scholarship and teaching.

Michaéla Schippers is Endowed Professor of Behaviour and Performance Management and the scientific director of the Erasmus Centre for Study and Career Success at Rotterdam School of Management, Erasmus University Rotterdam, the Netherlands. She received her PhD from the Psychology Department at the Free University in Amsterdam.Her current research concentrates on team reflexivity, team diversity and team leadership, as well as goal setting, academic performance (study success) and the use of team charters to improve student team performance. Other current projects concern knowledge sharing within teams and networks, virtual teams, new ways of working, behavioral operations management and social exclusion/inclusion.

Ina M. Sebastian is a Research Scientist at the MIT Sloan School's Center for Information Systems Research (CISR), where she studies how large enterprises transform for success in the digital economy. Her current research areas are collaboration across organizational boundaries in ecosystems, digital strategies and organizational redesign and digital workplace and talent management.

Beatrice Van der Heijden is a Full Professor of Business Administration, in particular Strategic Human Resource Management at the Radboud University, Nijmegen, the Netherlands, and Head of the Department Strategic HRM. Moreover, she occupies a Chair in Strategic HRM at the Open University of the Netherlands, School of Management, at Kingston University, London, United Kingdom, at Ghent University, Belgium, and at Hubei University, Wuhan, China. Her main research areas are sustainable career development, employability and aging at work. Van der Heijden is Associate Editor of the *European Journal of Work and Organizational Psychology* and of *Gedrag & Organisatie*, and Co-Editor of the German *Journal of Human Resource Management*.

Nick van der Meulen is a Research Scientist at the MIT Sloan School's Center for Information Systems Research (CISR). He investigates digital business transformations, particularly concerning how leading organizations manage information and technology to enable new ways of working that drive performance.

David Weir is Professor of Intercultural Management at York St John University, having held Chairs at several universities, including Glasgow, Bradford, Northumbria Liverpool Hope, Essex, Ceram and Rennes. He has researched and published extensively on Management and Leadership, especially in the Arab world, and is a Foundation Fellow of the Leadership Trust and a Companion of the Chartered Institute of Management. He is currently working on issues related to craft in spacing and timing, new styles of work, storytelling, poetry and auto-ethnography. He is a performance poet, most recently with the Dithering Wobblies.

Christina Wessels works as a research associate in Germany and received her PhD in Management from Rotterdam School of Management, Erasmus University in 2017. Her research interests lie at the intersection of organizational behavior, information technology, and organizational psychology, and include topics such as the changing nature of work, flexible working practices, job crafting, digitalization, employee well-being and performance.

Index